The Braided River

For Keith

The Braided River

Migration
and the
Personal Essay

Diane Comer

OTAGO

Published by Otago University Press
Level 1, 398 Cumberland Street
Dunedin, New Zealand
university.press@otago.ac.nz
www.otago.ac.nz/press

First published 2019
Copyright © Diane Comer
The moral rights of the author have been asserted

ISBN 978-1-98-853153-3

Published with the assistance of Creative New Zealand

Editor: Paula Wagemaker
Index: Barbara Frame
Front cover design: Lisa Elliot
Cover photograph: Randy Hanna
Author photograph: Ebony Lamb

Printed in China through Asia Pacific Offset

Contents

Here is the time for the *sayable, here* is its homeland.
Speak and bear witness.

—Rainer Maria Rilke

Acknowledgements

A true debt can never be repaid, for which I owe my migrant writers my deepest thanks. This braided river is made possible through the gift of their personal essays, which have carried me across oceans and back again. I wish to thank each of you for your writing, your time and your steadfast belief in this book. Your courage in the face of difficulty sustained me through earthquakes, hemispheric shifts and the loss of language. My gratitude for your generosity and inspiration is past words.

For supporting the research in true transnational fashion, huge thanks to Lyndon Fraser and Jennifer Clement. For listening to me in a dark time, I want to thank Thomas Wright. To my favourite doctoral women, Sonia-Ingrid Anderson, Julie Johnson, Lorraine Ritchie, Lenore Hoyt and Marguerite Tassi, many thanks. For help landing the fish, cheers to the Splinters, with special thanks to Kate for her manaakitanga. To the poets and writers in my life who gave careful consideration to the words, I am grateful to Susan Benner, Coral Atkinson, Dianna Troyer, Bern Mulvey, John Price, Sonia Sundstedt, Harry Ricketts, Laura Klein and my sister Lisa Zimmerman. Heartfelt appreciation to my wonderful editor and friend Paula Wagemaker for her thoughtful editing of the manuscript, what a gift. Other friends supported me with art, letters, books, cups of tea, smacks up the side of the head and sheer belief in me: thank you to Gilaine Spoto, Kathy Kise, Geoff Vader, Daniela Dragas, Wayne Christianson, André Krebber, Wendy Logan and dear Brent Johnson. Grateful acknowledgement to my home crew who keep me in the middle of the boat, and especially to Selwyn for the river image.

To our dear friends in Sweden, whose kindness and generosity knew no bounds while we lived there, Inger Pettersson, Vicky Gatzouras, Åse Nygren, Ulrica Skagert, Jörgen Samuelsson, Jessica Enevold, Anna Svennson-Stening and Micke Dahlberg, *tack så mycket*. Know you and yours are always welcome in the land of the long white cloud.

To my son and daughter, Kitt and Rilke, thank you for being so patient and understanding throughout the shifts in our lives. May you always know where home is.

Finally, I could never have come to the present without him: the river under the river throughout this journey is Keith, who brought our family back to where we belong.

Introduction

The Headwaters of the River

My migration to New Zealand began in 2007 when my husband and I, with our two children, left the United States to come to Christchurch. I hated New Zealand at first. Alone, freezing in our rental house while my husband and children were at work and school, I wrote endless emails to friends and family detailing my unhappiness, no doubt putting many of them off visiting us for years. I needed a job, if only to be warm. As is often the case with migrants, my skills went unutilised at first. I felt disheartened not being able to teach at university level as I had done for years in the US and Sweden. I worked at one temporary position after another: receptionist, learning advisor, web page builder, dogsbody. And then I began teaching a community education course on the personal essay.

By chance or choice, the class attracted adult migrants who wrote essays of remarkable depth and scope about their migration experiences. Perhaps the loss of home prompts migrants to want to write, for 'it is a reality to those with the experience of exile that leaving home, creating absence, and dislocation is essential for the writing act to proceed in the first place, and to become meaningful'.[1] I felt a flash of recognition when Gareth, a Welsh doctor who had migrated to New Zealand in 1974, wrote: 'Emigration is surely a synonym for farewell.'

My family and I had said farewell two years earlier to our friends, family, house, work, dog and a lifetime of connections, and I was still in a state of grief. One night in tears I smashed a wine glass on the table, asking my husband when we would be recompensed for everything we had given up to come to New Zealand. He didn't have an answer, but this Welsh migrant did, and his sense of loss, endured and then shared in his personal essay decades later, radiated past the individual to touch me and a larger audience. I realised migrants possess an affinity for the genre whose hallmark is to try, to weigh and to test, even as migrants have tried, weighed, tested and been tested by their chosen country.

One golden summer evening, the last day of term, as I stood in the University of Canterbury's beautiful old homestead of Okeover with its high ceilings and French doors opening onto the green lawn, I knew in all my years of teaching I had never taught such a remarkable class. No matter what writing prompt I gave them or how high I set the bar, they cleared it. On that last day, I looked at these 12 students, half of them New Zealanders, half of them migrants from Croatia, Thailand, Switzerland, Wales, the US and Uganda, and realised they were a microcosm of the population of New Zealand, a country with a strong history of migration, both past and present. That first class showed me that the synergy between migrant and the personal essay was akin to dry kindling, strike match. Why were we all here? I wondered, and suddenly I had a purpose again: to see where migration and the personal essay coincided.

I had come to the right country. According to the 2013 census, more than a quarter of New Zealanders were born overseas.[2] Everyone who has arrived on Aotearoa New Zealand's remote shores – from Polynesians several centuries ago, to the first British and European colonials in the 1800s, to myself – came as a migrant. Māori are tangata whenua, literally people 'born out of the land [whose] spiritual and epistemological connections are strengthened and renewed by occupation of particular lands, intimate connections born out of the practices of everyday life over a sustained period of time'.[3] Although successive generations of Māori have bonded with the land they named Aotearoa, 'migration and mobility have been part of Māori experience from the earliest movements to the present day'.[4] Migration remains a powerful metaphor, not only as globalisation, climate, social and economic change continue to drive movement, but also because 'our most ancient metaphor says life is a journey'.[5]

I was a serial migrant and migration had shaped much of my life, but I was also a writer who had been studying, writing and teaching the personal essay for over 20 years. What I found is that migration and the personal essay form a braided river of possibility that deserves to be explored in depth. Both the migrant and the writer set out from what they know towards what they do not, in life and on the page. Charting that voyage of discovery is an endeavour they share in their quest for understanding.

Like the braided rivers that flow across the landscapes of Aotearoa New Zealand, much of what migrants discover and learn about their new country lies well below the surface narrative and remains unstudied from their own reflective and analytical perspectives. The forces that determine migration and how individuals react to and potentially write about it have an interwoven external narrative and a deep, wide undercurrent that carries the story towards its conclusion. Our lives have channels that entwine, divide and rejoin as they course towards their end, but underneath is another story, because 'We now understand that braided rivers consist of much more than active surface channels, and that the river flows across an alluvial gravel bed, which may be many metres deep and possibly kilometres wide.'[6]

We can't see much of the river that flows across the alluvial gravel bed of our lives, but we can sense it. And if we try, we can write about it. As both a migrant and a writer, I wanted to use the personal essay to look beneath the braided surface narratives to explore the lived experience of my fellow migrants in New Zealand. Giving voice to individual lives is the personal essay's forte, offering a powerful form of reckoning and witness. With its critical tools of reflection and analysis, '[the] personal essay does, after all, put one more directly in contact with the thought and feeling of its author than do other forms of literature'.[7] The genre provides a method of inquiry well suited to plumbing the more resonant depths of migrants' knowledge and experience and gives a more nuanced understanding of the existential landscape of migration.

Whether migrant or not, life flows on, slow or fast, and we don't always pause to reflect on the other river running beneath the surface channels. Caught up as we are in the current of our lives, we rarely perceive life's design until after the fact, because 'the design is what that life, without ever being able to predict or even imagine it, leaves behind'.[8] However, we can discern and grasp much of what is hidden below those braided river channels through writing, for 'Always behind the actions of writing, painting, thinking, healing, doing, cooking, talking, smiling, making is the river, the *Río Abajo Río*; the river under the river that nourishes everything we make.'[9]

'To theorize, one leaves home'

This book explores the river under the river in migrant lives, mine and others, here in New Zealand. We cannot easily see where a river originates, yet it does start somewhere, even as migration does. For migrants it often starts before they actually leave home, which accords with anthropologist James Clifford's observation that 'To theorize, one leaves home.'[10] I had always been leaving home, first as an army brat uprooted throughout my childhood and adolescence, and then as an adult moving between Sweden, the US and New Zealand. All my life I knew the one place where I could ground my sense of displacement was in writing. When I realised the inherent potential between the personal essay and migration, I found a rich and untapped vein and began laying the foundation for this book, gathering personal essays written by migrants, none of whom was a published writer.

Migration is a contested and sensitive issue on both individual and political levels, not only in New Zealand, a country whose population is rapidly growing through migration, but throughout the world. As our planet becomes more populated and resources scarcer, as climate change disrupts our landscapes and lives, the polarity between host and migrant, native and stranger, will become more critical. 'The twenty-first century,' says American philosopher Thomas Nail, 'will be the century of the migrant', and we are indeed seeing more migrants than at any other point in recorded history.[11] Ongoing political, economic and environmental instability will surely see those numbers rise even higher. Migrant personal essays testify to what happens in the contact zone between self and other, sharing the lived consequences of being perceived as an outsider. Their writing provides real-world lessons the globalised world would be wise to address.

Over the course of two years, amid multiple earthquakes in Christchurch, I invited migrants to write about their experiences during community education courses I created specifically for them. The course design applied Søren Kierkegaard's maxim – we live forwards but understand backwards – to migration. I sought migrants who wished to dig past the surface narrative to what had informed their migration on emotional and existential levels, who wanted to explore John Berger's premise that 'Emigration, forced or chosen, across national frontiers or from village to metropolis is the quintessential experience of our time.'[12] That quote, floating in italics in the course description, headed a list of potential themes to consider:

From Y to NZ: The roots of there to here
Departure and arrival: Thresholds
Nearness and distance: Between countries and cultures
Sense of place and displacement: Where is home?
Family and familiarity: The absence or presence of both
Loss/gain: The balance sheet of migration
Fictions of nostalgia: Missing X, Y and NZ
Who are you here? Negotiating migrant identity
Returning: You can't go home again, or can you?

The course was inexpensive and drew adult migrants of all ages, from a variety of backgrounds and many parts of the world. The random demographic of each term's class challenged the assumption that the personal essay is the province of the middle-class, well-educated older writer: the course attracted migrants from their twenties to their eighties, and while it included doctors and lawyers, it also included individuals who had left school at 16. Together, these individuals – keen to explore their migration in writing – and I shared a commitment to a narrative journey across years, oceans and seismic rifts as this book came together.

'Que sais-je?': *What do I know?*

The experience of migration is one of discovery, an essential element it shares with the personal essay: 'the essayist takes the reader on a journey, defining and commenting upon a real-life experience in a detailed and insightful manner that leads to a broader understanding of life and a greater sense of meaning and self-fulfillment'.[13] Both writer and migrant test and weigh experience for what it means, and this shared process of inquiry and analysis makes the personal essay an effective genre for assessing the actual stakes of migration for each individual. The essay allows migrants not only to explore their own stories but also to consider the meaning of them: 'the essay, in fact, focuses on achieved meaning to a greater extent than those other forms we typically call literature; essays foreground meaning along with represented experience'.[14] By looking past the surface narrative, the who, what, where, when and why, the facts that can be gleaned from any immigration survey, migrants can reflect on their own experience in order to create meaning and thereby uncover the deep structure of their lives.

The idea that the migrant narrative has universal import is particularly relevant in a globalised world, given that we'll see more rather than less migration in the future as the economic, political and physical climate continues to change. For those of us wanting to understand what this increase means on both an individual and a global level, the personal essay provides a powerful method of inquiry. The genre possesses the versatility and rigour necessary to study the complicated and changing landscape of migration 'because it combines theory and personal reflection. A multiracial theory, inspired by the personal essay, can make an individual story universal, because only such a theory can show us that we are, and are not, so different'.[15] Migrant personal essays offer real-life examples and insight into this contested space between self and other.

The nexus between migration and the personal essay drives an innovative and illuminating approach to studying what migrants experience first-hand. Michel de Montaigne, considered to be the progenitor of the personal essay over four centuries ago, understood that the process of inquiry is central to the genre. For Montaigne the essential question was always '*Que sais-je?*' or 'What do I know?' He adopted this question as his motto and explored it in essay after essay.[16] The question is also a fundamental one for migrants as they forge connections in their new environments, both in life and on the page. The migrant's own line of inquiry shapes the essay's mental and emotional journey, while the wealth of life experience provides endless subject matter to explore. The result is a record of discovery in writing: 'It is not sufficient to say that the essay is an explorative genre or that it is a form of meditation and discovery through discourse. We must also acknowledge that the essayist marshals rhetorical strategies with the intention of conveying to a reader the experience of personal exploration and discovery.'[17]

Given its ability to convey personal exploration and discovery, the essay possesses a striking affinity with migration, an experience that challenges almost every aspect of life – family, work, identity, friendship and connection – on both the most mundane and profound of levels. When writing personal essays, migrants reflect on the lived experience of migration, the learning curve of which is initially steep and the effects of which are ongoing and ultimately lifelong. Finding one's way through writing, or writing as a method of inquiry, can track both outward-directed and inward-directed discovery and so has clear parallels for how migrants find their way in a new country. Through the personal essay's quest to answer Montaigne's signature question, 'What do I know?', the migrants in my classes and I had the opportunity to assess the real cost of migration: that borne by the individual.

For two years I worked with migrants who wanted to write about their experience of coming to New Zealand. Each term a new constellation of migrants from around the world met to write essays and discuss them over cups of tea and biscuits or Korean pancakes and kimchi. They arrived in the class as strangers but by the end of eight weeks, having travelled together on paper and in discussion around the seminar table, they knew one another well. I wasn't surprised they bonded over the shared experiences of migration and writing, because the personal essay fosters a sense of intimacy and connection with the reader.

But what deepened that bond was what disrupted the classes – the Christchurch earthquakes of 2010 and 2011. When the university cancelled the course and refunded the students' fees, the group insisted on continuing and hosted the class in their homes, migrating from week to week around our broken city. When I had the opportunity to study at Oxford for a term they urged me to go, saying the class would pick up on my return. When our family was forced to relocate to Sweden for work, another casualty of the earthquakes, these migrants carried me through that sunless and despairing time with their steadfast belief in this book. And when our family returned, miraculously, to New Zealand from Sweden, they welcomed me back, one of them saying, 'New Zealand always knows who will return.' The generosity and determination of these migrant writers never flagged and for that I remain in their debt.

The river under the river

The Braided River distils the experiences and thoughts of 37 migrants who between them wrote over 200 personal essays. The migrants, from 20 different countries, were aged between 25 to 80 and had arrived in New Zealand at different life stages. They are contemporary migrants who came by choice, even if that choice was conflicted for some of them. The United Nations distinguishes voluntary migrants from forced migrants (refugees), the latter displaced by conflicts, famine or development, or natural, environmental or human-made disasters: 'Migrants are people who make choices about when to leave and where to go, even though these choices are sometimes extremely constrained.'[18] Given that only 3.4 per cent of the world's population lives outside the country of their birth (258 million people in 2017), the choice to migrate is atypical.[19] Migrants are the exception, not the rule, to how and where the rest of the world lives.

The migrant writers presented here came to New Zealand between 1940 and 2007; the youngest came at age eight (the only child migrant) and the eldest at 60. All of them experienced directly how migration alters the course of one's life, and their essays are rich in their evocation of this profound sea change. As Rudyard Kipling noted: 'All things considered, there are only two kinds of men in the world – those that stay at home and those that do not. The second are the most interesting.'[20] Interesting or not, migrants are individuals who have embarked on a decision that has lifelong consequences for them.

By investigating their own histories through the personal essay, the migrants who feature in this book disclosed the real roots of their migration, the very things that might not be gleaned through surveys or interviews. The exploratory nature of the essay reveals deeper causes as to why migrants voluntarily choose to live in places where they may face a loss of identity, language, family, work and culture. Migration affects employment, housing, friendship, finances, citizenship, social benefits – an entire host of things that determine and alter one's life course. And as the world becomes more global and transnational, with more movement across borders and oceans, the choice to migrate extends beyond the personal to inform national and international concerns.

All migrants have a set story they tell to explain why they come to a host country, but the personal essay elicits the origin and meaning behind that journey. Migrant essays ground these very large abstractions of family, identity, home, distance, loss and belonging in specific, concrete examples. What exactly do migrants miss when they say they miss home? How do geographical and temporal distances affect their connection with those they love in other countries? Where do migrants feel they belong? How does migration affect their sense of identity? These questions demand consideration and reflection from the perspective of those living with the difficult answers. For migrants, 'the personal essay offers the potential for expression that remains provisional, unsettled, challenged even, but which still conveys as strength of feeling for the places where we live and work, and which we sometimes leave behind.'[21]

Migrant personal essays can sound the hidden and turbulent riverbed of experience, articulating what is often unknown and unexplored. French philosopher and author Hélène Cixous highlights this premise of writing as inquiry: 'What interests me is what I do not know. And it leaves me first of all silent … I know that a search, or an exploration will unfold in this direction.'[22] The migrant's own exploration in the essay leads to insights that might not otherwise occur. The past becomes present and manifest when the depths below the surface of our lives resonate and are understood in writing. Suddenly *what do I know?* becomes *what I do know*, a transformation from question to answer as the river under the river appears.

The stranger who comes to town

Every migrant is a stranger who has come to town, and their story of migration encompasses two master narratives. One adage, attributed variously to novelists from Tolstoy to John Gardner, holds that all great literature is one of two stories: a man goes on a journey, or a stranger comes to town.[23] Migration embodies both narratives. The migrant goes on a journey *and* is the stranger who comes to town. The personal essays of the migrants I collaborated with speak directly to how these core narratives have operated and are operating in their own lives and, while grounded in individual experience, they express universal themes. Even if we never leave our birthplace, the journey is an archetypal root/route metaphor for life itself as we follow its course from birth to death.

We do not need to migrate to feel displaced, without connection or support, because whenever we feel and are treated as other, we *are* the stranger who comes to town. As Salman Rushdie understands first-hand, the migrant perspective 'is written from the very experience of uprooting, disjuncture and metamorphosis (slow or rapid, painful or pleasurable) that is the migrant condition, and from which, I believe, can be derived a metaphor for all humanity'.[24] With the two master narratives informing their writing – the journey and the stranger who comes to town – migrant personal essays address one of the most fundamental questions humans face: what does it mean to be at home in the world?

For the migrant, the journey of the stranger who comes to town is a quest for meaning, and perhaps also a search for home. Both entail a process of discovery that the essay shares. Just as migrants discover their new countries while living in them, so too do 'essays discover themselves in writing'.[25] Migrants find that their sense of place and identity is altered irrevocably by migration, their previous lives displaced and transformed, maybe even translated into a new language. As they live in their new country, they learn to negotiate or renegotiate an entire world, things both ordinary and far-reaching. They look for a way to connect, to make sense of experience in the same way 'the writer voyages to understanding in, through, and by means of the writing'.[26]

More than simply a path to understanding, the personal essay allows us to share our own individual part of history that otherwise would be forgotten. The memoirist Patricia Hampl underscores the importance of this endeavour: 'in the act of remembering, the personal environment expands, resonates beyond itself, beyond its "subject", into the endless and tragic recollection that is history'.[27] The essays explored here radiate past their individual subjects to reflect a part of New Zealand history that might go unwitnessed. Each one of these migrants committed to my classes because, struck by the possibilities of the form, they wanted to write about their own experience. As Livingston, a Scottish doctor, wrote: 'Time, perhaps, for an essay.'

With its dynamic of writing as inquiry, the genre is ideal for documenting the experience of coming into a new country as a migrant. The personal essay takes what is solitary and individual – the writer's own thoughts, feelings, memories – and gives it permanence; but more than that, it shares its relevance. The tests of fortitude and perseverance recounted in the migrant essays mark the stages of the journey of the stranger who comes to town, and that testing is uniquely suited to the genre because 'the essay is the crucible in which personal experience is tried and tested, weighed and judged for its meaning and significance'.[28]

We can learn more about the effects of migration in the personal essay than are revealed in the broad strokes of policy and economics. Through their essays, migrants articulate an experience that is both

under-represented and inadequately researched: 'Personal essays
quite facilely mingle the creative with the critical, the subjective
with the objective, and the emotional with the analytical. For voices
of the marginalized, the previously silenced, this is perhaps the
most appropriate vehicle of expression.'[29] The recognition of being
marginalised, of being treated as other, of not having a voice or language,
is familiar to migrants, and the personal essays informing this book
share, in direct and moving prose, how and why these experiences
affected them. The essays remind us that it is individuals who migrate,
not policy, not economics. As English statistician Austin Bradford Hill so
aptly put it, 'statistics represent people with the tears wiped off'.[30] Migrant
essayists are the vulnerable observers of their own lives, even as I have
been the vulnerable observer of theirs in this work.

Through their essays we also see what the world looks like from the
vantage point of the stranger who comes to town. This awareness of
simultaneous dimensions of culture, setting and often language enriches
the migrant's world view, allowing (and sometimes forcing) the migrant
to see and appreciate more. Critical theorist Homi Bhabha argues that
'the truest eye may now belong to the migrant's double vision'.[31] While
that vision may not be objective or impartial, it is enlarged by its multiple
perspectives, and the personal essay is primed to capture this double
vision, an awareness of past and present, foreign and familiar, near
and distant, as it traces individual consciousness in writing. The essay
becomes a record of what is known and what is discovered in writing as
we 'locate the essay as that crossing between self and other, experience
and meaning, process and product, form and formlessness'.[32]

The journey of the stranger who comes to town also occurs at 'that
crossing between self and other', and it is this that makes the personal
essay a valid narrative to study in a globalised world. For how we accept
or reject others has consequences that are individual, national and
international, and all migrants experience being perceived as other.
More so than native inhabitants, migrants are aware of what it means
to cross frontiers of culture, landscape and language where they must
adapt to the world they encounter. What migrants learn in that contact

zone has consequences for them and for the host country, given that 'to experience any form of migration is to get a lesson in the importance of tolerating others' points of view. One might almost say that migration ought to be essential training for would-be democrats.'[33] Everything turns upon the mutual reception of self and other, of migrant and native. In short, migrant personal essays reflect those encounters in the contact zone.

In keeping with the importance of tolerance, Huang, a Taiwanese migrant, declared in one essay: 'I want to be a good Ambassador for my culture so that more Kiwis see a multicultural society as a blessing and not a curse.' She recognises that not all New Zealanders share her positive perception of a multicultural society. As Māori scholar Jo Smith points out, the relationship between Māori, Pākehā and migrants is problematic: 'the differences between collectivities within the settler state, including those of migrants, are never resolvable.'[34] While the other will always remain unwelcome to some, migrant essays charting the journey of the stranger who comes to town provide vital and important lessons in our collective humanity. They inscribe something that is both elemental and ethical in the encounter between self and other, namely, 'To recognize the Other is to give.'[35] Just as we give meaning to experience in the personal essay, we can give recognition to the other, and thereby connect to a world much larger than ourselves.

What self and other must give is a welcoming and an acceptance of the other's differences. The recognition of the other is what grounds and integrates migrants in their new country, and without that recognition migrants will remain strangers no matter how long they live there. Noki, a Dutch migrant in his sixties, succinctly said: 'So who and/or what we are is defined in our relationships with others.' Stranger, neighbour, colleague, friend, lover, these are the infinite shades of connection along the continuum of human relationship between self and other.

Migrant personal essays confirm Martin Buber's aphorism that 'all actual life is encounter.'[36] When the self recognises the other, that person sees him or herself as significant in the eyes of someone who is other to them, and the encounter becomes meaningful. We feel this exchange each time we forge a connection with someone or something, which is analogous to when we write and find resonance and correlation between disparate things. What the essay explores is 'the intimate and mysterious connection that exists between the known and the unknown, between the telegraphic attenuations of the names we give things, the descriptions we offer – superficial, partial – and the significance that's coiled intricately within them'.[37] Only the individual can find these hidden connections, the significance between the known and the unknown, by tapping into the deeper parallel world, the river under the river, that writing reaches. If self and other maintain their separate existence and never meet, then the chance for connection is lost, as is the possibility for meaning and significance in that which remains unwritten.

Migration is a complex and fraught experience, and the personal essay is well suited to capturing that experience, as 'actions or events that were inexplicable or obscure or emotionally laden in the moment become more clear, not just with time and reflection, but with the actual, physical process of writing'.[38] The personal essay reaches into what hooks the writer most deeply, something that Daisy, an Irish nurse, intuitively understood: 'It is as though,' she wrote in one of her essays, 'throughout life, here and there, we put down reef anchors and these little anchors dig in ever more deeply each time their line connects directly to a real time experience.'

The moment when our experience connects us to the writing is always charged for both writer and reader, again because this is the moment when self meets other. As Cixous explains: 'The origin of the material in writing can only be myself. I is not I, of course, because it is I with the others, coming from the others, putting me in the place of others, giving me the other's eyes. Which means there is something common.'[39] That recognition of what is common and shared, especially when it acknowledges the other, is at the centre of our humanity. This is one of the great powers of literature, and it underpins our desire for stories, both to write them and to read them.

The shared language of migration

When I first came to New Zealand I thought I was a veteran migrant. I had grown up in a military family and lived in Europe, the Caribbean and the US, moving every three years if not more often. A fellow conscripted child, Jennifer Sinor, observes: 'Military children pride themselves in their ability to recover from loss. They wear their relocations like badges, or scars.'[40] I was in my forties when my own children migrated to New Zealand with my husband and me. They were five and eight at the time. Five years later, multiple and devastating earthquakes shifted not only the city we were living in but our lives, forcing us to migrate to Sweden to ensure financial stability. Suddenly I found myself voiceless, stripped of much of what gave my life meaning: language and connection.

Sweden taught me the profound lesson of being both the vulnerable observer and the vulnerable participant. Submerged in a language I didn't understand, I shared what non-native language speakers experience when they migrate to a country. Twenty of the migrant writers who participated in this book are non-native English speakers and they all addressed the vital importance of language, something I took for granted when I lived in New Zealand and shared the dominant host language. Sweden redressed this critical oversight in my perception of what many migrants face when they migrate. In Sweden, language revealed itself to me in its core importance. As Argentinian writer Alberto Manguel reminds us: 'Language is our common denominator.'[41] But only if that language is understood. Language is the river that runs through and braids everything together, the life blood of culture and connection, contact and communication. Fluency is just that, the ability to flow with and within the language, immersed and yet buoyant. During our year and a half in Sweden I realised I would never be at home in Swedish the way I am in English.

Writing this narrative in my native language carried me through the sunless months in Sweden, but haltingly, as I struggled to express experiences that by their very nature the poet Rilke calls 'unsayable'.

Throughout this time my migrant writers upheld me on the current of their writing, by giving voice and concrete examples for what resists articulation: belonging, identity, connection. English is the second or third language for half of the 37 migrant writers who agreed to feature in this book, yet they chose to write in English. For them and for me, English was not only the common denominator linguistically, it was also the shared language of migration.

Migrants' search for meaning is initially challenged by a sense of dislocation. Their ways of making meaning have been disrupted from their daily landscape, affecting their relationships to people, place and, sometimes most drastically, language. They must learn what things mean – not just ordinary things in their day-to-day living, but subtle codes of behaviour that inform cultural assumptions. In their new country they must also learn to negotiate an entire world of language, culture and connection, matters both obvious and obscure. According to Eva Hoffman, who migrated as an adolescent from Poland to Canada:

> Every emigrant becomes a natural anthropologist, observing, more importantly sensing such nuances, and the minute but not insignificant differences in cultural modes of being; differences, which I believe, may extend not only to the social or relational modes of expression, but to the meanings we attach to internal states; to what Michel Foucault called *the practices of the self*.[42]

These practices of the self are deeply ingrained and not easy to apprehend. It takes years to learn how to live in another country, culture and language. Migrants become familiar over time with their host country and, as aspects of living there resonate and are understood, they begin to grasp increased shades of meaning. The more their new country has meaning and connection for them, the more migrants feel at home in it.

For some this process of acclimation is straightforward and swift, and for others it is difficult and protracted. The migrants in this profile offer an entire spectrum of acculturation, even while their essays display a pattern for what gives life meaning: people, place, work, identity, purpose. Through their personal essays, they were able to chart a journey towards what it means to belong, to have a place to stand, as they reflected on these practices of self. Their writing not only reveals why they moved away from everything grounded, familiar and dear to them – their roots, their language, their familiar social norms – but also articulates how migrants cope with the ongoing repercussions of migration.

'Home,' says essayist and travel writer Pico Iyer, 'is not just the place where you happen to be born, it's the place where you become yourself.'[43] Migrants understand home is not merely place-based. Home represents an entire nexus of associations, memories, thoughts and feelings from which we generate crucial meaning. Migration alters our context for meaning because it 'not only involve[s] leaving behind, crossing water, living amongst strangers, but, also, undoing the very meaning of the world'.[44] The personal essay gives migrants a place to find that meaning in writing and to address where they became or become themselves, and how, when and why.

When I began this book on the personal essay and migration to Aotearoa New Zealand, I had no idea two major earthquakes would wrench apart the city of Christchurch and our lives. We had been living in New Zealand for five years and I thought we were settled, but the restless tectonic plates under the 'Shaky Isles' would provide a radical lesson in displacement. In the wake of these natural disasters we migrated to Sweden, where we lost roots, language and familiar social norms. But we also learned what is essential to belong. The story of that journey is one many migrants share: the stranger who comes to town. Where the stranger or migrant is accepted, a new home may be made with a new sense of meaning and purpose. When that did not happen for our family in Sweden, we returned to New Zealand to step back into a river that branched off and rejoined itself – the braided river.

Strands of the braided river

Every migrant journey begins in the hidden headwaters of a story, and my exploration of migration and the personal essay started there. New

Zealand's braided rivers originate high in the mountains, seeping from snowmelt and rainwater, trickling under rocks until they become visible. Similarly, the story of migration begins long before a migrant arrives in a new country. Tracing the reasons why someone chose to migrate means travelling back, against the current, to the headwaters of the river, and acknowledges that 'roots always precede routes'.[45] When migrants apply Kierkegaard's maxim of living forwards but understanding backwards to their migrations, their essays yield unexpected results even to themselves, for often the set answer they give for migration has much older origins than they thought.

Where the river originates is one source of knowledge; where and how it flows, above or below ground, branching or meandering, is another source. As migrants use narrative to track who, where, when and what they experienced along the way, they rediscover their past and make sense of it. The route of migration plots the journey of the stranger who comes to town. Here is where self and other meet, migrant and native, routed meeting rooted. Migrants are people who have crossed thresholds and frontiers, barriers between self and other, and they inscribe that route in their writing. They are both stranger and other to one another, something the host country does not always recognise. The writer Eudora Welty never left the American South, but she acknowledged the importance of the stranger's perspective: 'It may be the stranger within the gates whose eye is smitten by the crucial thing, the essence of life, the moment or act in our long-familiar midst that will forever define it.'[46] More than ever we need fresh eyes to see new ways of being and belonging in a globalised world, and personal essays capture what happens at the critical threshold of self and other. Those who have crossed the distance may know how to close or at least narrow it.

For many migrants in New Zealand, distance is one of the most striking aspects of life in this country. Most of the world's land mass and population lies in the northern hemisphere, where it is always the opposite season and a different time of day. New Zealand's remoteness affects everything from its unique flora and fauna to its economics and history, as well as who has migrated to its shores. New Zealand's distance from where migrants originate remains constant, even though transportation and communication have improved and become more affordable since the days of shipboard passage. How the migrants from my classes coped or were coping with the geographical, temporal and emotional distance of living here was a telling feature of their writing. Their essays demonstrate that distance attenuates and changes migrants' relationships to the people and the places where they were once known, familiar and belonged.

Belonging is the most elemental of human needs and the one most severely challenged by migration. Professor Brené Brown, who studies courage, vulnerability and empathy, observes: 'Connection is why we're here. We are hardwired to connect with others, it's what gives purpose and meaning to our lives, and without it there is suffering.'[47] Migration ruptures or stretches the connections to what matters most to humans: people, place, language, culture, the innumerable ties that bind us to the world. Migrants must find a way to connect, to understand and be understood in their new country, and in their essays we see them face this ongoing challenge. For me, living in Sweden threw the need for understanding and belonging into startling and painful relief, far more so than my time in New Zealand ever has. My sense of estrangement and displacement in Sweden was deeper than not sharing the language, and I finally understood that belonging is the river under the river, the force that gives meaning to our being here on earth.

Belonging is concrete and essential, not an abstraction, and our need to belong, to connect with others, is fundamental to who we are. Migrants must have meaningful contact and connection in the country where they live or they remain a stranger, forever other and outside the dominant culture. Migrants understand experientially what it is to perceive and be perceived as other, to feel welcome or not, and their essays offer eloquent testimony for what constitutes belonging: 'the personal essay turns out to be one of the most useful instruments with which outsiders can reach the dominant culture quickly and forcefully and testify to the precise ambiguities of their situation as individuals and group members.'[48] Understanding that dynamic between the dominant culture and the outsider is why migration must be studied from within the contact zone of self and other, the point of contact and conflict, on individual, national and global levels.

Migration influences and changes who migrants are, how they perceive and are perceived. An essential question relevant to everyone, migrant or not, is 'Who am I?' Identity and identification are at the crux of nation, migration and self. Identity is a problematic concept, yet it is rooted and routed in place and challenged by the displacement of migration. The process of identifying is where we forge connection and find meaning, and identity constellates around whether we belong or not. This question of who we are pulses at the most inarticulate level of our being, but it also causes the most tension, both internally and externally. Here is where the current of belonging joins the current of self-understanding; indeed, they are always entwined.

Migrants wrestle daily with problems of identity based on ethnicity, class, language, culture and any markers used to differentiate them as other. Where does acceptance begin? With ourselves or with others? The migrant personal essay makes it possible to explore these and related questions of acceptance and integration and to provide examples of negotiating this charged ground where questions of identity and belonging are posed, contested and answered. By looking back on their lives in writing, migrants present a way forward in a globalised world where, more than at any other time in history, people are able or are being forced to migrate.

The personal essay is one of the most effective tools available to inquire into the human condition, driven as it is by the all-embracing question '*Que sais-je?*', which Montaigne infused the form with from the outset. Yet even as the genre is rooted in individual consciousness, it moves outward to explore and connect with the world. The importance of connection to our lives and in writing cannot be underestimated. Connection is where we create meaning in the world and on the page. What the personal essays of migrants reify is how those connections are formed – where, when, with whom and why – and where they are not. The genre of the personal essay is the proving ground between migrants, their past experiences and their present selves. By exploring the encounter between self and other, migrant writers let us see the lived experience.

This book, then, is the story of strangers who came to town, who set out on a journey to be tried and tested by a new country, even as the essay tries and tests experience for its meaning. In the personal essay we see how 'the core of writing requires something that is very vulnerably personal, and yet at the same time very communal'.[49] Our willingness to be vulnerable in the essay and with one another is what creates an authentic connection between individuals. Perhaps there is no more important lesson than this willingness to trust in the difficult, something life and writing have always demanded of human beings.

The migrant's journey is that of an ordinary hero who leaves home to learn what it means to belong somewhere else or to fail in the undertaking. These migrant essays trace the root and route of that courage, of which migrants themselves may be unaware. Thanks to the remarkable individuals who shared their stories with mine, I can map the braided river of migration in our texts to find a way through both the interwoven surface channels that branch off and rejoin, and the deep, wide, subterranean river that few see until it is written. Long after the river of our lives empties into the sea, the personal essay resonates with the deeper story, the river under the river, the story only the individual can tell.

Chapter 1

Roots –
The River Under the River

*'Lucky is he who has been able to understand
the causes of things.'*

—VIRGIL, *Georgics*, BOOK 2

A small red postage stamp of Marco Polo is affixed to my Italian birth certificate: the mark of the traveller who returns, years later. The stamp fascinated me as a child. My parents collected stamps, but this stamp was out of place, not on an envelope or in a stamp album. Already my migrant identity appeared to be manifesting, the outsider in the family with Marco Polo and Italian documentation to prove it. I was born into the tribe of military nomads and before the age of 13 had lived in Italy, Texas, the Dominican Republic, Belgium, Missouri and New Mexico. I could speak Spanish and French because I had to, but the languages fell away when I no longer needed them. Yet I feel these languages deep within my memory when I hear them spoken, and my accent is good because I learned to speak them as a child. Spanish is a language of sunlight, heat, wide Caribbean skies, our Dominican housemaid killing a tarantula with a mop. French is overcast, grey, alone on an empty playground, the school buses long gone. But that is not where the story begins – the story begins long before we have our own words for it. As Italian philosopher Adriana Cavarero recognises: 'It is necessary to go back to the narration told by others, in order for the story to begin where it really began.'[1] The roots of migration always precede the route, and my roots were fiddle-footed from the beginning.

My migration began when my parents left their small Midwestern towns in the 1950s for the wider worlds of West Point and the university. My father originally wanted to join the navy, 'to see the world', but an older high-school classmate, seduced by the same dream, persuaded him to join the army instead, saying he would see his family more. My father used to sing, 'I joined the navy to see the world, what did I see, I saw the sea.' Clearly, he felt his more land-based choice was the right one. Intrepid for her generation, my mother spent a semester at the University of Puerto Rico to improve her Spanish, studying abroad when young Latina women did not leave the house unchaperoned. The blonde *gringa* got whistles and catcalls from the Puerto Rican men and dated US naval officers in blinding white uniforms on shore leave in San Juan.

My parents met at a party in Georgetown, the cosmopolitan heart of the nation's capital and about as far from their working-class roots as imaginable. The Korean War intervened, and they wrote letters. When my father returned from Korea, he gave my mother a strand of Mikimoto pearls and asked her to marry him. She is wearing them in the silvery black-and-white wedding photos where she radiates joy beside my father in his dress uniform. Her choice to marry him was deliberate. She didn't want to work outside the home, having worked her way through high school and university, and she wanted her children to be army brats because she believed they were at home anywhere in the world – one of the great fictions. She will follow his military career all over the world, and we three children will also trail in this wake. Because we moved so often in my childhood, at least every three years following my father's tours of duty, I craved roots and ended up in an unlikely location, the Midwest, for university. In hindsight, I realise I returned to the part of the country where my parents originated and to which they never returned, except to visit, homing in on their home, as it were.

The man I always thought I would marry joined the Marine Corps, a fiercer military tribe than the army whose mission, as he once put it, was 'killing people'. He sent me a strand of Mikimoto pearls he bought in Okinawa, an island saturated with World War II dead. 'You can't keep them,' my Midwestern boyfriend of the time said.

'Why not?'

'Because you live with me.'

For the time being, I thought. I reluctantly sent the pearls back. In a letter that followed the Marine told me he was getting married that summer in Sweden. I couldn't believe he was marrying someone else, a Swede no less. Seven years later I married the Midwesterner, thinking if I joined a rooted family – a family who had lived in the same place with their extended clan all around them – I would grow roots myself. But perhaps a frequently transplanted army brat cannot grow roots, or perhaps, like the banyan tree, my roots are up in the air, or perhaps people are home to me, not place.

When I was 33 my mother died and my life started over. The Marine and I divorced our spouses and I moved to Sweden to be with him. This was my first experience of love being the force behind my own migration. In my own silvery black-and-white wedding photos I wear the strand of Mikimoto pearls he gave me, the two of us standing on the windward side of O`ahu, halfway to New Zealand, the place we will come to in eight years' time. I can see now how my choice of partner became the root of movement, just as my father was throughout my childhood.

I have heard there are two kinds of army brats. Those who settle and never leave, and those who continue to move. Of my siblings, I'm the only one who continues to move, and my serial migrations seem to originate with my peripatetic upbringing and choice of partner. I'm also the only one in my family to have attended school in another language – French in my case. For migrants, 'roots always precede routes',[2] and our roots often propel us, as Ghassan Hage observes: 'to see one's ancestors, one's nation, one's community as only part of a route we are on rather than also part of our roots is a denial of their nurturing and propelling power'.[3] Both my parents left home, never to return, often living overseas, setting a precedent I would follow. The roots of my migration thus originated long before my subsequent moves all over the world, and I expect this is what many other migrants recognise when they explore their own narrative journeys.

Given that so few people voluntarily migrate, something must drive the choice to leave. The obvious answers people give for why they migrate – for work, for love, for family – can be gleaned in any survey, but what initially sets migration in motion often receives little attention, in part because it is difficult to apprehend or is ignored. The personal essay, with its inherent method of inquiry, grasps the elusive, deep-seated aspects of migration and 'allows glimpses into the lived interior of migration experience ... But it is more than this, for the individual experience is always richer, more contradictory, more than that which we represent as the experience of a group.'[4] By asking migrants to explore the root causes of their migration, we get answers only they can provide, driven by 'the lived interior' of their personal narratives. The answers often surprise them, as they realise that a few degrees in either direction and their entire life course could have been different. The personal essay allows them to determine if 'the events and accidents of life add up to a coherent story. That is every migrant's question.'[5] Writing lets migrants track that question past the surface narrative to channels known only to themselves, to find the river under the river.

'Migrations within living memory'

Our life's narrative has many strands, with most of its structure hidden well below the surface features. Adriana Cavarero points out that discerning one's life design is possible through narrative: 'The meaning that saves each life from being a mere sequence of events does not consist in a determined figure; but rather consists in leaving behind a figure, or something from which the unity of a design can be discerned in the telling of a story. Like the design, the story comes after the events and the actions from which it results.'[6] The personal essay offers us a way to look back and dig down past 'a mere sequence of events' to see the design inherent in the course of a life that may not be recognised. By stepping back from our lives and writing about them, we come to understand how chance, choice and the myriad other factors contribute to our life stories, for 'to live and understand fully, we need not only proximity, but also distance. This writing provides for consciousness as nothing else does.'[7] Migrants writing the personal essay can explore the real reason they undertook the journey of the stranger who comes to town.

For many migrants, the roots of their leaving their country lie buried in memory and because memory, is singularly our own, only the individual can trace memory back to its source and follow the wayward discursive flow of all that happens in a given lifetime. Memory and narrative are inextricably linked; indeed, our brain seems hardwired for it: 'The narratable self finds itself at home, not simply in a conscious exercise of remembering, but in the spontaneous narrating structure of memory itself.'[8] Because we remember our lives in stories, anecdotes, images – the infinite array of all that has happened to us – our sense of self is intimately linked to what we remember. The personal essay bears singular witness to what happens in an individual lifetime, tapping into the innumerable contents of memory. The writer can look back and see how experiences and artefacts that seem random and disconnected actually fit together. As Irish philosopher John O'Donohue reminds us: 'You cannot de-sequence your life. The structure of your life holds together. This is the unnoticed miracle of memory; it is the intimate mirror of the continuity of your experience and presence.'[9]

Few genres capture 'the intimate mirror' of our experience and presence better than the personal essay. The diary and letter serve a similar function, but their audiences are limited. In the personal essay 'the writer is acutely conscious of the reader and of having an audience that is an active part of the intellectual and emotional process'.[10] Acknowledging the audience as an active part of the writing process changes the dynamic of the exchange and opens the essay out to the other. The meaning derived from personal experience in the essay is not simply for the individual but is influenced by an awareness of the writing's larger import and implications, thus underscoring the importance of the genre for wider study.

The migrant writers featured in this book were keen to reach an audience through their writing – to give voice to what often gets overlooked in migration studies. American writer and activist Susan Sontag recognised that 'The influential essayist is someone with an acute sense of what has not been (properly) talked about, what should be talked about (but differently).'[11] The migrants all shared an acute sense that migration demands exploration from the perspective of those who understand the vicissitudes and rewards of the journey. Their essays stem directly from their own lives, providing the human context for what is so frequently seen in abstract terms: 'When we study migration rather than abstract cultural flows and representations, we see that transnational processes are located within the life experience of individuals and families, making up the warp and woof of daily activities, concerns, fears, and achievements.'[12] The migrants' essays testify to the 'daily activities, concerns, fears and achievements' that have informed their lives since they migrated.

In an interview based on his own migration experience from India to England, Homi Bhabha addressed the significance of studying migrant life stories:

> We're talking about migrations within living memory. And I think one cannot stress enough two things. One is the specificity of particular experiences. The other is the need to theorize narrative and identity, to try to make that theoretical work deal with the very specific configuration and conjunction of different cultural and social elements ... because life stories display that very particular weave of elements of lives lived iteratively, lives lived interstitially, and challenge those, like myself, who are interested in a theoretical understanding of these processes; they challenge us to think beyond what our concepts enable us to do.[13]

By foregrounding this particular weave of 'lives lived iteratively, lives lived interstitially', migrant personal essays offer a unique opportunity to contribute to the theory of narrative and identity, particularly migrant identity.

The personal essay bears the stamp of the individual's thoughts and reflections about the migration experience and tells a story about why and how that experience unfolded. That story is uniquely the migrant's own, and the personal essay articulates matters only the individual writer can. According to essayist Nancy Mairs, 'we are each the stories we tell ourselves about ourselves, and no one of us can authentically tell another's story.'[14] The experiences distilled in the over 200 personal essays I've read provide a wealth of narrative through which to explore Homi Bhabha's 'very particular weave' of 'migrations within living memory'.

Like the headwaters of a river, hidden underground until the river surfaces, the roots of migration remain hidden until the personal essay's line of inquiry discloses them. In tracing the origins of their respective migrations, migrants discover the individual and invisible channels that brought them to a country. The inextricable link between memory and narrative reveals that which eludes larger drift-nets of analysis, thanks in part to the nature of memory: 'Memory is attention which endures, which envisions both backwards and forwards, which can shine upon deep recesses filled and perhaps half-forgotten long ago; it is made up of intuitions, as well as representations, feelings perhaps but faintly perceived, odors, sights, sounds, hesitancies, judgments – all thoughts that go into the making up of mind.'[15] For migrants, it is this digging down into their own memories that reveals what led them to live elsewhere.

Narrative also provides this opportunity to look both forwards and back in memory: only by looking back on our past can we understand how we arrived in the present. Narrative is critical to our sense of lived time because it helps us bind memory and history. As French philosopher Paul Ricoeur said: 'Time becomes human to the extent that it is articulated through a narrative mode.'[16] Because the personal essay makes it possible not only to remember but also to recognise, it allows us to grasp in writing what we did not understand at the time events occurred. Through the essay, the writer discovers what the experience meant: 'In the essay, experience is weighed and assayed for its value and meaning, which derive from reflection, meditation, or contemplation.'[17] For migrants, the personal essay uncovers how the root led to the route; it lets them investigate and detail how their respective migration journeys were set in motion long before they left their countries of origin. The surface narrative tells one story, but the depths reveal where the story – the journey – began.

In my own migration narrative the convergence of two people – my parents, who left home for the greater world embodied by the university and the military – led to a constant uprooting and instilled in me a restless quest for where I belong. Given this ceaseless movement over four decades, spanning two continents, two hemispheres, five countries, and seven different states in the US, never staying more than seven years in one place, it's not surprising that I'm drawn to study migration, and to study it in a way, namely writing, that allows me to ground my sense of self and my world. Julia Creet argues that 'migration rather than location is the condition of memory. Between times, places, generations, and media, from individuals to communities and vice versa, movement is what produces memory – and our anxieties about pinning it to a place.'[18] But what if instead of pinning memory to a place, we followed its course as we would follow a braided river, above and below ground, the channels separating and joining, flowing to a destination we cannot foresee? For this is the movement of the personal essay as well, exploring experience for its meaning, with its unexpected sparkle of revelation.

More than any other genre the personal essay addresses the individual meaning and experience apparent in the narrative because we can explore the story that is singularly our own. Through the act of writing we can capture what is fluid and moving in our lives, and 'in telling the story of who we are, we tell the story of where we have stood. While place is important, it is narrative that makes place possible.'[19] For migrants, place is not static as it is for those who never leave their home ground. Migrants shift place and landscape, and perhaps linguistic landscape as well, often radically, but migration does not negate the reality of having stood somewhere previously. Indeed, this reality gives migrants an ability to see things people with long-established roots rarely see. This awareness is of the kind described by the Polish social theorist Zygmunt Bauman: 'Rather than homelessness, the trick is to be at home in many homes, to be in each inside and outside at the same time, to combine intimacy with the critical look of an outsider, involvement with detachment – a trick which sedentary people are unlikely to learn.'[20] This inside/outside, involvement/detachment, is particularly well suited to the migrant personal essay, with its insider perspective of the stranger who came to town and perhaps made their home there.

The story of migration thus invokes the two master narratives: the stranger who comes to town and the person who goes on a journey.

But something sets the stranger on their way, long before they arrive in their new country – and that deeper story underlies all the set narratives migrants tell for why they came to that country. Given that who we are and where we start from will have ongoing repercussions for where we end up, narrative lets those of us who are migrants search as far back into our memories as we can or want to. From there, we can trace our coming to the new country and thereby reveal the origin and shape of the journey, for 'what is interesting in migration studies is the stories people tell about their trajectory. Because migration is always a journey.'[21]

By using narrative to look past our stock answers for leaving – for work, our partner, our family – we begin to realise and understand that deeper currents carried us forward. Too often the route overlays the root, obscuring it, such that our personal past 'may have been buried under a clichéd set of tag-memories or covered by a slick pattern of familiarity. The work of recovery – the cultivation of reveries – counters the dominance of sheer change, which is our shibboleth, and ultimately our bugaboo.'[22] We cannot halt the flow of our lives, but if we try we can step into that river and write about it, reaching past what is familiar and readily told to what shimmers forth onto the page from the depths of our experience and gives it meaning.

Our story begins where we do, in a certain place and time. '[T]he story of one's life,' writes Adriana Cavarero, 'always begins where that life begins';[23] with migrants, the story always begins elsewhere. Migrant narratives originate in another country, another culture and perhaps another language. The essayist can trace those roots across both time and space. Where we've been informs where we are now, and in the personal essay 'memories of space traversed and time spent are conflated and brought to bear on the present in a highly personal, idiosyncratic manner.'[24] As migrants, we can tell our story from different vantage points, depending upon the age we were when we migrated and the age at which we write about our experiences. Where we step in the river, whether early or late in our lives, determines how much time has elapsed between our past and present selves. Accordingly, in our essays, we can step into a new place in the narrative and 'use the vantage point of the present to gain access to what might be called the hidden narrative of the past. Each is, in its own way, an account of detection, a realized effort to assemble the puzzle of what happened in the light of subsequent realization.'[25] By inquiring into the roots of our own migrations, we discover and reveal these hidden narratives of the past, the very things that slip through the larger categories of analysis applied to migration – history, politics, economics. From among the Heraclitan drift of image, emotion and memory, the essayist sees the associative, nonsequential connections that do not appear in surface narratives but in the writing where meaning manifests.

The search for meaning is central to human existence. The personal essay is ideally suited to this purpose because 'the impulse to write essays, as to tell stories, grows consistently out of a single source: the individual confrontation with the hard facts and particularities of the world – of place, of any aspect of life – and the resulting effort of the imagination to seek meaning in what it confronts.'[26] By interpreting 'the hard facts and particularities of the world' migrants have a means not only of drawing deeper significance from the journey that began long before they set out for a new country, but also of sharing that with others.

What we remember matters to us as individuals and to all of us collectively: 'memory, tempered by human feeling, is what allows humans to imagine both individual well-being and the compounded well-being of a whole society, and to invent ways and means of achieving and magnifying that well-being.'[27] The intersection of narrative and memory therefore has an ethical component, which perhaps partially explains why societies have always used stories as a form of instruction and illumination that implicitly asks, as the Inuit do, how does the story help? The story of migration is one of the oldest ones available to us. Whether a person goes on a journey or a stranger comes to town, what happens in the resulting contact zone has individual and global consequences for self and other.

The beauty of the pāua

The real question behind the roots of migration is, in essence, why are you here? It's a question asked, in one form or another, of every stranger who comes to town. To be asked 'Where are you from?', as migrants often are, even decades after their arrival, is to suggest, rightly or wrongly, that one is not from here, wherever 'here' is in the world. Exploring the roots of her own migration, Amelia, an Englishwoman in her fifties who married a New Zealander, opened her essay with a memory:

> As an eight-year-old in suburban London I received a gift, a bracelet. A silver bracelet with seven paua shell hearts attached. My uncle and family had travelled to New Zealand by boat for a holiday and returned with gifts for us all. The beauty of the paua, its colour and iridescence, fascinated me. Seashells from our British seaside holidays were dull in comparison. Was this the start of my journey to New Zealand where I now live? Or was it a secondhand book entitled *A Young Traveller in New Zealand* that I bought at a church fair on 10th February 1968 when I was ten that fostered the dream?

Amelia's words exemplify how the personal essay serves us best, by helping us to wrestle with questions and strive to answer them: in Amelia's case, what fostered the dream?

Amelia's older, migrated self reflects back 40 years to when she was eight and was given a pāua-shell bracelet. That memory in turn has her wondering if the bracelet led to her buying the book about New Zealand two years later. Her thoughts about the significance of the bracelet and the book exemplify the 'realized effort to assemble the puzzle of what happened in light of subsequent realization'.[28] Would she have connected these two images had she not asked: 'How did I get here?' What is striking in her opening paragraph is the specificity of the details: seven pāua-shell hearts on the bracelet and the inscription of the date when she bought the book. These two isolated but distinctive details are the first images she selects as portents of her coming to New Zealand, even though both predated her arrival by decades. As with the red postage stamp of Marco Polo on my birth certificate, only the individual can be privy to such disparate details and therefore able to connect the significance of these stray artefacts.

The personal essay forges connections that would otherwise be missed, and the writing is both creative and constructive because the specific details are not decorative but illustrative. They are pieces of a puzzle that make up the larger life narrative. The significance of the bracelet and the travel book could not occur to Amelia at the time she acquired them, for narrative – and perhaps understanding – is always retrospective. We cannot know what things will mean to us later. This facet is one of the perishing and marvellous qualities about life – its evanescence and strange ability to become resonant after the fact, especially in the personal essay: 'The essayist thoughtfully scrutinizes the world, drawing out significances which until then may never have been clearly seen or fully understood, creating and explaining new artifacts of intelligence through the alchemy of mind and words.'[29] Amelia understood this alchemy implicitly when she wrote in a later essay: 'We have a love affair with memories, tastes and sensations from the past. They are the very essence of our being. They travel with us globally and edge our daily existence. The best of the past sustains us and fuels our daily life.'

Our past is elemental to who and where we are in the present, as T.S. Eliot understood: 'Time past and time future / What might have been and what has been / Point to one end, which is always present.'[30] For migrants, the past leads to a future elsewhere: the pāua-shell bracelet and the *A Young Traveller in New Zealand* become harbingers of the journey taken but are understood as such only in hindsight. Amelia herself questions the connection: 'Was this the start of my journey to New Zealand where I now live?' But she remembers that compared to the dull seashells she found on her holidays in England: 'the beauty of the paua; its colour and iridescence fascinated me'. New Zealand, by extension, looks far more alluring in the eyes of Amelia the child. The pāua shell embodies a far way place whose fascination pulls her attention across decades, long before New Zealand becomes a reality.

From the bracelet, Amelia segues to meeting her future Kiwi husband in London 15 years later, a fluke she remarks on: 'One in a million?' We cannot underestimate the effect of love upon where we end up in the world. Russell King argues that 'love migration can probably be found in all types of migration.'[31] Over half the migrants featured in this book came to New Zealand because of their choice of partner. Unlike many migrant spouses, especially those who came in the two decades following World War II, Amelia was able to visit New Zealand before she moved there. She admits that 'a trip to New Zealand in December whetted … [her] appetite for this amazing country' and that she 'was wooed by Mount Cook', conflating her fiancé with the landscape perhaps.

In the 10 years prior to migrating to New Zealand Amelia and her husband lived in Gabon, the Netherlands, Australia and Syria, enjoying a luxurious expatriate lifestyle thanks to his work: '… living in hotels, lounging by pools, having a driver, business class air travel round the world up to three times each year. We asked ourselves, "What would life be like in the real world?" We had always agreed that we did not want the children to grow up as "Ex-Pats". Friends' children were always asking, "Where do you come from?"' And there it is, the idea of origin being essential to who we are and who we will become.

For migrants, the decision of where to raise their children has repercussions that extend beyond their own lives. Many New Zealanders who marry partners from overseas wish to raise their children back in New Zealand, and the collective belief, real or imagined, is that New Zealand is a wonderful place to grow up. This belief, however, is tested by what migrants experience in the new country.

When we first arrived in New Zealand in 2007 with our children aged five and eight, I couldn't see how this might be a better place for them to grow up. The reality of my daily life challenged the migrant trope that the new country will be better than the old one. Jobless, freezing in our Christchurch rental home and alone all day, I had ample time to focus on what was missing in New Zealand, rather than seeing what is here. Then I became parent help in my children's school, a school that boasted students from over 50 countries, thanks to the rich pool of parents working at the university, all mixed in with Kiwi kids. I listened to fledgling readers make their first flight off the page and helped twist Giacometti-inspired sculptures out of baling wire covered with aluminium foil. While I could see my children were thriving in New Zealand, I could not yet accept living here.

Only when I began teaching community education courses in the personal essay did I begin to have my own sense of connection and purpose. My students, both migrants and New Zealanders, fostered my appreciation for this country, and I began to write about migration to this far-flung land. And then, as though to test our resolve for being here, the earthquakes struck. A natural disaster with hundreds of ongoing aftershocks showed the mettle, generosity and fortitude of a people, and I felt bonded to this place. But then my husband's job became as unstable as the earth beneath our feet and we were forced to move to Sweden. The irony of this tectonic shift in perspective was both telling and powerful. Sweden threw migration into startling relief and would be 'the great teacher we have been saying we want. "No not this teacher!" we shriek. We want a different one. Too bad. This is the teacher everyone gets.'[32] I had been paddling in the shallow end and now found myself in cold, deep water, grappling anew with the loss of roots, cultural norms and a new and primal loss, language. What I could not know in those sunless months was that Sweden was not the end of the journey. What an unexpected gift our return to New Zealand was – a chance for me to see what is here and to embrace it.

Initially, my husband was the driver for our coming to New Zealand. He believed our children would have more opportunity there, more of a sense of possibility than the United States offered. I didn't share this vision when I first came here in 2007, but when we returned to New Zealand in 2013 I could appreciate how prescient his decision was. For our two children, New Zealand *has* been a good place to grow up. I experienced this first-hand during my daughter's school camp as I watched her try all sorts of mad Kiwi outdoor pursuits. What parent would not want her child to grow up in a country that teaches her how to navigate in the bush, cook on a campfire, build a bivouac, splint a broken limb, zip down a flying fox, shoot arrows, climb over obstacles, swim, kayak and abseil, all in the spirit of helping others and 'giving it a go'? Love-driven migration thus pertains not only to love of partners but also to love of children, and many migrants choose to leave their country of origin to provide a better future for their children. Maartje, a Dutch migrant who came with her family in 1963, acknowledged her parents in this regard: 'They came here to become Kiwis and give their children a better life, and I for one seized it with both hands.' Mary, a Scottish psychotherapist, echoed this idea 50 years later when she and her husband shared 'a desire for our son to live his early years in the carefree moment and learn life skills in a fine little country'.

For migrants with children, the timing of their migration can be quite sensitive. The older we are when we migrate, the more we're rooted in the language, culture and place from whence we came. Having disrupted our 13-year-old son by moving him to Sweden after the Christchurch earthquakes, I can testify to the disastrous effect of this on all fronts. He became depressed and withdrawn. The sunny, outgoing youth chosen to speak at his high school's open day to prospective students and their parents was gone. I understood why Amelia and her husband, with a newborn daughter and two young sons under the age of six, felt pressure to decide whether they were going to continue to 'live all over the world', much as I did growing up, or settle in New Zealand. She describes the tension of weighing the pros and cons of the decision:

> In the dark cold nights following our daughter's birth we were challenged almost beyond human tolerance. Do we return to Damascus or accept the job we had been offered in New Zealand? My parents watched helplessly the agonies we went through. Salary, housing, medical care, annual around the world trips, job satisfaction, lifestyle, family in [the] UK, family in New Zealand. The cries and demands of a new baby and two lively boys added to the noise in my head.

Although Amelia lists the competing claims of each job, she does not state what tipped the balance in favour of New Zealand. But then she does not need to, as the ultimate weight of the decision had been determined years earlier: 'We had always agreed that we did not want the children to grow up as "Ex-Pats".' The desire for roots for their own children is what led them across the world to plant them.

In a wonderful coincidence, the six-week-old baby they bring to New Zealand in 1995 is christened with water poured from a pāua shell and grows up to read and enjoy the second-hand book her mother bought, which had 'survived the travels and cullings of possessions that … occurred with every move'. But perhaps the most telling use of the extended metaphor of the pāua bracelet appears at the end of Amelia's essay: 'The bracelet has a missing heart. I believe it symbolically remains in the UK where part of me still resides.' With the missing heart, the writer finds meaning in something that could have seemed inconsequential to anyone else: a child's bracelet. As Patricia Hampl observes: 'We find in our details and broken, obscured images, the language of symbol.'[33] Amelia might not have understood the bracelet's symbolism until she began writing and seized on that one image from amidst her memories. She titled her essay 'Paua Power', recognising in retrospect the enduring power of love to determine our lives in ways we can never anticipate.

Both Amelia and her husband made sacrifices when they migrated for their children's sake. Her husband relinquished his lucrative career as an engineer and incurred his family's disapproval by returning to New Zealand. Amelia gave up her native country and regular contact with her own family. By sacrificing his route to financial success and her roots to place, they ensured their children would have both – roots and routes. As Rockwell Gray cautions: '… mobile and other-directed as many of us are, we tend to confuse our identities with our itineraries or our ascent on some professional ladder of success. When the lack of deep connection to a place and its traditions forces us to ask where we actually are, we are asking who we are.'[34] To offset the potential for the uprooted identity of expatriates, Amelia and her husband provided their children with a stable upbringing in New Zealand, where they flourished as a result. Neither she nor her husband could have known in 1995 how any of this would turn out. Only years later can they see the result of migrating to New Zealand, which she acknowledges: 'The children are freer and their endeavours get recognised more readily.'

Amelia's story reveals its design after the fact, an idea maintained by Adriana Cavarero. We can discern a pattern from a mere sequence of events when we follow the deeper narrative. Amelia's childhood fascination with other and elsewhere led to her being an *au pair* in France when she was 18, to her choice of a New Zealand partner at 25, to following him all over the world for 10 years, to finally settling in New Zealand. We can trace the trajectory of that journey through the pāua shell as well: from the pāua bracelet brought back as a gift from New Zealand, to the pāua shell christening a new life both literally and figuratively in the chosen country, to the missing heart she believes remains in the UK. The missing pāua heart emblemises the torn allegiance many migrants experience when they are split between countries, where some part of them remains 'back' there. Amelia's essay reveals how seemingly random and incidental moments in her own life – a comparison between the iridescent pāua and the dull English seashells – can lead to a Kierkegaardian realisation that life is lived forwards but understood backwards. We see how the individual roots of migration are subtler and more far-reaching than 'I married a Kiwi', and that the design inherent in Amelia's life becomes visible thanks to her tracing these deeper roots in the personal essay.

A stranger in my own town

The roots of migration are often set in motion by choices made for us, not by us, as is the case when children are sent away to boarding school. Older migrants who look back over 40 or 50 years can see how these early influences of education affected their migration. What one misses when forced to leave home can inform an entire life in a search to recreate what that first loss embodied. Hugh, an Irish doctor in his sixties who has lived in New Zealand for over a decade and is the son of migrant doctors in Northern Ireland, recalled his childhood in his essay:

> I had a very happy childhood and can still remember extraordinary details of the house and garden where I played with my younger brother and friends. In particular, I remember a colourful cherry tree, which doubled as a goalpost as well as various other sporting landmarks in the fertile imagination of a child.
>
> At the age of nine, it all changed rather unexpectedly when I was bundled off to boarding school in Belfast some forty miles away – my first forced

migration. This was just another adventure at first and I went willingly, but it gradually turned into a nightmare when I realised it was a long term arrangement which was to last for eight years. Only getting home several times a year for holidays, I soon lost touch with all my friends and I ended up becoming a stranger in my own town. Apart from seeing family and enjoying home cooking, homecoming was a mixed experience. By mid teens, I felt a bit like a displaced person with no fixed abode and roots that were withering by the year.

This initial loss of home determines the next 40 years of Hugh's life. He applies the migration metaphor to his own childhood, comparing being 'bundled off to boarding school' at age nine to a 'forced migration'. These words might seem like hyperbole, especially when the International Association for the Study of Forced Migration defines that term as people 'forced to migrate due to persecution, to flee war, to escape famine, or because of a major development project'.[35] He is none of these, and yet feels 'bundled off' like a package to an unknown destination, an occurrence that for him is not dissimilar to forced migration and is therefore indicative of his own lack of agency or control. The distance of 40 miles (63km) from home was enough to turn what might have been an adventure into a 'nightmare' when he realised it was a long-term arrangement about which he had no choice.

In the intervening eight years, with only occasional visits home during holidays, Hugh loses touch with all his friends and 'becomes a stranger in his own town', an experience that mirrors what migrants often feel when they arrive in a new country. The words that are most revealing, though, are those he uses when he returns to the migration metaphor: 'I felt a bit like a displaced person with no fixed abode and roots that were withering by the year.' He feels displaced in the very location we would expect him not to be – home. We cannot underestimate how integral place is to our sense of belonging, since one 'of the vital criteria of personal integrity is whether you belong in your own life or not'.[36] Eight years at boarding school eroded Hugh's feeling of belonging when he was home, and that sense of displacement sets his future migrations in motion.

Uprooting seems to lead to a strong desire for roots of one's own, or to keep moving. When budding migrant Hugh can choose for himself, can exercise agency, at age 17, he seizes the opportunity: 'I was ripe for my second (voluntary) migration, and, when I was offered a place at medical school in Edinburgh, I jumped at it. An opportunity to start a new life in a new country with new friends and freedom to shape my own life for once.' What is telling is the parentheses around the word 'voluntary', because they emphasise that the first migration to boarding school was not. For Hugh, like many migrants, the idea of a fresh start in a new place is a major draw, but the freedom to shape his own life is what gave the real impetus to his decision to seize the opportunity. The Jungian analyst Clarissa Pinkola Estés argues that the feeling of exile 'makes us yearn that much more to free our own true nature and causes us to long for a culture to match'.[37] We see how the initial loss of home sets the stranger on his way. Having been uprooted once, Hugh understands how moving elsewhere becomes not only possible but also attractive.

Now with a wife and three children, Hugh has been living in Scotland for 15 years when he becomes restless again: 'The path on which I had set myself was not proving as nourishing or rewarding as I had hoped or expected.' He invokes the journey motif – 'the path on which I had set myself' – but the indirect and passive phrasing indicates a lack of agency. Hugh's younger brother, also a doctor, has meanwhile migrated to New Zealand, having 'fought his own demons and fled to the furthest point on earth to escape them'. New Zealand as a place to start over is a common theme in the migrant essays. Inspired by his brother's tales of a new life in a new country, Hugh arranges a job exchange in New Zealand for six months, and the sojourn prompts him to begin again, just as when he left boarding school for medical school.

Hugh is in his late forties when he decides to change course by moving his family to New Zealand:

> I discovered that life didn't have to be as I was living it at the time, and, if I was willing to look over the other side of the mountain, or lose sight of the land and take a bit of a risk, there was a whole other world out there which was both exciting and stimulating again. Sure, there were new challenges and new skills to be learnt, but sometimes one needs something radical to shake you out of your comfort zone and re-awaken that spirit of adventure

and self discovery that always accompanies a migrant when he starts a new life.

Reminiscent of Joseph Campbell, who reminds us that the hero who resists the call spends the rest of his life in boredom and dread, Hugh urges the reader to set off on the journey of the universal migrant to 're-awaken that spirit of adventure and self discovery that always accompanies a migrant when he starts a new life'. The passage shows the essay moving from the individual, first-hand experience to the universal with ease, for 'at the core of the personal essay is the supposition that there is a certain unity to human experience'.[38] Whether we are migrants or not, we all set out on a journey of self-discovery, and 'losing sight of land' and taking risks are activities pertinent not only to migration but also to life.

Eight years after arriving in New Zealand, Hugh makes yet another transition. In a reversal of his father's migration 60 years earlier from farm to university, Hugh moves out of the city into the country. The house he builds facing the Southern Alps bears the name of the family farm where his father originated: Crossnacreevy. Perhaps his father's initial migration from the family farm to medical school prefigured his son's profession as well as his subsequent migration (ditto his brother's), and Hugh claims several times in his essay that migration is an inherited trait – his parents both had it, as did his brother. The journey comes full circle when his parents emigrate to New Zealand in their eighties, reuniting the family. Hugh has not managed, however, to recreate the home he lost in his childhood – but who can? He closes the essay with: 'If folk ask me where I live, I tell them New Zealand. If folk ask me where home is, I tell them a garden with a cherry tree, because home is not a place but a time when life was innocent, unknowingly secure, and full of wonder.' He returns to the cherry tree that was, for him as a child, the goalpost, both in imagination and reality. It is a symbol of lost security, innocence and wonder, which is how he defines home. The cherry tree and garden have vanished. For Hugh, home is not a place but a time – the time before he was forced out of the garden, like those first migrants cast out of Eden into the world.

'Make impulse one with wilfulness and enter'

Not everyone who's cast out into the world via boarding school feels
the loss of home as acutely as Hugh has. Whereas boarding school
uprooted and unsettled him when he returned home, making him feel
like a stranger in his own town, boarding school for Mary, a Scottish
psychotherapist in her early fifties, made her home even more precious:
'occasionally we were released from school and permitted to go home
so home took on a meaning that it would not otherwise have had were
you there day in, day out. The excitement and joy of arriving home after
a long car journey, turning into the driveway after months away and
glimpsing the house I loved through the trees, is about as clear a memory
as I have.' The verbs of confinement are noteworthy – 'released' and
'permitted' – in contrast with the palpable joy of seeing home again. The
personal essay gives immediate access to specific, individual memory as
the prose carries the reader alongside Mary in the car, 'turning into the
driveway after months away and glimpsing the house I loved through the
trees'. She tells us exactly what she feels. And shining in that last sentence
is her love for a house so rooted in memory that 40 years later she still
refers to it as 'the safe haven where I shelter whilst scary things happen
outside'.

As a practising psychotherapist, Mary is attuned to the powerful
archetype of home in her own life. That she returns to the house in her
dreams reveals how 'our psychic growth keeps roots in some tangible
localized ground'.[39] Her description of this remarkable house is almost
fairytale-like in its setting: 'Home was a big old rather intimidating-
looking house perched – precariously I thought, as a child – on a cliff on
the southeast coast of Scotland. At the back of the house, no more than
10 yards away, stone steps carved into the cliff face led steeply down into
the sea.' Home, perched 'precariously' in her child eyes, the perspective
offset by dashes, now has a stability and permanence in her adulthood.
Gaston Bachelard argues that 'the unconscious abides. Memories are
motionless, and the more securely they are fixed in space, the sounder
they are.'[40] Memories may be motionless, but the person who remembers

is not, especially if she migrates to the other side of the world. In the essay Mary's family home becomes anchored both in narrative and in time, to endure on the page, if not in reality. When her parents sold the house and died in their late eighties, Mary decided to migrate to New Zealand. Once those powerful anchors to place and family were gone, she may have felt free to reroot herself and her nine-year-old son half a world away. Like her son, she was nine when she was first uprooted to boarding school. Chance or circumstance inform these parallel departures, though perhaps, given her profession, she realised her son was still young enough to move without too much disruption.

Mary speculates that her migration might have genetic roots: 'Can it be to do with genetic inheritance? Us Scots are renowned for a restlessness, a pioneering spirit, a keenness to see what else is out there … My mother had that gene. She went to India aged 21. She joined the Voluntary Aid Detachment and spent a few years nursing overseas.' Mary's colloquial use of 'Us Scots' separates 'us' from them, the stay-at-homes, invoking a solidarity with the global clan of Scots, and perhaps it was coincidental that the class Mary joined had two other Scottish migrants and their Viking neighbours from across the North Sea, a Dane and a Swede. Cathrine, the Dane, also wondered if her desire to migrate was genetic: 'Is it because of my genes? This all absorbing feeling of curiosity has never left me.' But while many have 'a keenness to see what else is out there', not everyone follows the lure of the far horizon and migrates. 'What I still find surprising,' Mary acknowledges, 'is just how easy I found it, psychologically if you like, to "up sticks" and leave.' She credits years of confinement in boarding school with instilling a sense of restlessness and adventure:

> I can't overlook the influence of boarding school. Going out into the world is surely a normal response to years of confinement. I'm not sure the intent of those venerable school mistresses was to grow restless, adventure-seeking adults (I recall we were actually groomed to be 'young ladies'), but when you are removed at a tender age from all that is familiar, things are bound never to be the same again. Something is lost and something else takes its place.

For Mary, being 'removed at a tender age from all that is familiar' has to have a profound effect on an individual, something she grasps both personally and as a psychotherapist. The child may learn to cope and be resilient in the face of unfamiliarity, a characteristic well suited to a future migrant who will encounter other countries and cultures and learn to adapt. But it comes at a cost, as Mary notes: 'Something is lost and something else takes its place.' Anne Michaels addresses such recognition of loss in her brilliant novel about displacement, *The Winter Vault*: 'We become ourselves when things are given to us and when things are taken away.'[41] For migrants, often what is taken away is home and familiarity, which in Mary's case created a thirst for adventure and travel.

While her older siblings settled down and stayed at home, Mary 'got centre stage as the adventurer', but she then qualifies that remark with: 'Not being a particularly confident or extrovert child, going away from home required a certain amount of steeliness and spontaneity. Immigrant characteristics?' She could well be right in depicting steeliness and spontaneity as immigrant characteristics, given they occur in some guise in almost every migrant narrative. While spontaneity might prompt an individual to migrate, it is steeliness that sees the migration through. Mary concludes that no one contributing factor led to her migration. Rather, many diverse channels all fed into the braided river, 'no single origin, not one moment, not Fate or Destiny nor even a childhood dream. A random coming together of events and circumstances; of history and personality; of a desire for our son to live his early years in the carefree moment and learn life skills in a fine little country; a willingness to take a chance and live somewhere else.' Perhaps that final line is the most revealing.

Somewhere else. The allure of somewhere else is one thing for travel but quite another when someone chooses to live there. Mary's essay distils a key characteristic of migrants – the 'willingness to take a chance and live somewhere else'. Each of the migrant writers committed themselves to the risks of migration, and they also risked self-disclosure in the personal essay. Like the migrant who moves to a new country, the writer has no idea what she might encounter when writing. This willingness to take a risk and see where the writing leads is central to the essay as a mode of inquiry, as Phillip Lopate points out: 'There is something heroic in the essayist's gesture of striking out toward the unknown, not only without a map, but without certainty that there is anything worthy to be found. One would like to think that the personal essay represents a kind of basic research on the self, in ways that are allied with science and philosophy.'[42]

The essay's inherent willingness to test the validity and value of personal experience makes it an ideal genre to assess the stakes and rewards of migration. The emotional and existential costs of migration are exactly what cannot be quantified, and while theory and system hold sway in academic discourse, 'The lived individual experience which eludes system, and which the essay expresses and symbolizes, has an important place as well.'[43] The personal essay offers a way of structuring human knowledge that is most closely allied with individual, lived experience.

From its inception with French Renaissance philosopher Michel de Montaigne, the personal essay has been used to evaluate and understand one's place in the world, and for migrants that place has changed. Both the world and the essay become a vital contact zone that the migrant encounters, and what holds fast in the essay is the situation of the writer: 'The essay stands apart from both poetry and prose fiction, as well as other forms of academic writing, in its emphasis upon the actual situation of the writer, and thus upon the personal nature, the "situatedness" of all writing.'[44] For migrants that 'situatedness' is in another country, culture and perhaps language, and so the 'actual situation of the writer' is vital for our understanding of migration and its synergistic relationship with the personal essay. The migrant and the writer must learn what the experience means, on both a daily and a lifelong level, and the essay is adept at assessing that.

The aftershocks of migration, for example, may affect the individual decades later, as Maria, an older Dutch migrant realised when her husband was dying of cancer and she wished her family lived closer to help with his care. Maria lamented that migrants do not think of this eventuality, but how can they? When she and her husband arrived in New Zealand 50 years earlier by boat, they were not facing the end of his life on the far side of the world. She could not know then what she knows now. The poet Rainer Maria Rilke reminds us that 'the seemingly uneventful and motionless moment when our future steps into us is so much closer to life than that other loud and accidental point of time when it happens to us as if from the outside.'[45] At the time it occurs, we cannot always see 'the seemingly uneventful and motionless moment' when our future begins, but we can trace that moment back to its origin through the essay.

Sometimes, long before the migrant departs, the imagination of being other and elsewhere is already in motion. In a remarkable catalogue of her own migratory roots, Daisy, an Irish nurse who has lived in New Zealand for over 30 years, charted her journey away from her forebears through reference to poems, then maps and, from there, chance:

> There is something about our lot of Kellys that makes us mildly adventurous. The attribute is not necessarily a virtue; it is simply part of us – like our freckles and our love of food. I, for example, have always relished the exotic names of foreign places. At six I was captivated by an out-loud reading of 'The Destruction of Sennacherib'; at twelve by reading to myself 'The Golden Journey to Samarkand'; at eighteen I had a map of the world on my bedroom wall and an intention, one day, to see the South China Sea. In 1970 while preparing to live in Borneo I was diverted to Fiji. I didn't mind in the least. An exotic, golden and immense experience in their own right, the Islands of Fiji turned into stepping stones to New Zealand.

She opens with her Irish family being 'mildly adventurous', a trait they cannot help, like their freckles and love of food, but what shines in this passage is her own zest for the exotic and her embrace of what comes her way. She marks the rising level of her interest in foreign places at ages six, 12, 18, and then, by 1970, when she is 27, with actually living abroad. She is captivated on hearing Byron's poem at age six, long before she could have fathomed its meaning, and at age 12 by her own choice of reading, another poem flavoured with the far away and distant. Then the map of the world appears on her wall and with it her 'intention, one day, to see the South China Sea'.

Perhaps it's not surprising Daisy quotes Irish Nobel Laureate Seamus Heaney as an epigraph to one of her essays: 'Make impulse one with wilfulness and enter', for that is exactly how she has approached her life: by uniting impulse with will, or spontaneity and steeliness. When, as a nurse, she is on her way to Borneo but is diverted to Fiji, she is undaunted: 'I didn't mind in the least.' We see the joyous ribbon of enthusiasm throughout as she plots the stepping stones that lead from 'The Golden Journey to Samarkand' to Fiji: 'An exotic, golden and immense experience in their own right, the Islands of Fiji turned into stepping stones to New Zealand.' Looking back over 30 years, she writes: 'From the Atlantic coast of Western Europe, I came here to the South Pacific as flotsam and without significant intention. "Destiny hangs on a thread," it is said and yet it now seems inconceivable that life could have turned out differently.' She may argue that she came 'without significant intention', yet her willingness to follow where impulse carried her tells another story.

Daisy's migration has roots that exist not only in her vivid imagination and taste for exotic place names, for at age 12 she was sent to boarding school in Northern Ireland, 'to spend the next six years migrating from dormitory to dormitory with only a bed and a locker and share of a wardrobe to call my own'. That border crossing was not simply geographic but became cultural and emotional when her first six years of schooling in Ireland were invalidated: 'we had been taught all our lessons (except English) through the Irish language, our history stories were incorrect … Irish history from either or indeed any point of view was not taught except as incidental to European history. It took me a year or so to find a way to clamber over this soul-high threshold.' By age 12 Daisy is a migrant, having suffered the triple dislocation of roots, language and social norms. And when she returns home, she finds her younger sister now has her bedroom and she must use the guest room. Her displacement thus occurs in both locations – home and away.

Perhaps clambering over 'soul-high thresholds' at age 12 enabled
Daisy to take the later shifts in country and circumstance in her stride, or
maybe it's something more essential, a sense of the familiar when she is
far away. While at nurses' training in Belfast, she received a package:

> It had an Eire stamp and a Donegal postmark. It was neatly tied with string
> and secured with a dab of sealing wax. I opened it layer by layer and inside
> found, together with a familiar saucer and under a layer of damp moss, a
> wild primrose plant, root and all, in pale bud. The note said, 'I thought this
> might remind you of home, love Mum.' Together she and I were most at
> peace as we worked in her gardens. To this day, half a world away, I grow
> pale yellow primroses in mine.

Daisy does not say what she did with the wild primrose her mother sent
her, root and all, in 1962. Yet it takes root in the essay, as it does in her
New Zealand garden decades later, and we see how her mother, with
whom she had a difficult relationship, extended this image of affection
and connection, a memory of shared peace. The primroses of her
mother's garden in Donegal find a metaphoric and actual home in her
New Zealand one.

One evening in early spring Daisy brought a pale-yellow primrose to
class. Decamped by the earthquakes, our class was gathered in a kindly
Dutchman's living room, sharing stories of migration. Our various
routes had brought us from Ireland, England, Uganda, Slovakia, the
Netherlands, China and the United States. We passed the flower around.
From the red Marco Polo stamp on my birth certificate to the package
sent by Daisy's mother in 1962 and now this flower blooming in New
Zealand in 2011: I touched the pale trembling petals and thought how
far we had all come to be together in this room, with this flower, 'half a
world away' from where each of us was born.

Hero of the family

During each class I offered over the two years, I felt a sense of
congruence: a rare, chance gathering of migrants from all over the world
who wished to write about their experience. What struck me about each
of them was a bravery, a commitment to risk, and that very steeliness

Mary wrote of, both in life and on the page. The personal essay embodies those qualities because in this genre, as Leonard Kriegel argues, writers confront not only the world but also themselves: 'few other genres commit the writer's "I" so relentlessly and few other genres are able to force the writer to confront himself so absolutely. The personal essay allows writers to discover their own complexity – and that includes their hatreds, as well as the rawness and sustainability of their wounds. Among the legacies of the personal essay is that it has been used to describe so many different kinds of pain and self-discovery.'[46]

A moving example of the essay's power of self-discovery came from Werapong, who at 25 was the youngest migrant in the class by two generations. Despite his youth, he held his own with modesty and grace. His narrative reveals the roots of his remarkable poise. At age 15, Werapong's parents sent him from Thailand to New Zealand to attend high school and learn English. His essay reveals how he felt just before touching down in the new country: 'The flight to Christchurch was very full but I've never felt so empty in my heart.' Werapong is not a child being sent 40 miles away to boarding school, but an adolescent being sent to a completely different country, culture and language. He gives what may seem a stock response to why he migrated:

> New Zealand is my chosen country to pursue my future life journey. I carry the hope of my parents and the dreams of my grandparents with me to this new country. Things that could not have been achieved in the prior generations – will be achieved in mine. Despite my inability to speak the language, lack of knowledge of the New Zealand culture and not knowing a single person in this new country, I still wanted to be here more than anything else in the world.

As a Buddhist, Werapong has an acute awareness of ancestral pressure, borne out by his description of his father: 'My dad could easily fit into one of those images of the third-world children where neither he nor his parents had a choice about their four basic necessities – food, medicine, housing and clothes'. But his father loved learning: 'Every day he would walk for miles in bare feet on a gravel road through rice fields to attend what they called a "hut school". There were only three teachers in the school; the teachers only had high school qualifications.'

His father's example of dedication amid extreme poverty sheds a
different light on his son's stock response for migration – education for
self-improvement – especially if one factors in the fees for international
students at high-school level in New Zealand ($13,000 a year in 2018,
plus room and board). Again we see how the roots of the migration
begin long before the individual leaves the country, as well as how
parental sacrifice enables the route itself to be possible.

Werapong describes his first night in New Zealand with candour,
and even though 10 years have passed, the emotion is immediate and
concrete:

> The first night in New Zealand was the longest night of my life.
> Homesickness seems to knock on the door as soon as I was alone.
> Memories come back – it's eight thirty now – Mum and Dad must be
> watching our favourite TV programme. I wonder whether they miss me as
> much I miss them. I could hear my own heart beating clearly. This is the
> first time I ever heard it – Thailand must be so noisy, I thought to myself.

The memory starts out in the past tense – 'The first night in New
Zealand was the longest night of my life' – but instinctively Werapong
shifts into the lyrical present and personifies his homesickness knocking
on the door. The prose switches into an even more immediate and
interior level of address: '… it's eight thirty now – Mum and Dad must
be watching our favourite TV programme'. He can see what is happening
at 8.30pm, thousands of miles away in Thailand. He doesn't name the
programme as it is the presence of family, not the show itself, that
matters. He invokes their shared ritual to console himself in his parents'
absence. Then he asks the poignant question all migrants ask themselves:
'I wonder whether they miss me as much I miss them.' The question is
just one of the unanswerable questions migrants face, and having asked
it, Werapong immediately acknowledges something extraordinary and
visceral: 'I could hear my own heart beating clearly. This is the first time
I ever heard it – Thailand must be so noisy, I thought to myself.' He hears
his own hammering heart because he is not at home but frightened and
alone in a bedroom in Christchurch, New Zealand. Both references
to Thailand have the phrase 'must be', as though his insistence that his

parents 'must be watching' their shared favourite TV programme and that 'Thailand must be so noisy' underscores the missing familiarity of family and country. They must be there – even though he is not.

Perhaps Werapong's youth made him so forthcoming and unguarded in his prose, but it is also the hallmark of the essay to show vulnerability. We see 'the real possibility in the personal essay to catch oneself in the act of being human'.[47] Werapong does this beautifully when he reveals his vulnerability at the time of this memory:

> 'I miss home! I miss Mama and Papa! I shouldn't have come here!' I shouted inside my head.
>
> 'Go to sleep, it will be better tomorrow. You are here for a reason, you are here because you chose to be here,' I heard a small voice inside my heart responding to my head.

Alone and frightened, he reverts to someone much younger than age 15, and instead of calling his parents Mum and Dad as before, they become Mama and Papa. The exclamation marks intensify his anguish, and now the heart that was beating in fear enters into a dialogue with his head, which is shouting out in protest at being in this foreign country. He dramatises his mental state at the time, that of a frightened child, and even though he claims his migration was voluntary, the reality is painful. His closing image describes the emotional cost of this journey: 'I drifted to sleep on a wet pillow – tired, homesick, fearful but full of hope and optimism. Things will always be better tomorrow.' His wet pillow reveals he cried himself to sleep, depicting the very thing not often considered in migration studies: 'the tears of migrant people are what we often overlook and/or fail to understand'.[48]

Werapong will graduate with honours and become the youngest chartered accountant at one of New Zealand's top accounting firms before being seconded to their European offices in London, Dublin and Copenhagen, all before the age of 25. If we follow the route of his tears, we see they originate in his parents and their hope for both themselves and, in turn, for him. His essay enacts what Hélène Cixous describes: 'I go back up the stream of tears. When I begin to write, it always starts from something unexplained, mysterious and concrete. Something that

happens here. I could be indifferent to these phenomena; but in fact
I think these are the only important phenomena. It begins to search
in me.'[49] The personal essay also starts from 'something unexplained,
mysterious, and concrete' that begins to search in the individual.
The search becomes part of the writing process, but it originates in
'something that happens here'. Here may be the here of the present, or
a here in the past. If, for example, we go back up Werapong's stream of
tears, as he does, we see they originate in choices his parents made, and
their route leads to his root/route:

> It is extraordinary to discover that two of my greatest qualities are
> something I derived from the things I didn't choose and could never
> have chosen – they belong to my parents' choices earlier in their lives.
> My father, who did not choose to be poor, chose to love his learning,
> and he transcended his peers by focusing on this personal characteristic
> throughout his life. My mother, who did not choose a broken family, chose
> to hope and remain optimistic about her own life. Both my parents seem
> to have transferred their passions and dreams to me without me nor they
> realising when it began or how the process was done.

This is the moment of recognition, which the personal essay discovers
through its route of inquiry and inclination. Perhaps being Buddhist
accounts for Werapong's awareness that the future enters him long before
it happens, and perhaps his willingness to begin with tears, with sacrifice
– his parents', his own – reflects a willingness to realise his life course
begins long before his own sense of purpose manifests. At 25 he already
understands that we become ourselves when things are given to us or
taken from us. Sent thousands of kilometres away at age 15, Werapong
gained a path to self-actualisation his parents could never have imagined
for themselves but did envision for him. Even his name, Werapong,
which means 'hero of the family', reveals their hopes for his future. He
sees his hero's journey, which all migration narratives are to some extent,
with great modesty, realising he is part of a greater and more generous
chain of being: 'Love connects things – love connects what we can
choose with what we can't. My parents' love for each other has remained
the most powerful thing that ever happened in their lives – they used
each other's strengths to build their business and lives together. But the

most essential notion of all – their love acts as a connecting bridge to me – transferring what I didn't choose and made me who I am today.'

As a Buddhist, Werapong understands that 'love connects things – love connects what we can choose with what we can't'. We cannot choose our parents and we cannot choose the times we are born into, but we can choose what and whom we love. Aware of his own place in the chain of cause and effect, he writes: 'Although I don't have a say in whatever choices my parents made in the past – I am gratefully blessed for the consequences of their choices. The challenge remains for me on what choices I now make – so that my children and grandchildren would feel blessed for the choices that will make them who they are in the future.' His shifting verb tenses reveal how his present choices will make a sense of blessing possible for his yet unborn children and grandchildren. The future is predicated on the past. His route will become their root, even as his parents' routes became his own.

Voyaging toward understanding

Sometimes the route not taken by the parent is thrust upon the next generation. While it is natural for parents to want to improve their children's future through education, on occasion the parents' own thwarted desires to travel and live elsewhere prompt them to send their children to boarding school or overseas, setting the future migrant in motion. Susan, an American in her fifties, wrote: 'I believe the start of my forced exile from my homeland began when my mother was sixteen and her parents sent her to Stephens College for Girls, a small school in Missouri.' Her mother thrived in boarding school and later majored in geography: 'She always had trips in mind and with maps at hand she researched countries of interest, explored train trips in faraway places and questioned people where to go for adventure.' But then her mother married and projected her frustrated dream of travel onto her daughter. For Susan, however, it was a 'forced exile' from her homeland:

> While I was growing up she would send me to places starting with summer camps. From Girl Scout camp to church camp to girls' camps in Minnesota,

I would be packed off for part of each US summer. With each trip I wanted less and less to leave home. The separation anxiety I suffered in grade school grew even greater. For someone who never wanted to leave home I was sent away a lot!

How sad that a child who never wanted to leave home was sent away so often. The exclamation mark punctuates Susan's amazement in the present that this would happen so often in the past. She admits, 'I had trouble individuating from my mother since I was a little girl.' This loss of agency extends into her twenties, when her mother decides Susan should be an *au pair* in Copenhagen, resulting in a negative experience that keeps her from travelling out of the United States for a decade.

In her thirties Susan started working in Antarctica for six-month stints, and this pattern continued for eight years. This time, however, she chose for herself where and when she would go, exemplifying how 'Moving to a foreign place and international travel are archetypal situations for protecting and expressing the need for freedom and independence.'[50] Susan no longer experienced a northern hemisphere winter or the binding hoopla of the family Christmas. She now lived in a perpetual summer, and what greater summer camp could there be than Antarctica with its seasonal employees, all about as far away from home as one could get:

> Antarctica is the place where misfits meet like misfits while working for a common cause. We go there under the guise of supporting science in the vast tundra. Yet the truth is we are drawn there to meet other like-minded people. In a cult-like society, the runaways and the travellers, the wanderers and the adventurers all converge at the end of the earth, in Antarctica.

Antarctica seems to appeal to 'the runaways and the travellers, the wanderers and adventurers', a destination for those who clearly don't want to be at home, at least for six months out of the year. Most notably, Antarctica is Susan's choice, not her mother's: 'The travel bug that was within her had possessed the wrong person, me. I was doing all the travelling she dreamed of doing.' The child who had been sent away every summer against her wishes now departs for each Antarctic summer. Then, at the age of 42, 'finally putting on my big girl shoes, shoving my separation anxiety aside, and running away from home', she moved to

New Zealand to marry a Kiwi whom she met in Antarctica. Thus, her eight-year sojourn at the ultimate out-of-the-way summer camp led to her finally leaving home. The route became the root.

The desire for freedom and independence is at the heart of what prompts many migrants to leave home in a more dramatic and far-reaching fashion than that experienced by other people. For migrants, home does not exhibit as strong a hold and 'the centrifugal force of desire and the response to the call of the Other becomes more compelling.'[51] What gives the individual a sense of belonging in their family or country of origin is a complex subject. For example, Taegen, an Englishwoman in her early seventies, wrote: 'I question how much of my persona brings about the pathways my life takes – why me and not others. What is it about the sense of "belonging" and staying within the corral versus stepping outside and searching and seeking?' She sees the roots of her migration as being part of her persona, an inborn desire for 'searching and seeking'. This is the personal essay's nature as well, as G. Douglas Atkins notes: 'In such essays the writer voyages to understanding in, through, and by means of the writing – a true essay, one is tempted to say, is an attempt to learn.'[52]

The idea of voyaging to understanding in writing has clear parallels with the migrant experience. Any stranger who comes to town must attempt to learn to live there if they hope to settle, and perhaps my unwillingness to learn to live in Sweden is one reason I could never belong there. I think the 'soul-high thresholds' our family faced in Sweden – linguistically, culturally, existentially – would have taken years to surmount, though. Where the stranger feels welcome, the voyage to understanding becomes reciprocal in the rich exchange between migrant and native.

Sometimes our voyage towards understanding ends in the realisation that we don't belong somewhere, whether in a country or in our own family, as in Taegen's case. For her, 'belonging' and 'staying within the corral' are linked, and from the beginning she refused to stay put: 'From an early age I was off and away, always going down to the river to play, breaking the ice in the puddles in the street, staying over at my best friend's home – especially when I was upset with my father and his dictatorial ways. My independence was learned at an early age.' Her home, the original corral, was more confining than welcoming and explains why she does not see belonging as positive. As an adult her range became greater: 'Once again as soon as I was free to choose I was off to explore all the big city of London had to offer, then my first foray to the European continent, and then further afield to South Africa to live and work.' Critical here is the phrase, 'as soon as I was free to choose', and what she chose was to go elsewhere. While not all migrants are free to choose where or when to go, what is compelling are those who, given the choice, do not stay in their country of origin. In her thirties, a blind date with a Kiwi led to Taegen's second marriage and a new life in New Zealand: 'Off to the antipodes, additional family, new friends and a whole new way of being. I had never been so happy in my life … there was so much joy in the belonging I felt the balance began to tip in favour of the new life I had begun.' The belonging she did not feel in her own family was finally grounded in her new, blended family, half a world away. The root that led away from home became the route to belonging in New Zealand.

The desire to escape

Strong ties to family and place of origin are no guarantee people will remain where they grow up. This likelihood prompts an important consideration as to the nature of roots and identity, namely that neither concept is necessarily rooted in place. As the wily Gertrude Stein noted: 'Our roots can be anywhere and we can survive, because if you think about it, we take our roots with us.'[53] What is critical, Susan Stanford Friedman observes, is that 'identity depends centrally upon narrative, whether it is an effect of rootedness or routedness'; for migrants, 'identity developed through routes involves an experience of leaving roots, of moving beyond the boundaries of "home" (however that is defined or problematized)'.[54] Personal essays offer a way to anchor that fluid identity in narrative.

Sometimes, despite a strong identification with one's home, migrants feel compelled to leave. Gareth, a Welsh doctor in his seventies, grew up in large, close-knit family, the memory of which is still vivid 35 years later:

> I can smell the sulphur from the slow burning, buried coal on the old river wharf; I can look up at the mediaeval nave of the abbey ruins; I can feel the wind as it blows over the tops of Hirfynydd, Mach Hywel and Druma mountains; but most easily of all I can hear the voices of the past, of parents and sisters, and uncles, and aunts and cousins, of preachers and teachers.

Yet he left all that and his comfortable medical practice in Wales for New Zealand. He speculates why: 'Did the war time atmosphere of excitement, anxiety, restriction, deprivation and fear foster a desire for escape into a new world? The other children were all born after the war, were not exposed to the same atmosphere and never seemed to have the desire to escape.' For Gareth and his cousin, both born before the war into privation, the initial escape was 'from what, in prewar days, would have been the almost inevitable employment in heavy industry or coal mining'. Higher education again proved to be the route out: 'We both could have gone to the University of Wales in Cardiff, forty kilometres away, but went hundreds of kilometres away to Edinburgh and London. Today it would seem like a minor decision but we had moved into a new world and, in fact, we had emigrated.'

Looking back over 50 years, Gareth can see that what now seems a 'minor decision' and a short distance was, in fact, a migration: 'My departure in 1957 meant that I left behind industrial South Wales with its particular culture, its chapels, its song, its rugby, its self-righteousness, its once radical socialism and arrived in a university world of questioning, argument and freedom.' Freedom – there it is again – freedom from what 'all adds up to an enormous pressure to be *Welsh*'. He began to question and feel circumscribed by his cultural identity once he could see it from the outside. Having a taste of freedom in this new world made it impossible to settle in the old one. His cousin later emigrated to the United States to work as a priest with drug addicts. Gareth, after a stint in the fens of England and believing he could still live in the old world of Wales and practise medicine, found it otherwise:

> We had been in Tenby for eight years and I could look forward to another thirty years as the local GP. My family and I would be respected and we would be comfortable. The inevitability of it all, the certainty of security, the bonds of respectability, the terrors of conformity were all too great. We would be crushed between the weight of our culture and past and the granite millstones of our comfortable future.

Curiously the very things that might embody home for some – respectability, comfort, security and culture – are what drove Gareth's migration: 'Our lives seemed settled but the restlessness, the minor dissatisfactions, the searchings surfaced again', and these proved strong enough to persuade him to move his wife and young family to a rural practice in New Zealand, to start over in a new world, 'which was twenty thousand kilometers in the future and twenty-five years in the past'. As Hélène Cixous points out, it is the unexplained, the mysterious, the concrete, that goes searching in us. As 'the searchings surfaced again', what terrified Gareth was 'the inevitability of it all', the 'terrors of conformity' and that he and his family 'would be crushed between the weight of our culture and past and the granite millstones of our comfortable future'. He uses the masterful rhetoric absorbed in Welsh chapel, invoking powerful cadences that build as he piles one abstraction on top of another like so many millstones, to explain his own bid for escape from these very strictures. Here the pressure of roots becomes the root of migration. Like fossils under pressure becoming the coal his family mined in Wales, Gareth undergoes a metamorphosis. He becomes what Salman Rushdie affirms all migrants are: 'metaphorical beings in their very essence'[55] – in other words, transformed.

While some migrants respond to the pressure to leave, others feel a pressure to stay where they are, and their desire to travel and live elsewhere is discouraged. Sabina, a young Dutchwoman who came to New Zealand at age 36 in 2008, was quite direct about this:

The reason for moving is the hope that it will make things better. The grass is greener on the other side of the hill. This commonly used saying by the Dutch has a quite negative ring to it. It encourages you to stay put and treasure the things and the life you have, instead of wanting something else. And, so I've learned, the grass indeed isn't always greener. But the longing for the other side of the hill to see for myself the colour of the grass is always alive within me.

Her longing to see 'the other side of the hill' is strong enough after a visit to New Zealand for her to quit her job as a journalist and sell her house, even though she's learned the grass is not always greener elsewhere. Her migration is greeted with suspicion by those left behind. They suspect her of running away and think she 'must be mad'. Indeed, she titled her essay 'Mad', because unlike the postwar Netherlands that prompted the wave of Dutch migrants to New Zealand, the Netherlands she leaves is prosperous and thriving. Consequently, she shouldn't want something else but should 'stay put and treasure the things and the life you have'. But she did not – she chose to migrate. Yet again the need for individual freedom figures prominently and she declares: 'My new country has given me freedom and space.'

Sabina traces her desire to live elsewhere to her childhood: 'The childhood dream of living somewhere else made me travel and just the near thought of moving and starting again, that it is possible, makes me happy.' She can even point to the exact moment when she knew she wanted to stay in New Zealand: 'How I clearly remember that moment in the bus to Christchurch airport at the end of the holiday, the signs at the last roundabout: left Picton, right Timaru. I wanted to jump ship. I wanted to stay in New Zealand, where you could wander near the sea and feel perfectly alone but not lonely.'

Not everyone is given such a clear sign of which direction to take in their lives. Her emphatic statement – 'I wanted to jump ship. I wanted to stay in New Zealand' – unequivocally affirms her desire, and in three years she made it a reality. Unlike the 28,000 Dutch migrants who came to New Zealand earlier because of the privations of World War II,[56] Sabina gave up a job and a home of her own to migrate towards 'the thing I needed all my life: lots of space and some sort of freedom'. We see

that she values freedom more than security. Greg Madison argues that
for voluntary migrants, 'Self-direction (self-creation) in life prevails over
the importance of belonging and security, in fact *anything* seems worth
sacrificing in order to maintain the freedom to choose for oneself.'[57]
Piet, an older Dutchman who migrated in 1959 with his wife, can see
the rewards as well as the responsibility of this freedom: 'The shift to a
country far removed from our parents and close family definitely made
us more independent in our actions and thinking than would have
been the case otherwise … [it] gave us greater freedom from traditional
constraints too, but also the responsibility to get it right by ourselves.'

Sabina, recognising her place in the great Dutch chain of migration,
hosts her final lunch with her parents at the historic Hotel New York in
Rotterdam: 'From here many migrants left for America, my aunt left here
in the fifties like so many other Dutch people for the States, Canada or
Australia and New Zealand as well.' One way Sabina differs from earlier
Dutch migrants is evident in her hyperlinking all the place names in her
essay. She presumes her text will be read online, and maybe she is right,
since in the future more texts will be encountered that way. Yet even
with her awareness of the likely habits of future readers, she sees that her
own migration may have older roots: 'My dad left his place to travel and
challenge himself when he was eighteen. My mother was born in a town
where many people left for better futures and so I sometimes think my
urge to go far was already written for me in some way.' The route always
has roots. She realises her own 'urge to go far was already written for
[her] in some way'. How often the migrant narrative begins long before
the individual leaves the home country to see if it really is greener on the
other side of the hill.

Sabina's essays, influenced by her background in journalism, are
rich in both description and investigation of why she migrated. Even as
she explains why she was drawn to New Zealand, she lists the pressures
pushing her away from the Netherlands and her justification for
choosing to migrate:

> Not happy about my home, my job, my life, the traffic jams, the crowded
> beaches and malls, the rapid changing politics that paints my country

sometimes as stone mad and crazy, all these thoughts and feelings drove me
away. If this is my life in this country for the next forty years, it will drive
me mad.

The list of everything driving her away is quite specific, for example,
the crowded beaches compared to the solitary idyll she paints in New
Zealand, where 'you could wander near the sea and feel perfectly alone
but not lonely'. She is undeterred by the naysayers remaining in the
Netherlands: 'I left the questions about are you sure and what will the
others think far behind me.' Clearly a woman who knows her own mind,
she is unafraid of pitting her decision to migrate against 'my home, my
job, my life, the traffic jams, the crowded beaches and malls, the rapid
changing politics that paints my country sometimes as stone mad and
crazy'. We see in her refreshing honesty the power of the personal essay:
'The attractiveness of the "I" that stares out at the world is that it knows
two things: the first is that it is unsheltered, the second is that it is the
writer's own eye that must measure what it sees in that world ... How
that eye sees and what it chooses to look at is central to what the personal
essay does.'[58] In many respects the unsheltered 'I' that must measure what
it sees in the world is fundamentally the migrant's eye, the I/eye of the
stranger who comes to town. Risk-taking and assessment are inherent
in both the migrant and the writer, and the personal essay is a record of
both.

The unsheltered I in the personal essay rests solely on the one who
sees and assesses what she encounters in the world. This singular first
person is all essayists have to rely on, and yet no one grasps first-hand
experience better than the individual herself, for 'the essay stays closer
to the individual's self-experience than any other form except the
diary'.[59] What redeems the personal essay from solipsism is its outward
gaze, where the writer turns what is private and reflective, hidden or
remembered, and finds meaning not just for herself but for others. The
writing shares what might otherwise never be observed and, by making
the personal accessible, also makes it relational: 'We, readers of personal
essays, are placed in a privileged position, where we have access to
the vulnerabilities, uncertainties, and processes of skepticism at work

in the mind of a writer, as it is represented on the page.'[60] Where self meets other is where understanding begins. Likewise, when migrant meets native is where understanding begins or breaks down. Our understanding of migration will be enriched by taking an inward turn that then reaches outward in the personal essay.

To say yes, go

The roots of migration begin within the countries, cultures, families and times we are born into, over which we have no choice. But even within these broad constraints, children born into the same family do not all migrate: something else comes into play. For voluntary migrants there is a choice – to marry, to work, to stay, to move, something that says 'yes, go' – and yet the impulse to go has earlier roots. Something sets the migration in motion long before the individual crosses from one place to another. The story of migration begins long before we do, even as our own narrative begins long before we do. The journey and narrative precede us. We are en route years before we migrate or write. We pick up whenever, wherever, and go. The pāua-shell bracelet, the boarding school, the war – whatever the catalyst, we are set in motion whether we want to be or not. And yet there are moments when we do choose: to love someone, to leave, to start over on the other side of the world under different stars. Look at this tiny red stamp of Marco Polo on my birth certificate. Of course it's a symbol, proof I was born elsewhere to parents who left home and scarcely looked or went back. Marco Polo, the Venetian merchant, my secret patron, set me on my way and, like me, returned. Now I am telling a collective migration story, making a very particular weave out of the gift of these essays. Underneath the larger braided river of our lives is the root of why we came to New Zealand, long before any of us had words for it. These are some of them.

Chapter **2**

Routes – Writing Between
Two Shores

'*Everything changes and nothing remains still.*'
—PLATO, *Cratylus*

The route contains the route, bounded by both time and space. Time moves relentlessly forward, the river will empty into the sea, and our life contains our death, wholly our own, marking the end of our story. But the route emerges moment by moment, subject to choice and chance. I didn't know when I began writing this book that the earth would shear apart multiple times, that a sound like that of a freight train shrieking towards us in the middle of the night was going to alter irrevocably the trajectory of my family's lives. I remember thinking, after the first quake struck Canterbury and no one had died, that we were living in a state of grace because we had been spared.

But that was not the end of the story. The tectonic plates have their own narrative route that unfolds in larger planes of space and time. Six months later a different fault opened up and destroyed downtown Christchurch, killing 185 people and changing the course of an entire city. Homes, livelihoods, lives: gone. Many people chose to leave. Or they were *forced* to choose, which was our family's story: we could stay until my husband lost his job, which now looked increasingly likely, or go to Sweden, where work and the unshakable Baltic Shield of the Scandinavian peninsula awaited us. The route contains the route, and Sweden – cold, immovable, unyielding Sweden – would ultimately provide the route back to New Zealand, but at the time I could not know that.

Sweden was a forced migration, impelled by tectonic plates and economic realities. I didn't want to go to Sweden, but knew we had no choice. When we first left New Zealand for Sweden, I felt like a horse wearing blinders that shielded me from all that would make me shy and baulk on the road forward. I could not see what was behind me or beside me, only a narrow path ahead.

As the months wore on the blinders fell away, revealing the true emotional cost of migration. Stripped of roots, language and culture, I was forced to confront migration in startling, painful reality. The result was as seismic as anything the quakes wrought. I realised where I belonged, and it was not Sweden. Not for me, nor for my husband, nor for our children. The effect was revelatory and transformative – route changing – for our lives and for my writing. I would never have understood how essential language is for migrants had I not been bereft of it in Sweden. Like the air I breathed, I had taken language for granted. Hélène Cixous, herself a migrant, explains that 'at some point, for someone who has lost everything, whether it be a human being or a country, it is language which becomes a country'.[1] I had not lost everything, but I had lost enough. Language became the country I now lived in.

In Sweden I woke up to the same sunless day, over and over again. I watched my children struggle in the local school, saw my husband worn down by bureaucratic inertia and commuting, and I tried to write, hating my life. I remember lying on the floor of my study, tears leaking into my ears, our New Zealand-born German shepherd lying beside me, his furry brow crinkled with worry. I didn't know how I could continue this book, but I kept writing, day after day, month after month, about distance, identity, belonging, nudging the narrative forward, not realising all these pages were going to come together and that Sweden was not the end of the story but part of it.

For writing, like life, is written forwards but understood backwards. We cannot know how writing will lead us to understanding until those words are written. And herein lies the beauty of melding time and narrative, because together they allow us to arrive moment by moment, word by word, to an understanding of the route that has taken us from where we have been to where we are now. Writing in Sweden I was following a braided river, not knowing it was drawing me to where I belonged, half a world away. New Zealand's braided rivers course across the Canterbury Plains from the Southern Alps to the Pacific Ocean, branching and rejoining for kilometres on their way to the sea. Their Māori names are incantatory: the Rakaia, the Hurunui, the Waimakariri, the Waitaki.

That spring our family decided to return to New Zealand, and here was where the river rose up from its hidden headwaters to glitter toward its destination. What we had encountered in Sweden made us reconsider the route we had chosen and clarified where we did want to live again: New Zealand. Not every migrant is given a second chance to get it right – to realise, yes, this is where they want to live – and, as occurs in the personal essay, to experience a moment of profound recognition.

Living in Sweden made us realise we belonged in New Zealand, something we could not have grasped without having lived in both places. Rockwell Gray observes, 'we cannot know who we are without knowing where we have been; and recall of all those now absent places is necessary to a full sense of dwelling in the present. To dwell is to be embedded, and to be embedded is to belong through a history of having belonged in many places before.'[2] We may not feel we belong everywhere we live, though where we live does teach us where we do and do not belong.

For migrants to settle and feel they can belong there must be an affinity between the place and the individual, and what engenders that is inexplicable – much like the attraction between people. Belonging is always reciprocal: we welcome and feel welcomed where we live. Migrants must confront an entirely new frame of reference for work, housing, daily life – the vast array of the ordinary that has become unfamiliar. And the culture and language may be entirely or subtly different from what they know. Without a reciprocal sense of welcome, the route of migration becomes even more demanding.

What migrants learn over time teaches them how to proceed in their new environment, as the route behind informs the route ahead; for, as Lydia Fakundiny notes about the essay, 'The route is mapped in the going.'[3] So too do migrants' routes get 'mapped in the going' as these individuals trace their experiences in writing, and what manifests is not nearly as straightforward or linear as one might expect. The personal essay shows that factors which slip through the larger categories of analysis are pivotal to the migration route, and often are seen only after the fact. Two routes therefore occur simultaneously – the route itself and what one learns along the route.

The route, moreover, appears differently when we look back on it and realise how chance and choice affect outcomes in ways we cannot perceive at the time. If there is a design in our lives, it only emerges afterwards, when we can see the connections. Narrative, Adriana Cavarero agrees, is a means to uncover that design, for 'the pattern every human being leaves behind is nothing but their life story.'[4] The personal essay is an ideal genre to apprehend our life stories – to find the deep currents and interwoven channels that shape the course of our lives.

Exploring the route

The route of our lives has both intention and accident, and while not everything is causal, it may be connected. As a method of inquiry, the personal essay enables writers 'to discover the nonsequential connections that allow those experiences to make larger sense; they are about circumstance becoming meaningful when seen from a certain remove.'[5] We realise how the root, the deeper narrative of our past, intersects with outward circumstances, and that bringing those strands together in writing allows a larger pattern to emerge.

Our lives acquire a richer meaning when we understand how the past affects the present. Susan Stanford Friedman says that 'Routes are pathways between here and there, two points of rootedness.'[6] But routes are also pathways between then and now, and movement is ongoing and influenced by what came before. Where do we step in a river that keeps moving? We can only step in from this present moment, informed by the past and the places we have been, our route mapped in the going, unwinding from what has happened along the way.

When migrants begin to explore their respective routes they see how random occurrences – an expired visa, a bankrupt company, a chance encounter – all factored into their migration. Migration scholars recognise that 'No single cause is ever sufficient to explain why people decide to leave their country and settle in another.'[7] Or as Gareth, the Welsh doctor, put it, 'the theory of obliquity suggests that the achieving of a complex goal is always by complicated and indirect routes'.

Thus, the route we think we are on may not be the route that unfolds, as Elizabeth, an Englishwoman who was the driving force behind her family's migration, realised: 'what I thought I was risking were exchange rate fluctuations, living on the beach versus in a hillside suburb, never seeing older members of my family again. A new life being better than an old life.' The route proved quite different from what she anticipated: 'looking back, I wonder if all along my subconscious really knew what the deal was. Knew there was a more fundamentally life-changing purpose to New Zealand. A kind of 12,000 mile rehab. A safe, far away, beautiful place, where the people are reserved and don't ask too many questions. Where no one I knew would watch my psyche's planned but embarrassing surrender.' New Zealand became a place to nurse and heal herself, something she could not have known when she chose to migrate there for work. The root/route overlaps and intertwines when migrants delve below the obvious narrative for the reason(s) for their journey.

For migrants that journey is both literal and existential. Acknowledging the entwined nature of roots/routes, Māori trace their whakapapa (genealogy) back to the ocean-going waka that brought their ancestors to New Zealand centuries ago.[8] Like most migrants, they were voyaging towards the unknown and brought their cultural memory forwards in the form of narrative. According to historian Philippa Mein Smith, 'Polynesians carried their stories with them, peopling each island with their own genealogy to establish a cosmological and social order.'[9] Contemporary migrants also bring a cultural memory with them embedded in things tangible and intangible, and especially in language. Individual memory migrates, too, and that root informs the route. As the Chinese migrant writer Ha Jin observes, 'no matter where we go, we cannot shed our past completely – so we must strive to use parts of our pasts to facilitate our journeys'.[10] How migrants use the past to help them find their way in a new country is part of the new narrative route they are charting.

The personal essay explores the movement from the known to the unknown and follows where that leads. Just as we cannot know where the route ends, we cannot predict how the writing will progress, and so 'the essay might be considered a journey into the unknown, a voyage of discovery'.[11] Migrants arrive in a place not yet mapped or rooted in memory where they must learn to negotiate everything their life touches: work, home, family, language. How migrants navigate that route, both in life and in the essay, addresses how strangers learn to cope with a new environment, both immediately and long term, because migration is an ongoing dynamic, even though the experience of being a stranger lessens over time. The learning curve is initially steep, and while it tapers off as the migrant becomes more familiar with a country, it cannot be hastened. Mary, the Scottish psychotherapist, recognised this aspect of the migrant's route when she wrote: 'The experience of a new friendship/country must be tended, like a small seedling, if it is to put down roots and flourish. One cannot hurry, it takes time.'

The personal essay reveals what migrants learn along the migration route that enables them to put down roots and feel they belong. In writing, the testing and weighing of individual experience provides vital information about the contact zone between migrant and native, a space of increasing relevance in a progressively more mobile and globalised world. Migrants are the vulnerable participants in their own lives, and their willingness to share that vulnerability on the page is part of the genre's empathetic appeal. But more than that, the personal essay shows the ways in which migrants are changed by what they experience. It is this combination of self-disclosure and self-understanding that is central to the form: '[T]he task of the writer of personal essays … is not only to tell us what happened to him but to show us how what happened was transformed by memory. The personal essay is at its most powerful when it gives us the writer realizing how he has been permanently, inextricably changed by all that he has witnessed. The eye he casts upon the world will never again see as it saw before consciousness itself was changed.'[12]

Migration is, by its very nature, transformative: migrants are changed not only by what they witness but also by what they experience first-hand. For those who have crossed oceans, cultures and languages, for these strangers who come to town, the personal essay is a cogent means of charting the journey in which they can actively reflect on the route taken and what they found along the way.

The seeds that flourished

Doug, an American sculptor in his sixties, has lived in New Zealand since 1990. He recounted the arc of his migration, from stranger to friend, by opening with Constantine Cavafy's famous invocation to the journey: 'As you set out for Ithaca, ask that your way be long.' Doug's memory of the poem's opening lines is looser than most translations, but he seizes its essence, because Cavafy's poem celebrates the journey, not the destination.

Doug was 27 when he first encountered the poem, and it unsettled him: 'I'm just a vagabond kid on the road. This isn't the stuff of an Odyssey. Is this an admonition?' He crisscrossed the United States several times and then, like Odysseus, returned home, where a random date with his future wife in a coffee shop set his migration to New Zealand in motion: 'There it is. New Zealand. Like the woman in the coffee shop, waiting for you.' The magnitude of their meeting registers in hindsight: 'When we reached her door I stepped over the threshold. That step was bigger than the one across the Pacific Ocean.' Here the root and route converge, for it was she and her eventual job in New Zealand that would coincide to determine the journey. Doug closes his essay with the realisation: 'The journey was long, at last. We've fashioned lifetime friendships in two worlds.' Time and distance – both inform that statement. Only the migrant who has lived somewhere else for at least 20 years can vouch for having forged lifetime friendships in two worlds.

Doug recognises, with the backward Kierkegaardian glance, what enabled him to develop friendships in New Zealand: 'that silly little grin you wear out of small town America will reap rich dividends where you're going'. When he first arrived he had no idea he would be welcomed and would make friends so easily. The essay offers the gift of looking back and seeing what paved the way: 'I made friends the first day. A dozen the next week. Good heavens, being American is terrific social currency. It hangs on you like the sign that reads: "I'm from Whidbey Island, ask me." This is the key, your admission ticket, your moveable feast. I can still freeze the gazes of shoppers in a supermarket check-out line by just opening my mouth. What fun.'

The breezy ease of Doug's bonhomie is apparent in both his prose and how readily he made friends. His openness is infectious – he 'made friends the first day. A dozen the first week.' His shift to present tense shows that for him the 'terrific social currency' of being American does not devalue over time: 'This is the key, your admission ticket, your moveable feast.'

Doug's delight in his arrival in New Zealand shines decades later, and his use of the present tense makes it fresh and spontaneous, for 'the lyrical present in nonfiction creates a sense of timeless immediacy, generates for both writer and reader the feeling the prose is being composed on the spot'.[13] He acknowledges that, unlike non-native speakers or those from other ethnicities and cultures, he has an advantage: 'After all, I'm white, middle class and speak English, besides being American.' For migrants, the route of acceptance is determined by the ground on which they arrive, and how receptive that environment is to the concept of other.

When Doug first heard his wife considering a job in New Zealand, he was enthusiastic about the idea:

I'd been hearing about Utah, Iowa, South Carolina, Los Angeles. I'd vetoed all of them.

'Here's one in a place called Christchurch, New Zealand. How do you feel about New Zealand?'

'I'd die to go to New Zealand.'

Keen as he is to live in New Zealand, it's not surprising he embraces the country and its inhabitants. He sees the journey as both one-way and permanent, writing: 'Here we go. A shipping container. The bearer of all our earthly possessions. They're crammed into a box setting sail from all of our life to the rest of our life.' The rest of his life has not yet occurred of course, so when he and his wife set out they cannot know for sure that this will be a one-way journey; not all migrants stay permanently in the country they migrate to.

In the essay, past and present overlap and the migrant can see how the route turned out and what was learned from it. The writer finds meaning that might not have occurred to him when he first experienced something, in part because now he can see how the disparate pieces of his life fit together: how the woman in the coffee shop was, like New Zealand, waiting for him. The route of the essay unfolds from what has happened and what we make of it: 'What form an essay does take on, then, is determined only by the thinking and experience of the essayist; it hews closely to the way that life and thought naturally intermingle, to the way that the mind finds pattern and meaning in memory and experience and turns its findings into words.'[14] Pattern and connection emerge when we look back, because now we can see how our lives have progressed and how far we've come.

The personal essay furthermore encourages the revisiting of thresholds that might now have more significance. Doug shows this act of second sight when he returns to the memory of his first glimpse of New Zealand from the air as he flew in over 20 years ago:

I think it's about 5:00 A.M., other side of the dateline. The sky is blood red. Thomas has been asleep on me for hours. I haven't slept. My shirt is soaked. It feels wonderful. There it is in all its splendor. The green hills rise up to meet us, then fall to the sea. The distant land. Look at it, Kathleen. Our new country. Is this a fairy tale? This moment of descent carries all the seeds yet to flourish. We've landed. It's September and spring again. We haven't even suffered a winter.

He's not sure of the time but he vividly recalls the colour of the sky. His son, aged two, has been asleep on him for hours, soaking his chest with drool, a detail both intimate and ordinary. Even though he has not slept on the 12-hour flight, 'It feels wonderful.' New Zealand emerges below, and the image of the land welcoming them is personified by the phrase 'the green hills rise up to meet us'. He urges his wife beside him to see it as well: 'Look at it, Kathleen. Our new country.' Now the land is not distant but identified and claimed as their own. The possessive 'our' signals this arrival as a shared migration experience. The image of the green hills, his first sight of the land, prompts him to ask, 'Is this a fairy tale?'

The answer to that question, with its implied happily-ever-after ending, is given 20 years later when he writes, with retrospective awareness: 'This moment of descent carries all the seeds yet to flourish.' Like airborne seeds from another land, he and his family arrived in their new landscape in time for a second spring, the season of hope, rebirth and renewal: 'It's September and spring again. We haven't even suffered a winter.' They have leapt a day and two seasons ahead to a place that looks welcoming, not only from the air but also on the ground. He presents the moment with the revelation that he could not have experienced at the time. Writing the essay provides the epiphany as the memory of flying into New Zealand is transformed by what he now knows: that the seeds did bear fruit.

The next passage shows the young family disembarked and the perspective reversed. Instead of looking down on the land from the air, they look up at the sky above them: 'Then in equal parts exhaustion and elation, we're standing on the Canterbury Plains, looking at that ever-consoling Nor'wester arch. There it is, Thomas, those quilted clouds, knitted together like a furrowed brow of heaven, winking down on you. Imagine. You're only two years old. You get to grow up and spend your life here.' 'The distant land' and 'our new country' now become the Canterbury Plains, named and known when this passage was written, though not on the morning of their arrival. The scene is overlaid with local knowledge Doug did not possess when he looked up at the New Zealand sky for the first time. Twenty years ago, he would not have identified the nor'west arch as such, a cloud shape unique to the Canterbury Plains, nor known it would become 'ever-consoling'. The consolation comes later, from all the times he looks up and sees that cloud bank.

Irish poet John O'Donohue calls memory 'the place where our vanished days secretly gather.'[15] For Doug, those vanished days and skies inform 'that ever-consoling Nor'wester arch'. He depicts a past moment infused with a knowledge and emotion it didn't have then but does now. The narrative route has backtracked and seen the cloud through 20 years of sky, to uncover what was yet to have meaning for him. The personal essay gives present understanding to a past memory, revealing not just the route but what Doug learned en route while living in New Zealand.

Perhaps the greatest marker on Doug's journey is that his two-year-old son Thomas is now a young man. Instinctively, in a move to connect the narrative past with what it later revealed, Doug speaks directly to his son, pointing to the memory of the sky: 'There it is, Thomas, those quilted clouds, knitted together like a furrowed brow of heaven, winking down on you.' The personified sky 'winking down' on his small son is like a benevolent deity. From the greater vantage point of their shared lives, the father can address his past and present child: 'You get to grow up and spend your life here.'

One of the 'seeds yet to flourish' is now known to have done just that: with the double vantage point of the past and the present in the essay, Doug can place the toddler and the young man side by side, knowing that the route thus far has turned out well for his son. Like many Kiwis, his son will work abroad in his twenties, but come home to New Zealand to raise his family.

Between two shores

Migrants understand and interpret their experience relative to where they are in their migration journey: before they leave the country, when they are newly arrived, or days, months, years or even decades later. The personal essay is geared for such exploration, driven by its desire to inquire and appraise experience for its significance. Although the migration route is bound by time and space, writing allows for re-vision, to re-see or see in a new light, or even see what was overlooked. As the brilliant essayist George Orwell notes: 'it can also happen that one's memories grow sharper after a long lapse of time, because one is looking at the past with fresh eyes and can isolate and, as it were, notice facts which previously existed undifferentiated amid a mass of others.'[16] For example, the reasons migrants habitually give for migrating might not be the ones that drove them, or they remember details learned en route which they've forgotten or buried. As Gareth, the Welsh doctor, found, 'writing essays is a demanding, satisfying challenge that is also frustrating and emotionally charged. Frustrating when the words do not match the memories and feelings; emotionally charged when the words disturb the dust covering the memories which I had, perhaps, hidden from myself.'

One virtue of writing is that 'objectified and held at a distance from the self, the written word makes possible a considered survey of the human mind and its contents: once a thought can be looked at once, it can be looked at twice.'[17] Writing allows us to see what came before and what came after, where we have been and where we are now, and to reflect on how we have been changed by what has happened. Through the essay, Elizabeth, the Englishwoman in her forties, sees the value of looking back and understanding who she once was: 'Now I know more about who I was back then, what I was trying to contain, the past I was recoiling from and the future I was hurtling towards, I see more in the photographs of that time. I see panic, denial, abstract hope, haste, pain. An inability to cope unless I was running, so that I could feel nothing but the sinews in my calves and the ache of my lungs.' Her unflinching self-examination in her essay reveals she was running away to New Zealand, husband in tow, because he is happy to be towed and wants to surf, and she has lined up an excellent job.

Three weeks before they emigrate she predicts in her journal: 'It is so obvious it will end in tears.' The route did not end in tears, but it was transformed by them: 'In New Zealand I lost absolutely everything – my marriage, my home, my savings, my identity and my ability to soldier on with platitudes. Yet in the rubble of my life I found myself – a self that for 42 years I only hoped might exist.' She lists everything she lost, underscoring them through the insistent repetition of the personal pronoun 'my': 'my marriage, my home, my savings, my identity and my ability to soldier on with platitudes'. One loss leads to another in a cascade of undoing and dissolution of things both concrete and abstract. Migrating to New Zealand was the catalyst for all that loss, but it also gave her a 'self' that for many years she 'only hoped might exist'. Had she not come to New Zealand, that self might never have manifested.

For Elizabeth, the route to New Zealand became the route to an authentic self. Only through the loss of an identity tied to marriage, home, savings and the ability to soldier on does she achieve this transformation. She realises that her story is one 'of layers. In my new land of plenty, each one was stripped back by life's twists and turns to reveal the one beneath.' In the process of stripping back those layers through writing, she understands that the route contains the route: 'I've achieved so much in six years. More than I ever could have done in England. I think if my marriage had gone wrong in the UK, I'd have been propped up by friends and irritated by family. And both would have had me looking outward, not inward for solutions. In New Zealand it was just me, bags of pain, bags of time, great resources and the most beautiful scenery on earth.'

Family and friends who knew her narrative from the past are not witness to the dissolution of her marriage half a world away. They cannot help shore up her marriage or her self from afar. She must reconstruct her life and herself, which is exactly what she does: 'I left England a sad shadow of the person I could have been. I return reflective, confident, authentic, deliberating, unafraid of disappointing others in order to remain true to myself.' When, in the end, Elizabeth returns to England, she freely owns her part in choosing the migration route that undid her marriage: 'I was the architect of the life which would unravel us.'

Elizabeth's prose throughout her essays is forthright and honest, in keeping with the genre: 'The personal essay has an open form and a drive toward candor and self-disclosure.'[18] The level of candour and self-disclosure can be highly variable, of course, but everything Elizabeth achieves en route towards her self-realisation is embodied in writing that is 'reflective, confident, authentic, deliberating, unafraid of disappointing others in order to remain true to [her]self'. If her migration indeed formed the route to her authentic self, then her personal essays offered a clear pathway towards recognition of this awareness.

For some migrants, the route of migration has the opposite effect. Instead of coalescing a sense of self, the migrant experiences a sense of erasure, muteness and disappearance, a feeling I know well from my time in Sweden. Anna, a Swiss woman who married a New Zealander and migrated to his country in 1968, gave poignant expression to this idea: 'Sometimes I felt as if the person I had been was fading out of existence. So many of the things that had helped to shape me into who I was had been stripped away, my country, my language, my culture, the treasured traditions, my home, my family, my friends, and even my name. English speaking people pronounce it differently.'

What a catalogue of loss this is, with the powerful anaphora emphasising everything that is 'stripped away' from her: 'my country, my language, my culture, the treasured traditions, my home, my family, my friends, and even my name'. If ever there was a list of what a migrant gives up to follow a foreign partner to his or her home country, this is it. Anna begins with the large abstractions she has lost: her country, embedded in her language, culture and traditions. The list then deepens to more personal and grievous losses: 'my home, my family, my friends, and even my name.' Perhaps the most affecting thing she loses is also the most elemental and basic, her name. Forty years later the disbelief at her loss of name resonates – the last item on her list, even this is stripped away.

Little else stands in for us as clearly as our name, and Anna now understands that hearing her name pronounced differently contributed to her feeling that 'the person [she] had been was fading out of existence'. No longer surrounded by or speaking her own language heightens the sense of erasure, for 'people who move from one natural language to another are likely to undergo significant losses to their existing selves'.[19] Since no one remembers or shares her past narrative in the new country, her old self is in danger of 'fading out of existence'. Here the recognition and awareness offered by the personal essay are a means to prevent the disappearance of self, an insistence through words that prevents such erasure. Her migrated self must follow a route towards understanding and being understood, so that the world becomes resonant and meaningful again.

Our desire for meaning is essential to our well-being, and perhaps even more so for migrants who have left behind a world that held meaning for them. Unless we migrate with someone from our past, no one in the new country knows or remembers us as we were, and probably few if anyone share much of what once interwove our life – people, places, scents, tastes, sounds. Beth, a South African migrant in her sixties, produced a vivid list of what she misses in her home country: 'hot tropical evenings smelling of frangipani, the voice of hadeda shrieks, of bunny chows and the smell of rain on hot tar, of the Sharks rugby team and the No Tracy Chapman beggar'. These are the rich intangibles of a world she no longer inhabits, a world existing only in memory: 'Migrants, perhaps more than other people, are made by their memories of their birthplaces, their homeland, those left behind – interruptions in the life narratives that require resequencing, remodelling and reinterpreting as the newcomers incorporate and surpass their pasts.'[20] Migrants must find new frames of reference for meaning in their chosen country if they are to form any sort of attachment or connection, for that is the route of belonging.

Unlike those who never leave their home country, migrants cross a frontier into the unknown. They are stripped of the very things Anna the Swiss migrant detailed in her list: country, language, culture, treasured traditions, family, friends, home. Establishing similar links in the new country takes time, and it is this route that migrants map over days and years. Often the effort to understand things that do not yet have meaning is exhausting: language, culture, the innumerable things one encounters upon migrating to a new country. I felt this disconnect while living in Sweden, hemmed in by the dense forest of everything I did not understand: why no one made eye contact; why doors to houses opened out and not in; why there was no word for please; why they did everything in groups and travelled with their own bedding when they came to visit; and why, despite taking good care of its citizenry, the country felt neither welcoming nor generous.

Hélène Cixous observes that 'writing forms a passageway between two shores',[21] and this is especially true for migrants, who leave one geographic, cultural and linguistic shore for another. Every migrant crosses both a literal and an existential shore, and the personal essay acts as a passageway between the two, a route to where self meets world and self meets other. Emeritus Professor of English G. Douglas Atkins captured this idea when he wrote: 'In more than one manner the essay moves outward, the essay and its writer connecting with the world, with otherness.'[22] The movement outwards in the essay has a parallel with the route of migration, which is outwards from what is known and familiar towards what is unknown and other.

The passage between the two shores is even greater when the migrant must cross over into a new language and a culture very different from the ones left behind. In 1994 In Suk migrated from Korea to New Zealand where she found herself challenged by language, ethnicity, gender and marital status. Her essays show how difficult the route of migration can be as she journeyed from the known towards the unknown. As a divorced Korean mother, she experienced a powerful censure in her own country that helped set her migration in motion: 'I was alone, with my five year old daughter. I hadn't slept a wink for a few years. All the time there were questions, "Where will I go? What will I do?" trailed after me. The stigma of my situation burned within me.' When she sees the newspaper advertisement for immigration to New Zealand she realises an opportunity has appeared: 'All I could think of was to get away, miles away from where I was to start a new beginning.'

Three years later, In Suk receives permission to immigrate, yet she hesitates. Family, friends and colleagues question her decision: 'There were heaps of times I was asked how I would live with only a young nine year old daughter in a new country where I knew No One!' The exclamation mark and the capital letters underscore her fellow Koreans' shock at her decision. Eventually, despite knowing the risk, she leaves 'family, friends and an excellent job … taking flight on wings into the air with tears, dreams, hope'. She trades the emotional, concrete reality of 'family, friends and an excellent job' for 'tears, dreams, hope', those migrant tropes that might or might not smooth her passage to the new country.

On her arrival in New Zealand In Suk is confronted by the reality of her decision, not only for herself but also for her daughter: 'My daughter seemed to be excited, but my head was suddenly throbbing with anxiety with the thought of how to survive here.' She rents a small flat near a shopping centre, enrols her daughter in primary school and takes courses in English at the local polytech, but the immersion and her survival have an emotional cost: 'I withdrew from everyone because I felt I was deaf and mute.' Alone as she is in a foreign country, the experience of being without language is acute, and her essay distils what that absence was like: 'I felt I was deaf and mute.'

Eva Hoffman, who migrated from Poland to Canada at age 14, explains that 'being without language I found that when we do not have words with which to name our inner experiences, those experiences recede from us into an inner darkness; without words with which to name the world, that world becomes less vivid, less lucid'.[23] In Suk could comprehend the world in Korean, but the world in which she now lived was permeated with English, and in that world she was 'deaf and mute'. Hers was an experience I remember well from Sweden. I had no voice and could only glean the words I was slowly accruing in Swedish. Everything else flowed by in a stream of incomprehension. Few things are more daunting than migrating to a foreign country and facing the enormity of learning a new language. Stripped of roots, language and culture, In Suk acknowledges New Zealand as 'a world I could hardly understand except by enormous striving'. Her striving is borne out by her astute reflections within her personal essays.

In Suk's route towards understanding her new country was not just linguistic. It included a whole new physical and cultural landscape she had to learn to interpret. She describes one of her first evenings in New Zealand when the sense of alienation and strangeness pressed upon her:

When the morning went and the evening came, the nip in the air was filled with the quietness and darkness like a dead city. Where were the people? Where were the vehicles which boomed with hideous noises and a cloud of dust? The evening approached upon me, I turned on TV. The voices were flying over me like a ghost. I shuddered at the thought of the decision I'd made. There would be other trials waiting for us.

The sense of being haunted in this passage is unmistakable. In Suk likens the dark silence to 'a dead city'. In contrast, she wonders where the people, noise and clouds of dust characteristic of urban Korea are. Evening becomes personified: 'The evening approached upon me,' phrasing that could be due to second language learning but nevertheless gives the sense of being oppressed. She banishes the quiet of the evening: 'I turned on TV.' Even with the missing definitive article, her act of turning on the TV to provide some sense of connection with the outer world is understood and commonplace. The voices on the TV deepen her sense of being haunted and she extends the metaphor: 'The voices were flying over me like a ghost.' Language becomes disembodied and spectral when it is not her own.

Azade Seyhan observes: 'In many stories of immigration, the loss of voice leads women to encounters with voices and visions of ghosts.'[24] In Suk's muteness is conflated with the ghostly voices on the TV. Again she realises the ramifications of her decision, which are terrifying to contemplate: 'I shuddered at the thought of the decision I'd made. There would be other trials waiting for us.' The decision had been particularly difficult because it involved her daughter's welfare, even though this was part of its motivation. Back in Korea, In Suk was told '[her] daughter shouldn't be educated in Korea because of her direct personality'.

For In Suk, as for any non-native speaker, the route to integration in the new country is through language. Language embodies culture on abstract and concrete levels and touches on every aspect of the migrant's new life – written, spoken, heard. Language connects us, and when the migrant doesn't understand the host country's language, the sense of disconnection and alienation is profound. All the non-native speakers in this braided narrative chose to live in New Zealand, so agency provided a strong motivation to acquire the language. Moreover, the migrant's command of the host country's language is 'the most significant indicator of the ability to integrate with the local indigenous community and to come to terms with the local culture'.[25] Language was one of the reasons why Sabina, the Dutch migrant, came to New Zealand: 'The English language that I love is what made me go to all the countries where they speak it. And then I heard it one day in New Zealand where the English language suddenly has a nice ring to it.'

For Sabina, the route of language was positive from the outset because she enjoyed studying English in school. But for In Suk, who migrated in her forties, the route to language acquisition was difficult and she had to make a concentrated effort to master it: 'To integrate into the native society we moved to a Kiwi church. Tricky colloquial English is a forever task to be solved. Mingling with this was and is not easy. Whose problem is it? Nobody has the answer. This has made my high university's degree and good qualification buried. However, I have tried to learn English to survive here as a useful person who contributes to this society.'

In Suk recognises that learning '[t]ricky colloquial English' is 'forever a task to be solved', which the slightly awkward syntax tellingly reveals. The route to learning English is ongoing, as she confesses that 'Mingling with this was and is not easy.' Like many migrants, In Suk was deskilled when her university degree and qualifications were not recognised in the host country, or as she puts it, were 'buried'. The migrant's sense of worth and purpose is diminished when she is unable to work on the educational and economic level she once did because 'work provides a sense of esteem, self-coherence, identity, location in a social context, and, in Freud's words, "justification for existence in society"'.[26] As though echoing Freud, In Suk says with the humility that pervades her essays: 'I have tried to learn English to survive here as a useful person.'

In Suk did more than survive, though – she embraced the commitment necessary to embark on the route of migration: 'This turning point ought to be undertaken as vital milestone in my life and for my daughter like pilgrims.' Even with her slightly ungrammatical phrasing, she realises the importance of what she undertook and uses a metaphor appropriate for the journey, that of the pilgrim. The milestone has been vital, life-changing for them both, and especially beneficial for her daughter: 'Many circumstances surrounding my daughter led to outstanding solutions for her life.'

Overall, though, the journey proved to be more difficult for In Suk because her language acquisition lagged behind her young daughter's, which often happens with adult migrants and their school-age children. Immersed in the local Swedish school, my own two children learned Swedish fairly quickly because they had to, whereas I was alone all day, writing about being without language, and going into Gothenburg once a week to the polytech to learn Swedish in classes taught by a Hungarian migrant – hardly an accelerated language programme. But the truth was perhaps much simpler, for unlike In Suk, I did not want to learn the language of the host country.

Often feeling torn by the route she chose, In Suk considered going back to Korea: 'I was in conflict between returning home for my career and well-paid position or staying here for my daughter many times. My family, especially my mum, and Kiwi friends have encouraged and enforced us to keep digging the ground for us and other people by giving hope.' Her use of the word 'enforced' confirms how subtle and difficult language is, and yet she wants to imply she was given strength to remain in New Zealand thanks to family and Kiwi friends.

In Suk's selfless commitment to stay in New Zealand for her daughter's sake enabled her to overcome significant obstacles along her migration route, and she hopes that their example as migrants might help others. Her personal essays, with their modest but very real courage, embody what the genre can do as they move from the individual to the universal, for 'creative nonfiction is rooted in reality, but it seeks the symbolic character of art; that is, it seeks to discover the universal in the particular, and asks us to consider what it is that makes us human and connects us to one another'.[27] Both on the page and in her life, In Suk's example urges us all 'to keep digging the ground for us and other people by giving hope'. Her essays mark a passage between two shores, between

her formerly mute Korean self and her present-day English-speaking and
English-writing self. She has given voice to the migrant who arrives in a
country with nothing to connect her but 'tears, dreams, hope'.

Jigsaw pieces that fit

Migration is a passage between two shores, the known and the unknown,
and charting that route is something that informs a lifetime. 'Migrants,'
says Salman Rushdie, 'must, of necessity, make a new imaginative
relationship with the world, because of the loss of familiar habitats'.[28]
Forging that 'new imaginative relationship' is part of mapping the route
of learning to live in a new country. One of the difficulties I faced in
Sweden was that my life was unimaginable even while it was painfully
real. I couldn't bear the thought of living there permanently. Sweden
taught me that no amount of effort on my part would create a sense of
connection or belonging. We cannot will acceptance, from ourselves or
from others. Acceptance comes of its own accord, a gift of affinity and
resonance. We know when we feel it and when we do not.

I remember being stunned when my 11-year-old daughter, her
Swedish fluent after a year in the local school, said to me: 'I understand
everything, but I still hate it here.' I thought language would grant her
acceptance, but clearly language alone is not enough. We must accept
and feel accepted where we live to feel we belong, as John O'Donohue
acknowledges: 'True belonging is gracious receptivity'.[29] Without that
feeling of receptivity, no matter how long migrants live somewhere or
how fluently they speak the language, they will always feel at a distance.

One essential element that allows migrants to feel they belong in the
host country is love. It's far easier to forge a new imaginative relationship
with the world if there is something and someone to love in that world
as well. Love acts as a powerful magnet; it draws people together from
different cultures, languages and landscapes. Over half the migrants
whose essays inform this narrative came to New Zealand thanks to their
choice of partner. Of these 21 migrant pairings, 11 have New Zealand
partners and seven had to learn English as a result of that relationship:

love, not work, determined their migration route. 'Do not underestimate,' cautions Russell King, 'the libidinal factor in migration.'[30] For Maartje, a Dutch migrant, it was indeed love – the love between her parents – that brought their family to New Zealand in 1963: 'My mother loved my father so much that she followed him literally to the end of the earth. They took this step together and never looked back; they appeared to have no regrets.'

Taegen, an Englishwoman in her seventies, followed her partner to New Zealand in 1982. She had met her future Kiwi husband on a blind date in London: 'I moved to this side of the world for the love of a man. New Zealand was not a country I even thought about visiting let alone living in. I had travelled a great deal, I had even settled in another country for three years. South Africa.' Love plotted the route of her migration to a country she never considered visiting, 'let alone living in', despite her having migrated once before. This love also affected the lives of her two sons, aged 12 and 14, whom she brought to the other side of the world in the hope of blending them with her new partner's family of four teenage children. 'I sold my cottage, sold off or packed up our belongings, all to begin the journey to the next stage of our lives. It was a gamble. We loved where we lived, we were to leave behind many friends, new schools, a great job (a natural history photographic library), and I was making the decision for my two young boys (and my dog) based on the love for a very special person.'

Taegen gave up many things to embark on this route. Her sacrifice exemplifies the gendered dimension of migration, where 'women may also be more likely than men to make personal and professional sacrifices to join partners overseas.'[31] In her essay she recognises that her migration involved not only her concerns but those of her sons and, in a telling absence of personal pronouns, she bases this life-changing decision 'on the love for a very special person'. In both cases when she refers to the force driving her migration, with respect to its root and route, its origin and destination, she writes not 'my love' but 'the love'. The absence of the personal pronoun 'my' makes the power of love greater and more universal, a force strong enough to offset everything left behind. The object of this love, moreover, is a generic blank: 'a very special person'.

Taegen planned her route carefully, visiting New Zealand twice before deciding to migrate. Friends urged her not to sell her house but to rent it, leaving her with a fall-back if it didn't work out, but she did the opposite, thereby committing herself to the migration: 'My reasoning was that if I was half hearted about anything then it would never work. I was sure of my man – less sure about New Zealand, nervous about what I was imposing on the lives of my boys, sad about leaving my parents. So yes, apprehension but also a conviction that this was a wonderful chance for a new beginning for all of us.'

Here, she is sure of her partner, and in this instance she does claim him as 'my man'. But then that wonderful dash against which she stacks everything she is not sure about, and the list is weighty – the new country, her two sons and her parents. Her writing is effortless and swift in its declaration of the pros and cons of her decision: 'So yes, apprehension but also a conviction that this was a wonderful chance for a new beginning for all of us.' We can hear her refuting any naysayers about her chosen path in that 'So yes', which accords with essayist Edward Hoagland's claim: 'A personal essay is like the human voice talking, its order the mind's natural flow.'[32]

Yet that flow is crafted, not random as speech often is. As Phillip Lopate says of the form, 'there is still a good deal of selection and art in this appearance of spontaneous process.'[33] Taegen had an unshakeable belief in her endeavour, which no doubt helped her to realise 'a new beginning for all of us'. Her two sons 'never looked back', and for herself she writes: 'I had never been so happy in my life. I often used to comment: it was as though the world was made up of jigsaw pieces and somehow Bill's and my pieces had found their way from one side of the world to the other – to fit.' Again the dash appears, but instead of separating the clauses, it joins their two pieces of the puzzle. What her essay reveals is a radiant confidence and belief that this route will work out. She believed it 30 years ago when she risked everything for this man, now named, and it glows on the page decades later, even though she is now a widow.

The idea of fitting together like a jigsaw puzzle, as one piece finds its way across the world to be with another, is a good analogy for whether migrants can find a way to connect and to feel they belong. How well migrants fit with their new partners, the new country, the new culture or, perhaps most challenging, the new language, determines how smooth the route will be. Taegen's migration route was comparatively easy as she married into the New Zealand culture, spoke the dominant language and wished to live in the chosen country, as witnessed by everything she gave up to make that route possible. She not only adapted herself to the route but also made the most of it. For example, having come from the culinary abundance of Europe, when she saw the limited produce choices in New Zealand she took immediate action: 'Imagine my disappointment as I gazed at the few tired-looking vegetables offering me no choice. A large vegetable and herb garden were quickly established and what I could not buy I grew.' Her proactive response serves as an excellent example for how to make the route take root: adapt. The sentiment was one that Amelia, another English migrant who married a New Zealander, embraced: 'Discussing with the Vicar my thoughts on marrying an international ex-pat he asked, "How was I going to cope?" "Well," I replied, "adopt, adapt, adjust." So began the next 25 years of my life.' The adaptive and flexible nature of the personal essay is readily suited to chart such route-making because it 'is able to take off on any tack it wishes, building its own structure as it moves along, rebuilding and remaking itself – and its author – each time out'.[34] Migrants, too, seek to rebuild and remake themselves in a new country.

Not all migrants adapt and adjust as readily as others. Sometimes, even when the migrant is married to a native and speaks the language, such advantages do not offset everything they gave up and left behind in the home country. Livingston, the Scottish doctor who migrated to New Zealand at age 60, found migration problematic from the moment he first became aware of it as a possibility. He mentions passing brushes with New Zealand that included care packages received as a child from an uncle who lived in Greymouth, and his father's respect for All Blacks rugby: 'This warm awareness of New Zealand came into focus when I met Janet. New Zealand now had a persona which I loved. Had Janet come from, say, Latvia, I would have loved her no less but would I have been as comfortable?' Here we see a growing awareness of New Zealand with each feature of the country he encounters until the country becomes embodied, literally and figuratively, in Janet, his second wife.

By looking back, Livingston was able to see his migration route unfolding into deeper layers of connection. Though Sven Birkerts notes such unfolding with respect to memoir, it applies equally well to the personal essay: 'the search for patterns and connections is the real point – and the glory – of the genre'.[35] When we look back in the essay we can see patterns and connections that do not appear at the time they occur, as Livingston recognised: 'New Zealand came into even sharper focus when in 1994, this middle-aged couple had a daughter. It was then that the unimaginable – moving to New Zealand – drifted into my consciousness.' Suddenly, the prose distances itself in the third person, the personal names are dropped, and they become 'this middle-aged couple' with 'a daughter' (not 'our' daughter). It is as though the experience is happening to someone else.

I felt the same way when Sweden came on the horizon: a dissociative sense that this was not happening to me, even while the reality was drawing nearer. For Livingston, migration to New Zealand was an abstraction despite his 'warm awareness' of the country. But then 'the unimaginable – moving to New Zealand – drifted into my consciousness.' Like an iceberg drifting towards him, his younger self had no idea that this abstraction would become a reality – that the route he was on contained this route. The drift lasted 11 years before he and his wife acted on what, for him, had been 'unimaginable'.

In the UK the couple's daughter had been about to enter a 'notoriously bad local high school', and Janet, who by now had been living in Scotland for over 20 years, thought the family would be better off in her home country, New Zealand. Once more we see how love for partner and/or child determines the route of migration, and how often it entails sacrifice. 'Why did we come here?' Livingston agonises in one of his essays:

Why did we not just move somewhere else in the UK with better
schooling? Janet would have accepted that. How could I abandon again
my older children? I did not want to. But there was the strength of Janet's
simply stated belief that life for all of us, especially our daughter, would
be better in New Zealand. Her fairness in refusing to put pressure on me,
her insistence that it was to be my decision and that she would accept the
outcome, made her argument all the more potent.

His torment is evident in the rhetorical questions, 'why, how', as
though he cannot believe he made the decision when there were other,
easier choices. While it was his wife's desire to move back to New
Zealand, she insisted the decision should be his, and for him the choice
was painful. He had to sell his medical practice and leave behind his
aging father and two older children from his prior marriage. What
he gives up is therefore considerable. Nor are his reflections on this
proposed migration unconflicted: 'Even after two years of pondering the
decision, I was still not sure the move was right for me.'

Despite his misgivings, Livingston did decide to migrate. His
conclusion as to why he made this decision is wonderfully self-
deprecating: 'Then, of course, there is me and the way I am with my
tendency to try to avoid the grind of sorting out difficult personal
problems, preferring sometimes to extirpate them by drastic action –
like moving to the other side of the world, perhaps.' He mocks his own
character – 'Then, of course, there is me and the way I am' – before
following on with a ruthless analysis of his 'tendency to try to avoid
the grind of sorting out personal problems, preferring sometimes to
extirpate them by drastic action'. The sentence breaks in on itself with
the dash, and the drastic action 'is moving to the other side of the world,
perhaps'. It's hard to imagine a more extreme approach to rooting out
personal problems than moving halfway across the world. Rooting out
becomes his route, but with that final 'perhaps' he equivocates, almost
whimsically, showing he's still not convinced.

Livingston's wife and daughter went on ahead to New Zealand while
he wrapped everything up back in Scotland. While they were apart his
daughter fell ill with an undiagnosed malady, adding to his anxiety both
as a father and as a doctor: 'By early April and the time to leave, I was

emotionally exhausted.' He was such a wreck his sister realised he could not manage the journey from Lincolnshire to Heathrow Airport: 'When we arrived at the station, I was barely able to get out of the car, let alone haul my bags onto the train and across London. I can still hardly believe how bad I felt. She left me in the car, walked to a cash machine and over to a taxi which she arranged to take me to Heathrow one hundred and twenty miles and one hundred and fifty pounds away.' In recounting this moment of pure vulnerability he wins the reader's trust, thereby meeting Phillip Lopate's assertion that 'Some vulnerability is essential to the personal essay.'[36] Even when writing of this departure seven years on, he cannot believe how miserable he felt. His words reveal how fraught the actual route can be when the migrant is reluctant to leave.

Finally, Livingston is aboard the flight. Through the window of the emergency exit at the back of the plane, where a queue forms for the lavatory 'courtesy of alcohol, prostates and nerves', he watches England recede. In a memory riddled with ambivalence he looks back on both himself and his departure:

> So, there I was, my head swimming in this mix of emotions, looking out of a little window at the back of a big plane watching England slide away. What should have been unalloyed joy at the prospect of seeing my family was tarnished by my worry about my daughter. What should have been optimism about a new life was clouded in sadness, doubt and nostalgia. And, looking at the big handle which opens the plane door, the oddest thought flashed through my mind. That journey was my threshold.

Livingston torments himself by comparing what he 'should' feel with what he does feel. His unalloyed joy at reuniting with his family is tarnished by worry, and any optimism about his new life is 'clouded in sadness, doubt and nostalgia'. While New Zealand 'drift[s] into his consciousness', he watches England 'slide away' in actuality. And as he looks at the handle of the emergency exit, which he may have felt tempted to pull, he knows there is no going back.

At this moment the epiphany strikes him: 'the oddest thought flashed through my mind. That journey was my threshold.' This threshold separates the life he once had from the one he will now live. The migration is no longer an abstraction; it is real. As German philosopher

Martin Heidegger observed: 'The threshold bears the between.'[37] And it is not a stopping place, but exists like an irrevocable moment outside time and space when we realise we cannot prevent the flow of what's happening. Yet Livingston does stop it, right there in the essay, so as to acknowledge it: 'this moment is not the result of applying a preconceived method, but is a spontaneous, unpredictable discovery, though often prepared by careful attention and observation.'[38] Livingston bears witness to that threshold moment and gives it duration and permanence in writing, long after he is on the far side of the world.

'With no language but with hope'

Sometimes the migration route is not planned but inadvertent, the result of a fork in the road where the individual chooses something that will affect the rest of his life, even though at the time he is not aware of the impact of this decision. Anton, a Russian deep-sea navigator, found himself at such a crossroads: 'This is it. From East to the West. My company had gone bankrupt and the captain was drunk. I knocked on the door of the captain's cabin and asked him for my passport and then I would be off to the land of opportunities, thanks for nothing, see you later, bye bye.'

The bitterness he felt at finding himself suddenly jobless in New Zealand still stings in his prose over a decade later. Only 23, stranded in a country with no prospects, connections or language, Anton remembers his response: '... to escape my worries I put on my running shoes and I ran. Up the hills, through the university grounds, in the beautiful botanical gardens, anywhere, everywhere. It was like I was running from this very difficult decision I felt forced to make ... return to the uncertain life of the Russian fisherman, or should I take my New Zealand visa, and earn a living here, with no language but with hope.' Although he does not have a clear way forward, and although both paths are uncertain, hope seems to have been crucial to the decision he makes.

Adrift in New Zealand, Anton bumps into fellow Russians he has known since high school back on Sakhalin, an island of 450,000 people.

He explains the coincidence as 'The way the Russian community worked outside of Russia, as well as in Russia, was that you know a Russian who knows a Russian who knows another Russian and suddenly everybody knows everything about everyone else.' One such chance encounter with a former schoolmate boosts his determination 'to do what I really wanted, which was to try my luck with any casual labouring I could get'.

Having agency proves to be critical. He manages to find work, remaining in New Zealand despite parental pressure to return to Russia. His father, a fellow deep-sea navigator, travelled extensively for his job and had extolled the clean, green beauty of New Zealand to his son: 'My father loved to tell these stories many times.' These stories and the same career choice as his father led him to 'the beautiful island that I would dream of, and it happened, I am here. It felt exciting right from the beginning in the way that I had dreamed, so already I felt a connection to this place.' His father thus influenced both the root and route of Anton's maritime career and the dream of New Zealand.

While working as a fruit picker and sharing a flat 'with three Russians, three Azerbaijanis, two Englishmen, two Māori, and one French guy' (a veritable pack of migrant workers with the exception of the Māori flatmate), Anton was robbed of several thousand dollars that his father sent him. He felt he could not accuse anyone without causing arguments and ending friendships, but he is blunt about what this experience taught him with respect to staying in New Zealand:

> At times, in my home away from home, it's all good fun, but when you are cheated and have no voice, it is an ugly reminder that you are not safe here, not until you achieve the life that is acceptable, really until you latch yourself to a New Zealander with family and a social network, and make it home. Many of my friends I heard about, those living in Dunedin and Christchurch, had begun to do this.

The passage starts out in first person, 'my home', then shifts to second person, making the personal self universal, one who is robbed and has no voice. However, he also gives voice to that migrant self who had neither language nor agency at the time the event occurred.

Years later Anton's tone is still bitter, but the pain of the theft has turned from a reminder about safety to the need for connections and a sense of belonging: 'you are not safe here, not until you achieve the life that is acceptable, really until you latch yourself to a New Zealander with family and a social network, and make it home'. The word 'really' emphasises the route needed to achieve acceptance. Anton condemns those of his friends that he thinks have taken this route too readily: 'I felt that it was sacrificing your youth to just hook up with some woman you don't love, a friend of a friend's wife for example.' Again we see how the chain of association among Russians works – 'a friend of a friend's wife'.

Anton is correct that marrying into a host-nation family gives a migrant immediate access to the culture and community, accelerating the assimilation process. Mixed-nationality relationships provide 'relatively rapid and direct access to host-country sociocultural networks, where access would normally take years, decades and even generations to access'.[39] Birgitta, a Swedish woman who married a New Zealander, pinpoints this route toward familiarisation:

> In New Zealand, there was a large family, too, a family-in-law to stay with until we found a house. I would grow fond of the new Mum and there was no difficulty about that name as it was an English word, not used for my own mother. What was, sometimes is, *normal* in New Zealand, is still the life in that family, *what* they said, the *way* they said it, the food they ate, the plants that grew in their garden, their attitudes to everything. What would have taken years if we had lived by ourselves seeped into my conscious and unconscious minds during the first six weeks.

Birgitta received a crash course in New Zealand cultural norms from living with her in-laws for six weeks. Her education in local culture was relatively comprehensive: '... *what* they said, the *way* they said it, the food they ate, the plants that grew in their garden, their attitudes to everything'. Her use of italics specifies and clarifies, and even though over 40 years have passed since she first came to New Zealand, the memories still resonate. The list of what she learned exemplifies how the 'extended family, especially the in-laws, assumes the role of familiarizing the newcomer with the local culture. It is also the primary agent for conveying local values and practices'.[40] From the vantage point of decades, Birgitta can look back and state: 'What was, sometimes is, *normal* in New Zealand, is still the life in that family.'

Migrants who do not have the benefit of a family to familiarise them with 'local values and practices' must look for other ways to connect and make sense of what is happening on their own, even as the writer does on the page. Essayist Cynthia Ozick agrees: 'a genuine essay is made out of language and character and mood and temperament and pluck and chance … An essay is reflection and insight.'[41] These traits are exactly what aid migrants on their respective journeys – language, character, temperament, pluck and chance – all of which lead to reflection and insight, both in life and in the essay. Both the migrant and the writer are charting a route towards understanding as they find their way in life and on the page.

Looking back on his own route, the Russian Anton is able to piece it together: 'While I was working as a kitchen hand in Arthur's Pass village in 1997 I could not speak much of the language. I remember I was taught to say "Gladwrap" by one of the waitresses. This was a very small and close community and I was the only Russian there at that time.' Building on one word, one encounter at a time, the invisible overlapping strands of chance and connection led from Gladwrap to his eventually becoming a chef and marrying a New Zealander who was also working in Arthur's Pass. The essay allowed Anton to draw meaning from these disparate and seemingly random events, tracing a design that emerges only when he looks back on his route in the new country – a country he had arrived in 'with no language but with hope'. In the essay the subject is not simply the self: 'The subject is, rather, all that is undergone: it is a combination of experience, self and the meaning and significance ultimately derived and then passed along.'[42] As readers, we travel the path of reflection with the essayist and share in his discovery. In titling his essay 'Best Decision I Ever Made', Anton sums up his view of the route he took.

Acceptance of the other

Migrants are helped along their route by those who welcome and help them become familiar with the new country. In an effort to understand where they live, migrants must learn to negotiate the language and culture, accessible to those who understand them but almost impenetrable to those who cannot. As Eva Hoffman points out for new migrants like herself: 'What that first period of radical dislocation brought home to me was how much we are creatures of culture, and how much incoherence we risk when we fall out of its matrix.'[43] Learning an entirely new matrix of language and culture is a lifelong effort for non-native speakers, and cultural understanding can be daunting even for those who share the language.

Often what helps migrants achieve linguistic and cultural fluency is simple kindness, such as Piet experienced when he arrived from the Netherlands over 50 years ago: 'On a rainy day, when we couldn't do much work on the farm, Bob might tell me to stay home. He would then often come over and have an extended morning tea with us and took great pleasure in teaching us new words and how to pronounce them.' The fact that his boss took time and experienced pleasure teaching Piet and his wife English reveals how a native inhabitant can make a migrant feel welcome and sufficiently encouraged to learn the language. In Piet's case that welcome came from more than one person: 'We found NZ people very polite and we were never ridiculed for coming out with the wrong pronunciation. All they would do is then repeat a word unobtrusively as it should be pronounced.' Decades later his essay singles out this kindness to him and his wife for helping them both feel welcome as migrants.

Noki, a Dutchman who migrated in the 1970s, experienced something rather different: '… integration was a more "in your face" exercise. Having to educate difficult teenagers is certainly stressful in a strange country. Accent is made fun of, purposeful misinterpretation rife and the propagation of half truths par for the course.' Yet his willingness to take his pupils' ribbing in his stride and their interest in how things were done in the Netherlands shows a mutual effort to connect between the migrant Dutchman and his New Zealand students. Sabina, the Dutchwoman who migrated in 2005, revealed positive interactions with colleagues, no doubt facilitated by her fluency in English: 'Working will give you real Kiwi experience and it makes the settling down process so much easier. Colleagues will put in an effort to get to know you, they have patience to answer your questions about where to go, what to do and it helped me to check things out, to learn the general opinion and thoughts.' Again, the personal essay proves invaluable for assessing the lived experience of migration, as 'the essay blends perceptions of the world with thought about the significance of what is perceived'.[44] Each of these encounters between native and migrant shows how a real connection to meaning gets formed in the contact zone, where both parties come away enriched and knowing more about the other.

Accepting the other is central to the route of migration. As we cross from the known into the unknown, both in the world and on the page, we enter the place where they meet. Acceptance and resistance both occur in this contact zone. What happens in that encounter sets the route of inquiry and discovery in motion. Where there is a resonance or exchange the connection between migrant and native, between writer and page, manifests in understanding and recognition, as evident in this vibrant passage from the Irish nurse Daisy:

> I was introduced to pick-your-own strawberries, honesty boxes, pot-luck, bring-a-plate and of course, the bottling of fruit. I loved the lot; it was all so sensible; I took to the new ways of doing without hesitation. I made friends and was befriended; I picked up new words and new ways of saying words – bach, veges and shopping – 'mawl'. I gave things a go and got on quite well – so well that we had to up sticks and go home to explain to the family that we intended to return in due course to settle.

Being a native speaker was an immense asset for Daisy, but so too was her enthusiastic response to what she encountered. Everything in New Zealand, from fruit to friendship, appeared generous and open, striking a chord with her. Daisy's words demonstrate how quickly a migrant can become acclimated when the place and individual resonate with one another. Her willingness to 'give things a go', a Kiwi expression, was echoed by Kornel, a young Slovakian, who suggested: 'the clue is to embrace the good. To like the people, the air, the tastes and many particularities hidden here and there.' It seems that when migrants can embrace the good, when they feel a resonance between themselves and the country, they find a route towards understanding and belonging.

However, even when migrants share the language, they will not necessarily experience a feeling of accord in the new country, as Theresa, an Indian nurse, found: 'Here I felt like a zero.' Acceptance of the other operates on a continuum and is dynamic, dependent on when, where and who we meet along the route. Although Theresa continued to feel 'like a zero' in New Zealand, especially when others had trouble understanding her accent, matters improved for her when she made 'a good friend for life. I am sure that relation helped me in my job. Since then my transition was smooth and without much helplessness, because she was there always with helping hand.' Friendship helped Theresa secure employment, but she continued to meet resistance in the workplace due to her ethnicity and accent: 'There was a time (even sometimes now) I kept silent due to my accent.' The unwillingness of some New Zealanders to accommodate her accented but fluent English rendered her silent by choice, even years later.

The personal essay allowed Theresa to acknowledge her self-imposed silence, which might not otherwise be known or observed. We see that by giving voice to her silence through writing, 'the essay is an act of personal witness'.[45] She admits she still doesn't feel entirely welcome as a migrant, that 'a complete merging was impossible due to the physical differences'. And she is forthright about the emotional cost of migration for her and her husband: 'It hurts to see the changed values in my kids, because they don't feel they belong in India any more … but we do and the conflicts start there. But at the end of the day you chose it so you have to take it whether you like it or not, you pay for it.' The ellipsis, like her earlier silence, marks a breakdown in communication, only now it is within her own family, the children having adopted the values of the host country.

Theresa is resigned to but not happy with the choice she made, having felt ambivalent from the outset: 'my husband decided on New Zealand as our dream country to migrate, for which I wasn't really convinced'. The regret is even more painful because they migrated for the sake of their children and now feel they have lost them to the dominant culture. The route contains the route but the outcome is not always what the migrant would have wished, as Theresa confirmed with her customary bluntness: 'Love the food, made many great friends around, comfortable job but something vital is missing. Tried to pretend not but didn't work. Life is not what it was all hoped to be.' What is missing in all those sentences is the 'I' who had hoped to join in and feel fully welcome in the country where she now lives.

A path to knowing

Giving voice to experience that is reflective and understood, weighed for its value and significance, is the hallmark of the personal essay. Because 'each essay springs from an idiosyncratic vision, the essayist's personal slant derived from years of life and thought and experience', we learn the real stakes of migration for each migrant, their particular and lived experience, the route mapped in the going.[46] The effect of migration on emotional and existential levels can thus be weighed and reckoned in this genre, where experience and reflection intersect to create meaning.

In Theresa's essay there is no accent to prevent us from understanding her. Young Anton, with 'no language but with hope', finds his unplanned route rewarded through his perseverance, from Gladwrap to becoming a chef, and is now married with two children. The tears, dreams and hopes of In Suk lead to her realising in writing: 'More than fifteen years have now passed by. The trials of life have turned into treasure, bringing wisdom to me and my daughter and then to others.' Susan, the American, tallies up what she has learned on her migration route: 'I can only sum it up one way – moving away from friends and family – minus 500 points. Moving to a great country with a wonderful husband – plus 500 points. Learning about myself, appreciating all I've got and changing my perspective on everything – priceless.'

What is priceless is what migrants learn when writing the personal essay and, in turn, sharing that exploration with readers. Migrants can trace the journey of the stranger who comes to town and tell us what they discovered, what helped, what hindered, where there was a moment of revelation or a small kindness extended, what seeds did flourish in the end. As Patricia Hampl emphasises, if, through writing, 'we learn not only to tell our stories but to listen to what our stories tell us – to write the first draft and then return for the second draft – we are doing the work of memory'.[47] What our story tells us is therefore at the heart of the personal essay. In the essay we can weigh and reflect upon what happened along the way and find connection and meaning in experiences and matters known only to ourselves. It is, after all, our own personal route that we map in the essay. Each of us has a singular river unwinding from its hidden headwaters to the sea. No one else's.

As a method of inquiry where experience is assessed and tested, both in actuality and then in writing, the personal essay is the ideal genre to explore how we live forwards but understand backwards and to share that recognition with others. Our ability to look both forwards and back along our own lives and the lives of others increases our understanding of the route taken or not taken, and so has immense value for migrants who have left an entire world behind and forged a life elsewhere. The poet Jane Hirshfield observes: 'Because we have the human fate of exile-consciousness inescapably present in our lives, we also get to look back from the perimeter and from the imagined ends, before and after our individual fates. We are able to see what isn't necessarily our own first point of view. This need not be self-dividing or coldly objective. It can be an increase of the intimate'.[48]

The personal essay can reveal what has happened before and after our individual fates and thereby can share what is not necessarily our first (or only) point of view. The writer can both remember what happened and reflect on what it once meant and what it may mean now. Only the individual knows what came before to bring about this point of recognition and revelation: that moment is the writer's to realise in the text. This moment of wonder and recognition occurs in the essay because 'the doing, the writing itself, is both a path *to* knowing and a path *of* knowing'.[49]

The route of the essay, even as it follows the route of our lives, leads us to knowing more about our lives. When we write, we pause amid the ongoing flow of time. We can look back and discover what we may have missed in passing and follow that route from experience to meaning. We do not stop time's passage in the essay: we understand it. We can step anywhere amid the innumerable moments of our lives to look for connection and meaning in writing. Whole swathes of our lives pass unnoticed and unrecorded, but we can find meaning along the way when it occurs. The personal essay is not the only way to achieve meaning, but it's a powerful and eminently transferable way of conveying it.

Experience without meaning is valueless, but the moment we sit down to write, we begin to remember and forge connections between our past and present selves, as journalist and author Joan Didion emphasises in 'On Keeping a Notebook': *'Remember what it was to be me*: that is always the point.'[50] She remembers that point in a personal essay where the private recollection of self becomes public – and therein lies a critical difference between the personal essay and diaries, journals and notebooks. The personal essay is written to be shared, and the meaning is made for more than ourselves.

'The essayist,' notes David Lazar, 'accepts the reader looking over her shoulder – or it may enlist the reader as an accomplice, an intimate, in the process of self-examination, in the processes of asking difficult questions of any subject it turns to.'[51] When we acknowledge that we are writing for someone in addition to ourselves, the route travelled generates more meaning, not in a didactic, pedagogic fashion, but rather the meaning resonates and corresponds with what others have thought and felt. The writer accepts the idea of other into the experience, as does the migrant, and the writing moves beyond personal significance to something that desires to connect in our shared humanity.

Acknowledging our shared humanity is central to whether the migrant finds acceptance on individual, communal and global levels. When the stranger who comes to town accepts and is accepted, a sense of belonging may develop and deepen over time. Charting that route of acceptance, closing the potential distance between the two shores of self and other, is critical to the migrant. When migrants and natives become known to each other, both cease to be strangers to one another. As

John O'Donohue says, 'all our knowing is an attempt to transfigure the unknown – to complete the journey from anonymity to intimacy'.[52]

For those migrants who find a resonance between themselves and the country and its people, the route towards understanding its culture and language becomes easier. They are able to embrace the good and see what is there, rather than what is not, to adapt where necessary, planting their garden with what is missing, interweaving their lives and narratives with others who live there. Even when migrants have a strong connection and identification with their home country, they may compromise because the people they love are happy in the new one. This is the route Livingston, the reluctant Scottish migrant, followed and acknowledged: 'Yet, when I clamber over all the baggage – and sometimes it is not easy – I can see that I am happy with the move, people I love are happy with it and others I love have grown to accept it.'

Some migrants cannot adapt to the new country, culture or language, let alone flourish in the place where they now live. Their route towards acceptance is thwarted by self, by other or by both, as with Theresa, the Indian nurse, who has tried to be accepted but still cannot feel wholly so. Because these migrants never feel they truly belong, they remain a stranger from somewhere else where they were 'known, embraced, and sheltered'.[53] To have a sense of belonging, migrants must feel known, embraced and sheltered in their new country.

A sense of welcome

I had been known, embraced and sheltered in New Zealand, something I did not notice until I felt its absence in Sweden. Part of this was to do with language. I had no idea how much language embedded and connected us with others until I was without it. Language is home to us in ways that are deeply integrating, and I realised that to communicate in Swedish with the fluency and nuance I was used to in English would take an intense commitment – in a country I did not want to commit to at all.

But it was more than that. After my initial grief over everything we had left behind in the United States, I had made a real effort to live in New Zealand. I made friends, taught wonderful students, planted gardens, lived through earthquakes. I knew and loved many people and things, and in turn my family and I were known and loved. The rich connections with people and place that we had enjoyed in our own country we had made anew in New Zealand. We should have known that to give that up again, to move to Sweden, would be impossible for all of us. But sometimes the route has an unexpected turn in its unwinding: the joy of knowing where one belongs and the joy of returning.

Understanding comes in its own time, the fruit of its own ripening and occasion. Before we migrated to Sweden the country looked safe, free from earthquakes and financially stable, but the reality was wrenching both in terms of dislocation and on emotional and existential levels, a crash course in what it means not to belong somewhere. What I witnessed when I lived in Sweden is that while it accepts a percentage of migrants into the country, it does not necessarily welcome them, as the May 2013 riots across several immigrant suburbs in Stockholm demonstrated.

The route of migration becomes even more difficult when migrants do not feel welcome, notwithstanding the added challenge of learning a new language and negotiating the subtle nuances of another culture. In Sweden I would always be an outsider, no matter how long I lived there, held back as much by myself as by the chilly reserve of the culture itself. I was reminded of the Argentine writer Jorge Luis Borges, who, when old and blind, contemplated all the cities he had lived in: Buenos Aires, Montevideo, Geneva, Austin and Nara. Rejecting Nara, Borges said: 'I don't want to die in a language I cannot understand.'[54] The truth is, where we are understood, we feel at home, and for migrants part of that journey is the route towards understanding their new country, its culture and its language.

I will never forget standing on the train platform in Gothenburg en route to Copenhagen and New Zealand, and my 15-year-old son saying, 'I am never returning to this country.' I realised that the sense of alienation he had felt over the year and a half we had spent in Sweden had embittered him, and I was grateful our time there was ending. One of the great rewards of returning to New Zealand has been seeing our children continue to grow up in a place they know and love and are known and loved. They were five and eight when we first came to New Zealand. Five years later the tectonic plates shifted, and we uprooted them to move to Sweden. No one in our family was able to flourish in that cold stony ground. The route to Sweden led miraculously back to New Zealand, to a world so small and familiar we ran into the principal of our daughter's previous school when we arrived back in the country at Wellington airport. He chided us for being traitors and moving to the North Island, but his delight in seeing us again was genuine.

How different New Zealand appeared the second time I came here, when I chose rather than resisted the route. My husband quips that Sweden made New Zealand look good, but it's deeper than that. What I learned about self, other, identity and belonging has been tested and assessed in more than one country and has changed how I see migration and what allows us to take root in some locations but not others. I realise perception affects what we can and cannot see in the host country. In New Zealand I can embrace the good. Sharing the language is part of that embrace, but I also think the country has embraced us as migrants. We feel welcome here. That welcome makes the route easier, and the stranger who comes to town does not long remain one.

We cannot know where the route will end, any more than we know what word will flow next in the sentence, for 'writing by definition is beyond us. True writing is always going forward.'[55] So, too, does the migrant go forwards, learning more, adding to the understanding of the route, all the while not knowing what lies ahead. The route contains the route and reveals itself in the going. Our route brought us back to where we could thrive and have a sense of identity, where our children could keep growing up with a place to stand, a place of empowerment and belonging, something Sweden interrupted and highlighted as essential to well-being. For here, on the far side of the world, the braided river shimmers homewards to the sea.

Chapter 3
Closing the Distance

'What seems so far from you is most your own.'

—Rainer Maria Rilke, *Sonnets to Orpheus*, xxxiii

On the day we flew out of New Zealand the country was socked in by clouds. Early winter, a dreary day, not even willing to rain. New Zealand had vanished from view, as though pulling the door of the clouds shut. I felt numb from saying goodbye to everyone, hollowed out, and couldn't believe we were headed for Sweden. Below these impenetrable clouds, I imagined we had already crossed the Waimakariri, the first braided river on the route north. The plane kept climbing and suddenly we broke through the clouds into sunlight and could see the snowy peaks of the Southern Alps glittering in the distance. I thought of the Māori name for the country, Aotearoa, land of the long white cloud, and how it fits, especially when seen from above, cloud-hidden except for that sparkling spine of the mountains. I blinked back tears as my daughter said, her voice rising in hope, 'We can come back.'

We did come back, the braided river rejoined itself, and we understood things again – not in snatches as in Sweden, but whole swathes of meaning and comprehension. As John Berger says: 'Home is the return to where distance did not yet count.'[1] The distance we felt from what we understood and what we did not in Sweden was considerable, and while that disconnect would have lessened in time, as it does for all migrants, we knew we would never feel at home living there. We needed to live somewhere we knew and loved, and so we returned to Aotearoa, a linguistic, cultural and emotional landscape now familiar and navigable, a place resonant with meaning.

In New Zealand everything felt near again – friendship, language, connection. The 12 time zones and 17,000 kilometres between Sweden and New Zealand are temporal and spatial, but the real distance is between the known and the unknown, the self and other, and how we negotiate that in life and on the page. New Zealand's remoteness from the rest of the world had always struck me, but Sweden proved far more isolating; the distance felt palpable, as I did not understand the language.

For migrants, distance is not simply geographic and temporal, it is also cultural and linguistic. Meaning closes distance. When we're part of a language and culture that has meaning and resonance for us, our sense of connection enriches the world around us. Language, people and places draw nearer when we understand them, an idea that Marcela, the Chilean migrant, expressed so well in her essay: 'Meaningful nearness, I've discovered, transcends time and space.' The distance between self and world, self and other, diminishes as migrants come to understand and be understood in the host country. That distance in Sweden was always going to be too great to close. We would always be strangers there.

Humans need meaningful nearness, a sense of connection to people and place, and it is this that ruptures when people migrate. Migrants move away from so much of what has meaning for them – roots, language, culture – and finding them again, if they ever do, is part of their journey of learning to live in a new country. But even as migrants close the distance between self and other in the host country, they open up a distance between themselves and where they once lived. For them, negotiating these different forms of distance is an ongoing challenge.

Nearness and distance

Distance is a geographical, temporal and existential reality for migrants, affecting how they see themselves in relation to space, time, memory and actuality. For migrants, the geographical distance remains constant and fixed from their place of origin, while the temporal distance stretches with each passing year they live in the host country. Permanent distance and increasing time apart are the consequences of migration and can be difficult to bear. Migrants must strive to stay in touch with friends and family left behind if they want to offset the distance between them.

While distance can be measured in kilometres and years, the real distance tends to be emotional, and that distance depends on how near or far migrants feel from what has meaning for them in both the host country and where they once lived. The personal essay's method of inquiry can help us assess the effect of distance, whether geographical, temporal, emotional or existential, on how well these migrant writers have adapted to living in New Zealand, a country whose remoteness has helped form its physical, cultural and historical identity.

When we look back through the medium of writing we bring near that which is distant in time and space, which enables us to understand others and ourselves better. My fellow army brat and memoirist Jennifer Sinor holds that 'in telling the story of who we are, we tell the story of where we have stood'.[2] Because migrants have stood in more than one place in their lives, the personal essay allows them to locate their migrated selves through narrative. They can reflect on what has happened – when, where, with whom and why – and from there map the route of their understanding. From its inception, the personal essay has mined the rich contact zone between self and other, self and world, weighing and assessing personal experience for its worth. Michel de Montaigne recognised the tension and possibility to be found in testing things in writing, and since the time 'he sat down in 1580 to map himself, the essay has existed somewhere on a line between two sturdy poles of inner and outer, experience and meaning, "I" and "the world"'.[3] Negotiating the space between inner and outer, experience and meaning, self and world, makes the personal essay an ideal genre for charting distance in all its concrete and emotional particulars.

Migrants on their journey of the stranger who comes to town are crossing the distance between 'I' and 'the world' as they navigate the contact zone. Part of their sense of estrangement and distance comes from living in a world removed from much of what helps them navigate it: roots, culture and, perhaps most importantly, language. Closing that distance between self and other, self and world, is central to each migrant's journey towards understanding and being understood, but it comes at the expense of being distant from what has held meaning for them in the past, as Gareth, the Welsh doctor, clearly understood: 'We leave everything behind, family, friends, our culture and the environment which nurtured us and travel with the luggage of memories.' Thousands of kilometres away and growing more distant over the years is the world he once inhabited – a world resonant with meaning.

We want to share our lives with those we love, and for migrants in New Zealand the distance from family and friends often precludes this. Amelia, the Englishwoman who married a New Zealander, catalogued what distance had cost her: 'I have lost the opportunity to care for my own parents in their old age. I have lost the chance to celebrate weddings, christenings, birthdays, anniversaries and funerals of those to whom I am related or fond of. Tapes and CDs sent to compensate for the lost experience wait for months or years before I can bring myself to listen.' Her list is extensive and emotionally loaded. She has missed countless milestones in the lives of those she loves back in England, and she cannot bring herself to listen to what would connect her with those experiences. More painful, especially given she's a trained nurse, is not being there to care for her aging parents. After her father died, she wrote, 'The distance seems greater between here and England.'

Perhaps distance is exacerbated when so much of a migrant's life is neither seen nor shared by friends and family afar. My own children are growing up unseen by my sister and brother, and I wonder at what emotional cost. As the young Slovakian Kornel vented in his essay: 'Oh yes, this bloody distance, it does not create any nearness, it's a myth.' He mocks the idea that absence makes the heart grow fonder. If anything, distance, both temporal and spatial, makes absence more painful. With each passing year, our life in New Zealand goes unwitnessed by those who were once closest to us. I told my sister recently that she has not seen my son since he was eight, and now he's at university. The sorrow of those unseen years broke in my voice 12,000 kilometres away.

Distance with respect to New Zealand is all too real, both in time and space, and originated 80 million years ago when the New Zealand

archipelago splintered off from the ancient supercontinent of Gondwana
to drift in isolation. From the beginning New Zealand was its own
migratory world: the pollen record shows almost all of the country's
native flora arrived and evolved after the land mass separated.[4] Of the
world's largest islands, the unimaginatively named North Island and
South Island of New Zealand are the most remote from any continent,
reflected in the fact that 82 per cent of the country's native plant
species are endemic.[5] Given New Zealand's geographical isolation, it is
not surprising that the country was among the last land masses to be
settled by humans, roughly 800 years ago in what is argued to be the
final wave of Polynesian migration.[6] The combination of being remote
and unpopulated until the relatively recent arrival of humans makes
New Zealand a remarkable microcosm on many levels: environmental,
cultural, historical.

Change on an island, for good or ill, may happen quickly. The
concentrated proximity of New Zealand's island environment and
the nation's great distance from anywhere else affects everything, and
everyone, that migrates to it. The flightless moa, for example, endemic
to New Zealand and the largest source of protein when humans arrived
here, was hunted to extinction by Māori within 150 years of their
landfall.[7] The flip side of extinction is invasion. British and European
colonisers introduced many non-native species, both animal and
vegetable, sometimes with disastrous consequences. The possum, for
example, was introduced in the 1840s for the fur trade. In the absence
of natural predators it proliferated wildly and is now established
throughout 91 per cent of the country and wreaking havoc on native
bush and birdlife.[8] Nearness and distance are an ongoing and informing
tension for all life in New Zealand.

A nationwide mobile phone company, 2degrees, trades on the idea
that only two degrees of separation exist between any one person and
anyone else in New Zealand. Two years before she became my student,
Damira, a Croatian lawyer, signed our residency permit, illustrating that
idea perfectly. Similarly, in the summer that I returned to New Zealand I
met some of my former students, a mix of both migrants and Kiwis, for

dinner. Even though they had taken part in different classes, they found they knew each other through other channels. Gareth, the Welsh doctor, had treated Damira as a patient, and Gareth's wife had worked for Hugh, the Irish doctor, years earlier. According to English poet Harry Ricketts, who migrated to New Zealand in 1981, 'the country is really a village with one and a half degrees of separation'.[9]

That night at dinner, migrant and Kiwi, distance and nearness were drawn together because of the desire to write personal essays. Everyone at the table was pleased to see I had finally grown to love and appreciate New Zealand, having railed in the past about its distance, its isolation from the 'real world'. Janice, a New Zealander in her seventies, held her wineglass aloft, looked me right in the eye, and said: 'Welcome home.' I had crossed the threshold from stranger to friend in my journey to Sweden and back.

The willingness to meet stranger and other is something both the essay and the migrant share. Each crosses from the known to the unknown and is willing to engage the other in order to learn, for who better understands the tension between nearness and distance than those who have experienced both in their migration? Cultural critic Nikos Papastergiadis recognises this dynamic tension as 'through their actions and decisions, migrants enter into a constant dialogue between past and present, near and far, foreign and familiar'.[10]

It is this constant dialogue between spatial, temporal and cultural polarities that migrants explore in their personal essays, fleshing out and grounding these abstractions in their own migration narratives. For migrants, the known world of their past, which may be both temporally and physically distant, is always running parallel to, albeit underneath, their present experience. As David Lazar observes: 'The essay is by its nature a self-reflective form, a form through which the self's prism considers the world.'[11] Migrant personal essays include a culture, landscape and perhaps language from their past. Therefore, what comes through the self's prism is coloured by the migrant's cultural and linguistic background.

Cathrine, a Danish woman in her eighties who has lived in New Zealand for over 50 years, recognises that her Danish cultural awareness still informs her life today:

> I never felt a stranger. To me I have always been as much part of the landscape as any New Zealander. But my whole outlook on life is that of a Dane with a background formed by the Danish educational system as well as by family and genetics. Danes can fit in with any population anywhere in the world – so we believe. They take their culture with them, fit in with the new culture and never have the sense of displacement.

Her culture is embodied in her 'whole outlook on life', and has not faded in the intervening decades. Yet this strong cultural identity hasn't prevented her from feeling she belongs in New Zealand. 'I never felt a stranger,' she declares. She does not see these two cultures as mutually exclusive but running in tandem. Danes, she says, bring their culture with them and adapt to wherever they live – a claim that in her case seems true.

The price migrants pay

Past and present, near and far can be brought together in the essay. Often what migrants miss is more real and necessary to them than what is present. Teuaneti, a migrant from Kiribati, found herself newly pregnant and alone in New Zealand in the late 1980s. For this 'first time mother in a foreign land … no relatives around was quite upsetting and frightening'. Teuaneti always wrote her essays in Kiribati and translated them into English, and here her use of third person underscores the sense of distance and alienation she felt in New Zealand. But as soon as she expresses what she misses from back home, her prose switches into first person and becomes immediate, sensual, enriched with connection:

> I could hear and smell the sea yet too far to reach and touch. I could see the ripe breadfruits hanging onto the branches yet too high to pick and the aroma of the fresh grilled milk fish in the air that could not be tasted frustrated me. I found comfort and support by ringing relatives back home. Their voices on the phone gave me the satisfaction and contentment that I was not alone and that they were nearby.

Teuaneti's evocation of the rich tropical landscape of her island home –
the scent, sound, taste and beauty 5000 kilometres away – exemplifies
John O'Donohue's assertion: 'Wherever there is distance, there is
longing.'[12]

In memory, Teuaneti's world feels immediate and tantalising despite
being distant and impossible to grasp: 'I could hear and smell the sea …
I could see the ripe breadfruits [and smell] the aroma of the fresh grilled
milk fish'. She closes the distance between the place and the people she
loves in the only way possible for her, by phoning, and finds comfort and
connection in speaking to them in her native language.

In 1987 toll calls to Kiribati were prohibitively expensive, at $2.50 a
minute. Each of Teuaneti's calls lasted 20 to 30 minutes, and soon her
English husband expressed his concern over the ability of the young
family's budget to sustain these calls – even though, as Teuaneti attests,
'he noticed that not only was I radiant after talking in Kiribati on the
phone but also my appetite improved!' The brief nearness of speaking
with her family in her native language on the phone was enough to perk
up her spirits and appetite, but each call was transient, expensive, its
positive effect vanishing all too quickly.

To help assuage his pregnant wife's longing for her island home, her
husband invited two university students from Kiribati to dinner, and
'as soon as they arrived,' Teuaneti writes, 'my craving was gone and
the drowsiness vanished. They brought with them the most pleasant
fragrance and warmest ambiance that I could not describe.' The two
women embodied Kiribati in scent, presence and language – all that
she was missing. On noticing Teuaneti and her husband had a spare
room, one of the students asked if she could board with them. Teuaneti
immediately agreed. What her husband thought of this spontaneous
decision, made at two in the morning, is left unsaid. He had planned
to bring his mother-in-law to New Zealand for a three-month visit so
perhaps he found a postgraduate student an easier option.

Teuaneti, the migrant who longed for the familiar things of home,
revelled in the companionship of her fellow countrywoman: 'The aroma
of any dish she cooked in my kitchen was inviting to devour just like

my mum's. The Kiribati homely companion and the language made me joyful and healthy and surely it did likewise to the student. It was like home away from home.' Distance from home disappeared once Teuaneti had someone with whom to share the language and food of Kiribati. Together, the two women recreated home in a small but real way in her kitchen.

How near or far migrants feel to New Zealand and their country of origin changes, of course, over time and circumstances. The Dutch migrants who came to New Zealand after the war could rarely, if ever, consider phoning home, whereas now such calls are within financial reach. Piet, who emigrated from the Netherlands in 1959, confirms: 'Contact with … family and friends was only possible by letter. We never once talked to our parents by phone, as international calls were too expensive and we simply couldn't afford them. Wouldn't it have been wonderful if we had been able to use free video calls via Skype then!' The exclamation mark at the end of his sentence echoes across the 50 years of Piet's life in New Zealand. In the twenty-first century it is hard to imagine the emotional consequences of migration sustained by the Dutch who came in the 1950s and 60s, but his personal essay makes them resonate again as he remembers his longing to be near those he loved and had left behind.

For many migrants, particularly those who came in the postwar wave of immigration, the ease and relative affordability of global travel did not exist. For them, the distance between New Zealand and their home country was even greater given the financial impossibility of visiting home. Here the concretely circumstantial aspect of migration is altogether painful. As Piet explains: 'The gap between New Zealand and Holland seemed huge, and for a long time at least, unbridgeable. We were aware that going back would be impossible; it was beyond our financial means to afford the trip back for several years to come, even if we wanted to.' Indeed, 20 years passed before Piet was able to return to the Netherlands. By 1979 the money he had saved from his pension was enough to cover the costs of a visit for him and his family to his homeland.

Although my family first arrived in New Zealand in 2007, we could not afford to send all of us back to visit relations, a situation that rankled when my husband repeatedly travelled to the United States because of his work commitments and saw my family and friends. Kornel, the young Slovakian migrant, captures in his essay what I felt: 'Sure, absence can make hearts grow fonder, but then in the same fashion grows the frustration, that those hearts find it hard to hug whenever they want to.' En route to Sweden we stopped off to see family and friends in the United States, and I felt the emotional distance acutely when my then 10-year-old daughter flung herself into my sister's arms at the Denver airport, crying out, 'I missed you!' Too much time had passed. My daughter had lived half her life in New Zealand and they had not seen each other in five and a half years. Living at such a remove from those one loves is the price migrants pay for having left.

Except for the Pacific Island nations of New Caledonia, Fiji and Tonga, New Zealand's nearest neighbour is Australia, which at three hours' flight time is hardly close, followed by the next nearest landmass and continent, Antarctica, at six hours. For anyone who migrates to New Zealand, 'the tyranny of distance' is an ongoing and dominant feature of their lives.[13] Migrants will always be at a distance from whence they came, and while that distance remains constant spatially, it will stretch temporally as they age, and wax and wane emotionally depending on how each of them negotiates it.

Yet there are migrants who see distance not as a tyranny but as a benefit. Elizabeth, the English migrant, quipped in her first essay that one reason she migrated to New Zealand was because she couldn't 'emigrate to the moon, so New Zealand will have to do'. In her case, the distance was actively sought and became part of the journey towards finding her authentic self. No one back in England witnessed her emotional breakdown and reconstruction in New Zealand, though her personal essay leaves a record of it. Sabina, the Dutchwoman who came to New Zealand in 2004, similarly found New Zealand's distance from her home country a cornerstone of her decision to immigrate there:

Can't you go any further? Well, no, I say to amazed people looking at me when I tell I will go to New Zealand to stay and live there. 'If I go further I will be heading back and that is so not the idea of this move.' I like the roughly 19 thousand kilometres between the country I was born in and my new place of residence ... Before packing my bags for Kiwi land I did consider migrating to countries only a two, four or eight hours' flight away, but in the end the longest distance from home was part of the intention and challenge.

For European migrants, New Zealand is as far away as they can go, and in their essays they frequently characterise the country as 'the other side of the world', 'the end of the earth' or 'the bottom of the world on an island in the Pacific'. When people choose to move such a great distance away, that distance becomes a definite factor in their lives, not an abstraction, 'and the material, physical distance of those moves matters'.[14] Sabina, however, as a contemporary transnational migrant, ameliorates distance by jetting back and forth to the Netherlands and by texting, emailing and Skyping with friends and family on the other side of the world. Not surprisingly, she calculates the distance in flight time and enjoys and even seeks out the challenge of that distance. But nothing captures the reality of those 19,000 kilometres better than those who came to New Zealand via ship decades earlier.

'Half a world away from my own'

Chris was nine in 1953 when she and her family migrated from England. The journey took 33 days and they stopped only twice, once for the passage through the Panama Canal and once off the coast of Pitcairn Island, where islanders rowed out with souvenirs for purchase. 'Most exciting of all, one of them gave my brother and me a bunch of bananas!' Chris's youthful enthusiasm rings on the page 60 years after that gift of fruit. Caught up as she was with the high jinks and pranks on board and with learning to swim, her child's mind did not register the geographical distance until two years later when her grandmother followed the family out:

> The first time our geographic distance from 'the old country' became apparent to me was early in 1955 when Nana came out to join us. My father

pinned a large map of the world to the dining room wall and marked out her journey in daily increments. We had a tiny *Union Jack* attached to a pin and each day my brother and I would fight over whose turn it was to move it a notch along her estimated route. I was very fond of Nana and it seemed to take forever for that pin to reach Auckland.

Although Chris had made the same journey, the distance only became real as the anticipation of her grandmother's arrival slowly inched its way towards her on the world map. Time and distance are relative, depending on how they're experienced, passing swiftly for a child on board a ship and creeping slowly in that child's imagination of the same journey. In the personal essay, writers 'present the world's meanings not as they have researched them or reasoned them out but as they have lived them'.[15] For Chris, when the journey had an abstract rather than a lived dimension, its progress 'seemed to take forever'.

Maria, a Dutchwoman who made a similar journey in 1966, experienced the time and distance in a more existential fashion. Unlike the child migrant, she was keenly aware of what she was leaving behind. As she looked back almost 50 years, she knew what lay ahead. Her essay therefore speaks to both time past and time future; she understands the long-term consequences of living at a distance from loved ones:

> It had been a long trip, six weeks on the boat, a ship full mostly with emigrants to New Zealand and Australia. I am sure many regarded this trip as the cruise of their lifetime. A trip of pleasure, lounging in deckchairs, dips in the pool, playing quoits and other games, dancing at night, just like the TV's *Love Boat* series. Take the day while you can, because a new life was awaiting, a life of hard work to establish themselves. But it was also a life away from war-stricken Europe. Most of these activities did not capture me.

Writing this essay at age 76, Maria takes a very long view, and it's not surprising the words 'life' or 'lifetime' occur four times in as many sentences. In 1966 the journey took six weeks; now it can be accomplished in a day. Distance becomes manifestly more real when the ocean's horizon is all the migrant sees for weeks on end. 'It had been a long trip,' she writes before shifting into present tense to make an acerbic comment about her fellow migrants: 'I am sure many regarded this trip as the cruise of their lifetime. A trip of pleasure.'

In distancing herself in her essay from the other passengers, Maria shows she didn't enjoy the trip as she believes they did. She compares 'the cruise of their lifetime' with the TV series *Love Boat*, but admits, 'Most of these activities did not capture me.' She follows this dismissive statement with an almost biblical mandate to those migrants enjoying the voyage, initially speaking to them directly, 'Take the day while you can,' and with the benefit of hindsight acknowledges why: 'because a new life was awaiting, a life of hard work to establish themselves'. Again she distances herself from the reality she would experience, one she shared with many Dutch migrants.

Maria does recognise the push factor of the war in their migration, her own included. She had witnessed Jews being rounded up on her street in Amsterdam in 1943: 'I was nine years of age and never forget that Sunday. Our friends across the road disappeared forever.' Then everyone's cats vanished and fresh mince appeared in a shop, the strange coincidence betrayed by cat skins pegged on the shopkeeper's clothesline. She recounts seeing a man dying in the street: 'The man huddled in an old grey raincoat was lying on the cold footpath. Gushes of blood, escaping from his mouth, coloured the grey concrete tiles. A ring of people, including me, had circled around him and stared at the dying man. This man lying alone in the crowd; forsaken. Nobody said anything, nobody did anything. Everyone, numbed by the war, just stood there and stared. Death in the street had become common, the war had deprived ordinary people from empathy.'

Migrating to New Zealand will distance Maria geographically from the war, but not emotionally. Perhaps the horror of what she had experienced prevented her from enjoying what her fellow passengers found the journey had to offer. Fifty years on, Maria's isolation is still marked in her writing. She does not mention her new husband, with whom she was travelling. The journey as she remembers and reflects upon it shows a solitary woman, a migrant apart:

> Apart from visiting exotic ports, we were confined to the boat. Large as it was I felt enclosed and caged, even with the wide horizon around me. Though this was the part I liked most, watching the sea in all its moods

from near dead-quiet to restless and wild and stormy. Fascinating too observing the dolphins which playfully accompanied the ship, the flying fish glittering in the sun and petrels weaving up and down as well as the sun's brilliant coming and going. Yes I liked that.

What is most striking in this passage is the image of confinement amid immensity: 'Large as it [the boat] was I felt enclosed and caged, even with the wide horizon around me.' She takes more interest and pleasure in the natural world outside the boat than the human world contained within it, perhaps because the former embodied a freedom she couldn't share. The writer Kristen Iversen notes: 'Writing about an experience expands it and allows me to unpack and unravel the thorny knot of emotion that has kept a particular memory close over the years.'[16] Looking back at herself almost 50 years later, Maria can see that her journey to New Zealand marked the threshold between who she was and who she would become, and that despite moving forwards into a new life, she still felt trapped.

Images of entrapment occur at other points in her story of the voyage. When the ship docked in Auckland her aunt showed her around briefly, 'mostly window shopping, but it certainly exposed me to a different world, a world I had to live in from now on'. The confinement becomes enlarged and more abstract. It's no longer simply the boat, but 'a world I had to live in from now on'. Longing to connect with something familiar, she asked her aunt where the street cafés were. The answer was even more unwelcome:

'Street cafes? They have none here.'

'What, no street cafes?' What a dismal picture. Not to be able to sit there and watch the world go by. It began to hit home. This is not like my homeland, not like Europe. This is an alien world. I felt adrift.

The text differentiates 'a world' from 'the world'. Maria could no longer sit 'and watch the world go by': her world, the world of street cafés in Amsterdam. She invokes the idiom 'It began to hit home' just as she begins to understand she no longer is home. Not only was she confined to a world she would have 'to live in from now on', but that world also bore no resemblance to the one she'd left behind. This realisation dawns on her in larger proportions – 'not like my homeland' (the Netherlands), 'not like Europe' (her larger cultural and geographic context) – until she realises: 'This is an alien world.'

Maria's essay depicts the effect of distance in all its existential enormity. She had come so far across the oceans of the world yet felt most 'adrift' right from when she made landfall. She distils the moment of when the stranger comes to town – but she has come to town to live. The magnitude of the decision to migrate preyed upon her as she gazed at the ocean in all its moods from aboard the ship, where 'Large as it was I felt enclosed and caged, even with the wide horizon around me.' For Maria, as for many postwar migrants, the journey was one-way. There was no going back.

Maria opened her essay with an image of herself newly arrived in New Zealand and sitting alone in front of a stranger's fire. The camera of memory is in the corner of the room, looking down on her: 'There I was, in the lounge of a total stranger, sitting before a small wood fire, which warmed me at the front and cooled me at the rear. Half a world away from my own … worlds apart.' Distance and nearness both come to bear in this image, held in tension by the ellipsis, which acts as a symbol of the journey and the separation that journey has created. She is half a world away from everything she knows and loves, in the lounge of a stranger, another form of distance, and she is alone with herself and this realisation.

Throughout Maria's essay the word 'world' appears to stand in for what she has lost. She can no longer sit and 'watch the world go by' in a street café in Amsterdam, but instead finds herself in 'a different world' and 'an alien world' that is 'half a world away from my own'. 'World' implies the distance and the totality of what she gave up when she migrated – friends, family, language, the familiar life she once knew, the world that had meaning for her.

In the closing image of her essay Maria returned to the memory of sitting by the fire. Now we have the backstory, her courtship and marriage to a Dutchman who had lived in New Zealand for 14 years and persuaded her to join him there. She had sailed half the world to this moment where she found herself at a stranger's hearth while her husband and his neighbour chatted away in the kitchen, making tea: 'I stayed behind, sitting alone, very much alone at that moment. It was then that I fully realised what migrating to a country, so far away, meant.'

Maria's decision to open and close her essay with an image of such poignant isolation shows the power that moment still has for her almost 50 years later. Patricia Hampl rightfully says, 'Pain has strong arms,'[17] and it can clench us long after the event. Seated beside the fire on the far side of the world, Maria has an epiphany that will cast a long shadow on her memory: 'It was then that I fully realised what migrating to a country, so far away, meant.' That realisation is a moment that will affect the rest of her life, echoing for years across both time and distance.

For Maria, the distance remained both temporal and geographical. Five decades later, she can see that her journey to New Zealand differed from any journey she had taken in the past because its consequences would be lasting and painful, endured and enduring:

> I thought of all the times I had been away from home in my early childhood, even for prolonged periods from extended summer holidays till three, four months and even half a year, but I always happily returned home to my people and the world I knew. This was not another 'away from home' situation. There was no going back, at least not for a number of years. I would not see my relatives and friends for many years. I would miss all this. I would not be going home.

Her present-day self knows what she could not know when she gazed at the horizon from the railings of the ship, namely that the distance would stretch into years. As Tennessee Williams remarked, 'time is the longest distance between two places'.[18] Maria compares her migration to occasions when she had previously journeyed away from home. Although each trip was longer than the one before, 'I always happily returned home to my people and the world I knew.'

Here again 'the world' stands for everything she knew and that was familiar to her. But this time that world is the very thing she cannot easily – 'happily'– return to: 'This was not another "away from home" situation.' Now, as she writes from half a world away, separated for years from her family and friends because "There was no going back', her prose becomes spare and direct: 'I would miss all this. I would not be going home.' The finality gains emphasis from the repetition of what she will no longer experience and from what now faces her, expressed in terms of absence. Maria is all too aware she will not go home for years, except in memory: 'migrants and exiles remember being home. Ultimately, it is always a memory of absence, of where one is not.'[19] Home is where migrants are not, until they make a new one. Maria's personal essay exemplifies the fact that many migrants never stop missing home even when they've spent decades in the new country.

'Emigration is surely a synonym for farewell'

The magnitude of separation and distance from what they love dawns on migrants at different points in their journey. Some realise it when saying goodbye at their wedding or at the airport, others on their way to the new country. That realisation registered with Dorothy, a Scottish bride, as she travelled to New Zealand in 1966 with her new Kiwi husband: '[I]t finally struck me what had happened. I had left the land of my birth to live at the other side of the world. I cried and cried and my husband couldn't console me, offering me beer which I didn't want. He did not seem to understand what was the matter with me. In these days when travel was expensive I wondered if I would ever see Scotland again, or my parents.'

Dorothy's New Zealand-born husband was returning home and could not share or understand the sense of loss she felt crossing this threshold. Fully conscious of the enormity of her decision, she was inconsolable. As the essayist Scott Russell Sanders notes, 'We are slow to acknowledge the pain in yearning for one's native ground,'[20] but Dorothy, in her essay, also shows that the pain of leaving abides across time and distance. When she met her new in-laws at the airport in New Zealand, 'It brought new waves of sadness that they were so different from my parents, as in-laws are. I felt sad that I had exchanged my dear parents [for] people I hardly knew.' Here the stranger had come to town within the family unit, and the nearness of her own kin receded even as her husband's people drew close.

Other migrants tell similarly affecting stories set around the time of their weddings and departures for New Zealand from Europe. The distance and vantage point from which the migrant chooses to narrate the event will vary, but he or she will always be present in the essay, because 'the author will usually be standing foursquare in the middle of the essay or off to the side of the action (but still unmistakably there) – and of greater importance, the essay will be in large part about him or her and the author's reaction as it is told and interpreted'.[21]

Piet's prose, as he wrote about his wedding in 1959 in the Netherlands, is neutral and contained: 'Our pending emigration to New Zealand cast a bit of a shadow over our wedding day. We had a big reception, but it had strained and sad overtones. It was the last time that we would see many of our relatives and friends, so we had to say "good-bye" to many of them. Not knowing when, or if, we would see each other ever again.' Five decades on, Piet knows that he didn't see many of his family and friends again, but he never reveals how that absence made him feel, then or at the time of his writing. Here the distance is between himself and the experience, almost as though he is numb, which may be how he felt at the time and still feels now. He keeps an emotional distance from the event: the narration is pulled back and detached. All he tells us about his wedding is that the pending emigration 'cast a bit of a shadow' over the reception, which 'had strained and sad overtones'.

In contrast, Anna, the Swiss migrant, depicts a searing farewell as she parted from friends and family in the airport in 1966:

> I can still see them now, my family, my friends and my colleagues from work. They stand in a semi-circle in the airport departure hall, and I move slowly from one to the other saying good bye. When I get to my father he starts to cry. Not soundlessly like my mother, but with big loud sobs. I have never seen my father cry before. I am shaken. I didn't know he liked me so much. He hugs me tightly. 'Oh Dad, don't cry.' I try to comfort him. 'We will come back.'

Anna narrates the parting scene in the present tense with all its stark and powerful immediacy, and she is right in the middle of it. As she moves around the semi-circle saying goodbye she stops when she comes to her father, who starts to cry 'with big loud sobs. I have never seen my father cry before.' Her realisation of the depth of his feelings for her – 'I didn't know he liked me so much' – is as dear as it is touchingly naïve. Anna is at the centre of the experience as she tries to comfort him, but her words offer little comfort to a father whose daughter has married and is moving to the other side of the world.

The scene which follows shows her own misery: 'Through the blur of my tears I watch the runway rush past. Then we lift off. I am no longer on Swiss soil. I have a terrible sense of loss. I wish my husband would hold me, or take my hand, but he is looking straight ahead. His mother is on his other side. We sit in silence. We are given orange juice.' It's not just her father who is without comfort, but she, too, as she sits in tears beside her husband as the plane lifts off: 'I have a terrible sense of loss.' As Anna moves from the embrace of her father to the husband who does not take her hand, she crosses an impossible distance that will inform the rest of her life. Her tears as the plane leaves the ground of her homeland capture that sense of loss in all its acute and painful reality, resonating over four decades later.

Taking a more detached and abstract view of her journey to New Zealand, Birgitta, the Swedish migrant in her seventies, explores what she does and does not remember from that critical period in her life. In her essay she sees her distant self in the harried face of a friend about to be married:

> A friend was getting married recently. A week before the wedding I tactlessly asked, was she happy? She had worry lines on her face, no obvious joy visible, and she said she didn't have time to be happy: there were too many things to be arranged ahead. Perhaps that was my situation in October–November 1966, because I don't remember thinking much of my parents and my four siblings, nor my best friends, all of whom I was to miss achingly, in fits and starts, later. It's also true that the memory of the sadness discernible behind their smiles on my parents' faces became a permanent part of me.

Older now than her parents were when she married, Birgitta can appreciate their sense of loss and speak to it, knowing now what it cost them to see her migrate so far away. She recalls her own thoughtlessness towards her family and friends at the time, caught up as she was in the arrangements for her wedding and emigration.

Time becomes fused at this point in her essay – past, present and continuous. The months before her wedding in 1966 combine with present time, while all the years in between are encompassed in her recognition that 'the memory of the sadness discernible behind their smiles on my parents' faces became a permanent part of me'. The personal essay allows us to see how 'perception and understanding change with time as well. There is the girl or woman – the character on the page – who experienced the event, and then there is the older woman writer – the narrator visible or invisible – who is looking back on the event.'[22] As she looks back through the medium of writing, Birgitta comes to understand that the sadness her parents felt has become part of her, a palpable and permanent consequence of living so far apart.

For migrants who have a New Zealand partner, the distance between the two countries remains a constant in their relationship. When migrants can't travel to see those they love, the distance becomes exacerbated and enlarged. Kornel, the young Slovakian migrant in his thirties, addressed this in his essay: 'The distance remains permanent, especially if you couple up with a Kiwi. Both of us are constantly negotiating the geographical and personal distances. I wonder if one can ever master this, perhaps one just needs to man up finally. Geographical distance can be conquered if there is money, time and courage to travel the long haul distance. Geographical distance grows though if one cannot do this. Then consequently grows the personal distance.'

The 'distance remains permanent' because one partner is always giving up his country and language in this relationship. Kornel considers himself the more flexible of the two, as his language skills are better. He quotes a Slovakian saying in his essay: '[Y]ou are as many times human as languages you speak.' After spending two years in Slovakia, his partner learns that his mother is ill and they return to New Zealand where they remain for 10 years, despite Kornel's strong ties to his own family. Kornel gave up proximity to his family, knowing that the personal distance would grow if he couldn't visit them periodically. In 2015 he and his partner returned to Slovakia, which meant the burden of distance and language fell on his partner, showing again their acknowledgment of 'constantly negotiating the geographical and personal distances'.

A migrant's sense of loss applies not only to those they love who age apart from them, but also to those they love whose lives keep unfolding and which they do not actively share. Beth, who migrated in her fifties from South Africa and has lived in New Zealand for over a decade, captures what it meant to leave both her mother and her daughter, now in her twenties:

> But as most of my loss involves my mother and my daughter, it is through them that much of my rebuilding has taken place. I am no longer the mother that is available for all the little everyday crises, or the daughter who can visit and fetch and carry. I am the absent one. I am the lost one. And oddly enough, although I thought that this would affect me most in terms of my very old mother, it is my daughter Ingrid whose life I have most missed out on: career changes, house moves, heartbreaks and small triumphs, all lost to me. This loss has hollowed me out and defies all attempts at filling. It affects me terribly when we are apart, and in our desire to have only perfect times when we are together, it has undermined the ease and spontaneity of our pivotal relationship.

Beth's prose is beautifully balanced between the pull of her mother and the pull of her daughter. The clauses swing between the two relationships, but the loss comes down hardest on the daughter's side. Beth is unstinting in how she perceives herself: 'I am the absent one. I am the lost one.' Those stark sentences with their syntactic symmetry emphasise the distress that the distance from her mother and daughter causes her: she no longer shares their daily world.

Beth is struck, however, by the realisation that separation from her mother doesn't affect her as much as separation from her daughter. Given her mother lived to be over 100, perhaps this is not surprising. Beth's mother is at the extreme end of her life, while her daughter is at the relative beginning of hers: '… it is my daughter Ingrid whose life I have most missed out on: career changes, house moves, heartbreaks and small triumphs, all lost to me'. The list is both ordinary and grievous, and there is no compensation for this loss, which has 'hollowed me out and defies all attempts at filling'. Beth returns to South Africa every year. Her daughter has visited twice but refused to migrate to New Zealand, stating, 'There's no one for me to date there.'

Although Beth knows New Zealand's distance from South Africa is geographical, it nonetheless contributes to the distance she feels from her daughter: 'It certainly can't help being this isolated: "The Gateway to Antarctica" the sign at the airport reads. I could weep.' The loss she feels affects her not only when she is apart from her daughter, which is to be expected, but also when they're together, which is not: 'It affects me terribly when we are apart, and in our desire to have only perfect times when we are together, it has undermined the ease and spontaneity of our pivotal relationship.' When reunited they try too hard 'to have only perfect times' – perhaps in an attempt to redress what both distance and absence have meant for their relationship. The lack of dailiness in their lives 'has undermined the ease and spontaneity of our pivotal relationship'.

The two women are robbed of the easiness they once shared in each other's presence, something their ongoing nearness fostered in the past: 'I am no longer the mother that is available for all the little everyday crises.' The strained relationship shows how limbic (emotional) resonance breaks down over long distance, as neural science confirms: 'Letters and phone calls are a salve on the wound, but are insubstantial substitutes for the full-bandwidth sensory experience of nearness to the ones you love. To sustain a living relationship, limbic regulation demands sensory inputs that are rich, vivid, and frequent.'[23] Living 11 time zones apart precludes 'sensory inputs that are rich, vivid, and frequent' and impairs mother's and daughter's ability to be relaxed and spontaneous when they're together. Because Beth's daughter is her only child, the loss is concentrated in this 'pivotal relationship'.

Ten years after Beth migrated to New Zealand, her daughter, now married, announced she was expecting her first child. Beth lamented to me in an email: 'Will I even ever see her pregnant? Maybe I will get there after the baby is born. Maybe I will always be airplane granny. I have lost so much, now the loss has a terrible future progression.' Ten years is

a third of her daughter's lifetime. Having missed an entire decade with
her daughter, she knows all too well that she will miss more: 'Will I even
see her pregnant?' She sees the distance stretching temporally into the
future, and now, with the imminent birth of her grandchild, the loss has
become generational: 'I have lost so much, now the loss has a terrible
future progression.'

What an anguishing thought, to know already that she will see
little of this child as he or she grows up. Even while Beth recognises
the transnational nature of their relationship, 'Maybe I will always be
airplane granny,' she realises the limitations of that connection. Her
wistful appellation 'airplane granny' acknowledges that she will always
be coming and going, unlike those grandmothers who live nearby.
Again, distance affects the nature of the relationship: 'In their classic
study of American grandparenthood, Cherlin and Furstenberg (1986)
state that the three most important factors influencing the frequency of
grandparent–grandchild contact are "distance, distance, and distance".'[24]
When a parent or their child migrates to another part of the world, there
is always the challenge of closing that distance to be near a grandchild.

Loretta Baldassar has done extensive research on transnational
families living in Australia and Italy, a comparable distance to migrants
who come to New Zealand from countries in Europe. She observes that
'the event of migration, by causing physical separation, absence and
longing, causes migrants to feel guilty about their moral obligations to be
co-present.'[25] Whether the emotion is guilt or longing or a combination
thereof, migrants tend to make more of an effort to see their friends and
family 'back home' than vice versa. David, an American who migrated to
New Zealand in his late forties with his family, writes of these conflicted
emotions in his essay: 'Leaving family is even harder than leaving
friends. Many children have a granny down the street or an aunt across
town, as I did growing up. Leaving this behind is leaving part of one's
soul. When I told my mother we were moving to New Zealand, she said,
"You bastard, I knew you would," and she started to cry. She was right.
We are "bastards" for leaving our families, and we know it.'[26]

Migrants are bastards when our distant family members see us, or we see ourselves, as having rejected them by moving away, even though rejection is unlikely to underpin the decision to leave. The point is, we left, and it may be that the obligation lies with us to return, not with them to visit, a point Chilean migrant Marcela made when I lamented that my sister had not come to visit us at the time we were living in Christchurch. 'It is *your* expectation that your sister come to see you,' she said to me. 'It is not necessarily hers.'

I remember looking out at the rainy winter night as she and I stood in the empty classroom together, realising my sister might never visit us in New Zealand. The earthquakes were still in the future, so my family and I couldn't know how they would wrench apart the landscape of all our lives. Nor could we know that the shifting tectonic plates would eventually bring our family closer to New Zealand, by enforcing the emotional and psychological distance of Sweden and thereby bringing us back to where we now knew we belonged. We had yet to cross that distance in time and space: we live forwards and understand backwards, a distance we navigate our entire lives.

Bridging the gap

Migrants affirm that the geographical distance is manageable if both parties make the effort to connect across the years and kilometres, but the distance becomes insurmountable and emotional when they do not. Marcela, the Chilean migrant, proved to be particularly eloquent on this subject:

> Geographical distance can be simply measured, being the same from each extreme of a line. It is the emotional distance however, that can be an insurmountable breach for those left behind. Where relations have been separated, the physical distance may become an excuse for not wanting to bridge the time difference, to dissipate distance into total absence. Within their reach, by tapping of some keyboard, the effort to create and maintain closeness was not embraced by many of those who saw us leave.

Marcela came to New Zealand with her husband, who was pursuing his doctorate. She characterises herself in her essay as 'a side dish to the main course' because she sidelined her own career in botany to his studies and had to learn English. The density and complexity of her prose is remarkable, conveying an idea that is particularly hard to articulate: 'Geographical distance can be simply measured ... [but it] is the emotional distance ... that can be an insurmountable breach for those left behind.' While Marcela tried to cross that emotional distance with family, 'writing religiously to them as others do praying', her effort was not reciprocated by her husband's family: 'Replies didn't come; the silence became longer and more intense.' The silence and lack of response created a space between couple and family that seemed larger than the Pacific separating them.

The distance, Marcela continues, increased when her husband's family visited from Chile. She explains that there was and continues to be 'resentment from those who do not accept we now can express ourselves in more than the only language they know'. The one factor that has given Marcela and her husband nearness and access in their new country, language, has intensified the distance within the family, and despite the couple's efforts it has not been overcome. Her husband's family no longer communicates with them; the distance has become one of 'total absence'.

The Chinese-American writer Ha Jin recognises that learning another language can be seen as 'an act of betrayal that alienates him from his mother tongue and directs his creative energies to another language'.[27] Perhaps Marcela's in-laws felt this betrayal, while failing to understand that their son needed English to study and work in New Zealand. Learning English hasn't stopped Marcela and her husband from speaking Spanish at home and raising their son to be bilingual. In contrast, Marcela's mother, at age 79, came to New Zealand for six months, having never left Chile her entire life, and enrolled in English classes. She crossed not only the geographical and emotional distance but also the linguistic one, whereas Marcela's husband's family 'have banned us from contacting them again'. Losing all ties with one's family is a high price to pay for migrating to a new country and learning its language.

Perhaps it is inevitable that migrants start to vanish from the former home horizon. We are no longer part of the daily landscape we left behind. We have, as Marcela once said in class, 'no relevance back home'.

But if we have had relevance for years, any diminution of it is painful. I have often thought that I am the one who writes, calls, Skypes and makes the effort to stay connected with my family and friends, and that these endeavours are largely one-sided. Since I left the United States in 2007, I have visited my friends and family there three times. No family member has come to see us in either Sweden or New Zealand. Unless, as I have found, the letters, emails and visits are reciprocated, the distance stretches and becomes ever more difficult to bear, a situation that Loretta Baldassar also recognises: 'It appears that as long as family members work hard at "staying in touch" by making use of all the technologies available to them, they can maintain mutually supportive relationships across time and space.'[28]

However, no amount of calls, letters or care packages from home can replace actually seeing someone in the country where they now live. Only three friends from the States have visited us thus far in New Zealand, and for everyone else our life here remains an abstraction. As one friend quipped when I visited her in the United States as we travelled to Sweden: 'Was it five years? It feels like you've been gone five minutes.' I remember feeling that her remark devalued our life in New Zealand because for her that life had happened in neither time nor space. Having never seen us here, having never travelled 12 hours on a plane, she had no conception of where we lived and how we lived in New Zealand. She might have felt I had been 'gone five minutes', but that 'five minutes' was the woman she knew when I lived in the States, and not the one who had been gone for five years: time was indeed relative in this instance.

For migrants whose families do visit them, the experience can be deeply validating for both parties, as Piet found when members of his family visited from the Netherlands: 'The distance remained the same, but the gap between them and us seemed no longer unbridgeable and a bit closer. Our letter writing had more meaning too. They had seen things here for themselves and they were able to visualise now what we were talking about in our letters.' Before the visit Piet saw the gap as unbridgeable, and his phrasing depicts that. He could have written 'the gap between us', but by polarising the pronouns, 'the gap between them and us', he creates not just a sense of the actual distance between the families but also a sense of tension and opposition.

After the visit New Zealand remained just as far away for his family in the Netherlands, but now Piet's New Zealand life had real meaning for them: 'These visits have in my mind contributed to a greater bond with the family too. The family have gained a better understanding about our life here and an appreciation as to why we might like to live here rather than in Holland.' His family's response counters that of Marcela's in-laws who couldn't understand why they had chosen to live in New Zealand and who had rejected them because of that choice.

My sister finally 'saw' that we lived in New Zealand after the September earthquake in 2010. I was on Skype with her when an aftershock struck and she said, 'My God, I just saw your house move behind you.' That it took a 7.1 magnitude earthquake and its aftershocks for my sister to realise where we lived says something about the unfathomable and unknowable quality of a migrant's life elsewhere when it's not witnessed directly. One reason personal essays become a vital resource for exploring individual experience first-hand is that they make it possible to document a life even the migrant's own family may never see or share. In the personal essay writers cross the distance between themselves now and themselves then: 'Because it is grounded in the profusion of ordinary life, creative nonfiction is always written against loss. For both reader and writer, it provides a palpable reminder that our lives always exceed our most carefully crafted arrangements of them.'[29] It is this writing 'against loss' that allows migrants to express such painful realities about migration. As Gareth, the Welsh doctor, so succinctly put it: 'Emigration is surely a synonym for farewell.'

The memory of saying farewell to family and friends is one of permanent anguish, especially when migrants know they may never see those people again. Gareth remembers saying goodbye to his wife's grandmother: 'We turned and looked back once more, she waved, and we never saw her again.' She vanishes, and that disappearance pierces years later because he knows they won't see her again. She exists now only in memory and on the page, where 'writing is the moving trace of our temporality'.[30] Gareth's essay speaks directly to that experience of loss when one migrates:

> Each visit back home to South Wales ends with fewer farewells. Neither of our mothers were alive on our last visit and there were fewer relatives and friends to wonder if we would ever see them again. Yet the grief reaction, the sense of loss is as poignant as ever. And there is always the sense of guilt. Did we betray all those who loved us; did we turn our backs on our heritage when we landed in New Zealand thirty-five years and two days ago? No, we emigrated with their blessing and time and distance have, perhaps, emphasised our Welshness and allowed us to be New Zealanders.

Gareth is able, in his essay, to pinpoint to the day how long he has lived in New Zealand. Even more revealing is his admission that 'the grief reaction, the sense of loss is as poignant as ever. And there is always the sense of guilt.' Time has diminished neither his grief reaction nor his sense of loss; the guilt Loretta Baldassar observed in migrants is always there. When Gareth asks, 'Did we betray all those who loved us; did we turn our backs on our heritage?' what he's really asking is are we bastards for having done this? His answer is 'No, we emigrated with their blessing.' Moreover, 'time and distance' from Wales have 'emphasised our Welshness and allowed us to be New Zealanders'. In a tension between nearness and distance, the temporal and geographical distance from Wales has created this feeling. It is the absence of Wales that makes their Welshness more present. As John O'Donohue notes: 'The opposite of presence is not absence, but vacancy; where there is absence there is still energy, engagement, and longing.'[31] Gareth's personal essay is written against loss, but it also inscribes the braided river of two cultures, Welsh and New Zealand, which flow together rather than vying with each other.

Saying farewell doesn't necessarily get easier when migrants experience parting from loved ones more than once. For younger migrants such as Kornel, the obligation to stay behind for aging parents can be a strong pull:

> I left home in Slovakia several times by now, but somehow it is always heart breaking. At the very moment of saying goodbye to my parents, it feels as if an invisible hand grabs my heart and pulls it down. Like it wants

to hold it so I will not go. This is followed by a very fast movie of evaluation in my head … What am I doing? Is it really worth it? Life is too short and I am leaving my beloved ones behind.

Regardless of how often Kornel says goodbye, each parting 'is always heart breaking'. The emotional pull of his parents makes him question why he is 'leaving my beloved ones behind'. The present tense gives a fresh intensity to how he feels: the emotion is ongoing and undiminished. He can identify exactly when and what he feels: 'At the very moment of saying goodbye to my parents, it feels as if an invisible hand grabs my heart and pulls it down. Like it wants to hold it so I will not go.' The feeling is visceral, but he describes it metaphorically. English is Kornel's third language, but the image and emotion are concrete and universal. When he questions why he's leaving his beloved family yet again, 'a very fast movie of evaluation' plays in his head. Riddled with doubt, he asks, 'What am I doing? Is it really worth it? Life is too short and I am leaving my beloved ones behind.' Here again is that sense of guilt Gareth says is permanent.

Gareth and Kornel, separated by 35 years in age and dates of arrival in New Zealand, describe the same emotion on saying goodbye to their families. Migrants are marked by these farewells. How could they not be? Some migrants say goodbye to family and friends they will never see again, and that anguish is something they carry with them to the new country. In the personal essay, 'A genuinely unique, concrete, and particular angle of vision is manifest in all successful instances of the form. Even so, there remains the experience, *potentially* shareable by all of us, that the essayist assays, the general that exists alongside the particular.'[32] Anyone who's said goodbye to someone they love, knowing they may never see them again, understands the grief of such a parting. We don't have to migrate to feel such a loss. But a critical difference for migrants is that they live with the ongoing distance and separation from those they know and love and, as their personal essays reveal, that experience permeates their lives.

Migratory birds

The longing to be with distant family does not cease with time but it may lessen in intensity. Daisy, the Irish nurse who has been in New Zealand since 1975, expressed this idea in an essay addressing nearness and distance:

> I have no blood relation in New Zealand so when family things happen at home I expect to be overhung by that desolate too-far-away feeling. I always want to compress distance, time and cost to be there again, with my own, just for a little while. In the early days at such times I used to go looking for a good bit of bacon to boil (food is such a cultural anchor), come home disappointed and talk myself into getting on with life here. Now that both my parents are dead and casual conversation across the world has become cheaper and easier the far-away feelings come less often and seem less burdensome.

Writing from the perspective of almost 40 years in New Zealand, Daisy is all too familiar with 'that desolate too-far-away feeling' when 'family things' happen back in Ireland. She knows what her response will be to those 'things' and that it will 'always' be the same: 'I always want to compress distance, time and cost to be there again, with my own, just for a little while.'

Migrants know this yearning all too well, whatever its prompt – a birth, a wedding, an illness, a death, or simply just to be near those they love and have left behind. Every migrant wants to be 'with my own', but it is not always possible 'to compress distance, time and cost to be there again'. The personal essay attests to this longing, compressing into words a universal feeling of loss that 'carries a sense of consequence in the real world. Something happened. It matters. It matters that it really happened.'[33] The distance matters. It is real, and its effect on migrants is ongoing and long-lasting.

Distance affects how much truth is divulged between migrants and their families and friends. Not sharing the truth in part or fully is a stratagem that migrants and their families commonly use, as 'people think carefully about whether to tell faraway kin about health concerns or other personal difficulties so as not to "worry" them ... It suggests that when kin are physically absent, their ability to respond appropriately to bad news is limited by distance.'[34] When someone robbed Anton, the Russian migrant, he deliberately withheld the information from his father: 'I couldn't tell my father because he had wired me that money, and he would have felt helpless and angry … To tell him, to let him into my stress and anxiety about this money (it was a lot of money, $2,000 American), would have crossed that line, because how could I keep up the confident attitude of being comfortable with about 80% of things here in New Zealand?'

Anton justified his desire to spare his father worry and anger and to maintain the illusion that all was well in New Zealand when he wrote: 'I felt I was maintaining a good attitude when I spoke with my parents who were so far away from me. I didn't want to have my mother crying on the phone, and my father telling me I had made the wrong choice.' Distance from the truth and distance from his parents both came into play, thus protecting him and them. Sometimes the migrant's own family withholds information, as when Kornel's parents in Slovakia didn't tell him his father had cancer, though typically it seems to be the migrant who doesn't divulge painful realities.

The silence surrounding what a migrant experiences can exist for decades, as Anna, the Swiss migrant, reveals: 'I never told my parents about these difficult early years, and how miserable I had been. I did not want to worry them.' Her distance becomes twofold – distance from the family she has married into and distance from her own family back home. Wanting to spare her parents from concern, she cuts herself off from emotional support. Finally, decades later, her personal essay gives voice to her mute suffering: 'I never told my parents about these difficult early years, and how miserable I had been.' Would it have helped to have told them, or would she have felt worse, knowing they felt helpless to support her? Anna's answer speaks for all migrants who long for real contact from afar with those they love: 'You want to be able to touch them. You want to talk to them. You want to hear their answers. You want to see their faces, their eyes and their expressions. You want to see their real smiles and not just the remembered ones.' None of that is possible across distance. My own family and friends knew how unhappy

I was when I migrated, especially when I lived in Sweden, but there was little they could do to alleviate my misery from afar.

When my family and I migrated to Sweden, that period of our lives reanimated our sense of loss, severing attachments we had made over five years in New Zealand and compounding the earlier losses from the United States. Now we had left two places we knew and loved. The absence of language deepened the sense of isolation, creating a distance far outstripping the geographical isolation of New Zealand. Our children were older, 11 and 14, and their memories were stronger and clearer than when we went to New Zealand. They suffered from the separation of all that was familiar and dear to them, not the least of which was their native language. One morning in Sweden my daughter found a pair of drumsticks a New Zealand friend of ours had given her and she began to cry, expressing what happens to all migrants: 'We left everything behind.' I couldn't argue with that. In her young life, it was true. We pine when we leave those we love behind, and although love stretches across time and space, it doesn't necessarily help us feel close to those we miss.

Living at a distance from family becomes particularly difficult when migrants' parents start to age. Migrants feel even further away when they most want to be near to help. Piet the Dutchman wrote: 'As we matured ourselves, we became acutely aware of our parents' ageing frailty in their old age. That was a time when we felt the need to be with them, but the distance and travel costs prevented us from making this a reality.' Piet is now the age his parents were when he thought this, and his essay reveals that he longed to be with his parents in their old age yet couldn't be because of distance and expense. The emotional sacrifices migrants make will reverberate with anyone who wants to be present at the end of their parents' lives.

The reality is that we cannot care physically for family members when we are distant from them; neither can we care for them emotionally to the extent we might like. Limbic resonance breaks down over distance, as evolutionary biologists and neural scientists verify:

> Our society overlooks the drain on emotional balance that results from severing attachments. From the dawn of the species until a few hundred

years ago, most human beings lived out their lives in one community ... The convenient devices that enable extensive mobility are problematic because limbic regulation operates weakly at a distance. We have the means to establish a peripatetic lifestyle, but we will never have the brains for it.[35]

Even migrants who have the means to travel between New Zealand and their home country to care for their parents point out the emotional toll the distance takes. Huang, the Chinese woman married to a New Zealander, is one such migrant:

> Seeing family is so important because you leave a country and you leave family behind and a new life can't completely compensate for not having your loved ones close by. Not too long ago both of my parents passed away within six months of each other and that was a very difficult time because I spent a lot of time travelling between Christchurch and Taipei to nurse them and to attend to funeral arrangements.

Huang is forthright in stating that 'a new life can't completely compensate for not having your loved ones close by'. Her Chinese culture expects her to look after her elderly parents regardless of distance: 'Among Chinese families, caregiving is an essential element of filial piety (*xiao*) that demands service and obedience to ancestors, parents, elders, and officials.'[36] Huang had the time and the money needed to return frequently to nurse both her parents and to make funeral arrangements, fulfilling not only the expectation for filial piety but also the emotional need for closure across distance with her parents.

Like Huang, Daisy, the Irish nurse, felt a cultural imperative to visit her parents, and she illustrated in her essay the experience of those migrants who do manage a caregiving role for years despite the vast distance between them and their families. Daisy, herself childless, was able to return to Ireland relatively often to see her family: 'For a long time after coming to New Zealand I was a migratory bird travelling between here and the British Isles almost every two years. This is the mode for a lot of people who decide to live abroad while their parents are alive.' The image of the migratory bird is apt as she swaps seasons and hemispheres to look after her aging parents, fulfilling an expected role because 'Irish migrant women are often involved in providing care and support to ageing relatives in Ireland.'[37]

Irish sociologist Louise Ryan points out: 'Close geographical proximity and cheap travel mean that there is an expectation that migrants will go home on a regular basis especially when their families need them.'[38] But Daisy neither lives close to her family nor finds travel inexpensive; she is not working in the UK as many Irish migrants do. The average price of a return economy flight from New Zealand to Europe is between €1000 to €2000 and the journey takes a minimum of 24 hours.[39] Even though her sister lives near their parents in Belfast and her brother lives in England, Daisy has made the far longer journey to Ireland 'almost every two years', each time having banked all her holidays so she can stay for at least a month.

Daisy's biennial trips back home also highlight that 'migrant daughters, in particular, feel a responsibility to participate in practical "hands-on" care by engaging in extended return visits, not only to perform their filial duty but also to provide respite to siblings'.[40] Daisy's nursing experience also informs her visits, as she can evaluate the care her parents are receiving. Once her parents are no longer living, her filial duty, the force that pulls her back, fulfilled across the kilometres and years, will no longer be as strong, and the effect of distance will be, in her words, 'less burdensome'.

The shared narrative of loss

For migrants who wish to provide a caregiving role or be present when a parent dies, but cannot be, the emotional cost of distance is particularly high. Longing and regret colour this experience in all the migrant essays, but none is more emotionally wrenching than that expressed by Anna, the Swiss migrant. Anna had just returned from her summer holidays when her sister phoned to tell her their mother had died. Stunned, Anna asked, 'Died … Just like that …?' Her mother was in a nursing home, but not physically ill. With a young family to care for, Anna couldn't return for the funeral. Half a world away, she realised: 'I am no use to Mum now.' Longing to be with her mother at the end, the only way Anna could place herself there was through imagination:

I imagine myself sitting by her bedside, lifting a spoon of chocolate pudding (Mum had a sweet tooth) from a dish on a tray and placing it between her lips. I wait patiently for her to swallow before offering the next one, the way she must have done for me when I was little. I wish I had been able to feed her like that, even just once. I wish I had kept Mum's last letter, but I didn't know it would be her last, that she was losing the ability to communicate. It is six years since I've seen her. She still knew who I was then.

The essay allowed Anna to do what she couldn't do in real life – sit beside her aging mother and feed her chocolate pudding. The roles are reversed: she is the adult, her mother the child, and the past and lyric present coincide in an imagined vignette that is as moving as it is mournful because it never occurred. The parenthetical aside – '(Mum had a sweet tooth)' – is a nod to the reader, who is not privy to this information, but the rest of the passage acts as interior monologue filled with regret: 'I wish I had been able to feed her like that, even just once. I wish I had kept Mum's last letter, but I didn't know it would be her last.' The hindsight is grievous not only because of the actual geographical distance between them and the passage of time, but also because of her mother becoming distant as a result of dementia.

Not knowing that the letter from her mother would be the last one, Anna didn't keep it. Nor could she have known at the time that her mother would not recognise her in years to come. Anna's experience is a painful example of the unravelling of the relational narrative Adriana Cavarero observes: 'At once exposable and narratable, the existent always constitutes herself in relation to another.'[41] As Anna's mother's awareness of her daughter diminished, so too did her ability to offer any shared narrative back to her daughter, if not in person, then at least in the form of a letter. The chance for any narrative resonance between Anna and her mother ended with her mother's death: 'Put simply, the necessary other corresponds first of all with the *you* whose language is spoken in the shared narrative scene.'[42] The necessary other, in this case Anna's mother, the one who 'still knew who I was then' and 'whose language is spoken in the shared narrative scene', was gone.

Perhaps Anna's impulse to create a fictive co-presence with her mother as she sits feeding her chocolate pudding is an attempt to reconnect their narrative and their selves, both separated first by time and distance and then by dementia and death. As Maruška Svašek, a Czech/Dutch migrant living in Ireland, clarifies: 'The multi-sensorial dimension of co-presence, the ability to see, hear, smell and touch each other, and to interact emotionally within the same time/space frame, allow for a unique form of intimacy which is irreplaceable by communication at a distance.'[43]

This shared intimacy of co-presence is what migrants forfeit when they move away, and it is forfeiture that Anna addresses on the page of her essay. She can travel back in imagination but not in reality to her mother's bedside. Each of us is stripped of a shared narrative when our parents die, but Anna's lament in her essay aches at the distance and not knowing:

> I want to know whether it snowed when she died. It seems important. My sister doesn't know. She lives in another town. I want to ask whether someone was with Mum when she died, but I am afraid my sister might say no. I remember when Mum's parents died. She had nursed them both at home, right till the end. Poor Mum. I hold onto the image of snow. It is soothing. A still, white world … softly falling flakes …

Twelve time zones away in a New Zealand summer, Anna wants to know if it was snowing in Switzerland, a detail so small and ordinary but for her, important. She wants to know if her mother died alone but cannot bring herself to ask because she is afraid the answer might be yes.

Anna's rapid segue from her question into the memory of her mother nursing her parents 'at home, right till the end' is imbued with the guilt of her absence from her own mother's deathbed. And then, as though speaking to comfort herself and her mother, she says, 'Poor Mum', alone, and herself so far away. Anna returns to the imagined snowfall: 'I hold on to the image of snow. It is soothing. A still, white world … softly falling flakes …' Unable to hold onto her mother, in imagination or reality, she holds onto the image of snow instead. The image is peaceful, as though the snow can cover the loss and ease her mother's passage into the next world, a passage Anna was not there to share. The ellipses, like so many dots of snow falling on the far side of the world, trail off into silence.

In a telling gesture, Anna cashed in her savings – $600 in 1992 – to send as many orange roses as she could afford to the funeral: 'Orange was Mum's favourite colour.' The roses are transitory, but they must stand in for her at the service. How many people attending the funeral would have known that orange was her mother's favourite colour? This is the part of the shared narrative that must be held by another to be understood. The personal essay inscribes Anna's moving gesture of sending the roses and thereby makes them permanent. The flowers become the visual equivalent of Anna's desire to connect, to tell the story and show the meaning of the story. Such small but particular details – the roses and the imagined snowfall – show how the personal essay can bridge memory and imagination to reveal what losing one's mother feels like to a daughter who migrated so far away from home.

Towards the end of her essay Anna returns to the mundane world where, stunned and in grief, she finishes grocery shopping:

> I walk past all those shoppers who don't know that my mother has died. I wish I could wear a sign of mourning that people would recognise, tie a black ribbon around my sleeve, or pin a black cloth button onto my top, like we do at home. Then people would ask me whom I am grieving for, and I could tell them that a whole chapter of my life has just come to a close, that my mum has faded out of the book as if the ink had run out. But all I can do now is wheel the supermarket trolley to my car. I put the groceries in the boot and shut the lid. Then I return the trolley.

Anyone who has lost someone they love knows this surreal and dissociative state of walking around in a state of grief of which others are completely unaware. No one knows her mother has just died, but she longs to communicate this.

Again we see Anna's effort to bridge the distance between New Zealand and Switzerland, only this time the distance is cultural: 'I wish I could wear a sign of mourning that people would recognise, tie a black ribbon around my sleeve, or pin a black cloth button onto my top, like we do at home.' She wants to be able to express her unspeakable and unwitnessed sorrow to those around her, as she would 'at home'. How sad those two words 'at home' are, where her mother is no longer alive. In Switzerland those visible tokens of grief – the black ribbon, the black cloth button – would invite others to ask her who she is grieving for. That, in turn, would allow her to continue the narrative that her mother's death has silenced, for 'the verbal response to *who* someone is always consists in the narration of his or her life-story'.[44] Only the living can continue the narration about the dead, and Anna yearns for someone to ask her to do just that: 'I could tell them that a whole chapter of my life has just come to a close, that my mum has faded out of the book as if the ink had run out.'

Anna understands that the relational narrative with her mother is finished. Intuitively, she chooses the metaphor of a book, which embodies their shared narrative. Except the ink has not run out; it runs on in this extraordinary passage. Even if the other shoppers around Anna are unaware her mother has died, far away, possibly alone, we are aware of it through her essay, which captures her acute, individual sorrow – a sorrow that is not imagined, that is not fictive, but is as real to the writer now as it was in 1992 when her mother died.

Perhaps the personal essay, more than other genre, has this ability to recognise 'that every human being, whatever her qualities, has her unjudgable splendor in a personal identity that *is* irrefutably her story'.[45] Anna's personal essay gives us the narrative of a loss no one asked her for, through no fault of their own. The pathos of the final image of Anna putting the groceries in the car, returning the trolley, her grief without witness or comfort, shows how unbearable it can be to live at such a distance from those we hold most dear.

Placed experience

Nearness and distance are profound and powerful concepts that touch on everything from kinship, geography, time and narrative, to where and how we perceive the world. Migrants struggle to bring the distant world close, in language, on paper, on the phone, and perhaps rarest and certainly most expensive, in person. The old geography adage that 80 per cent of all information can be tied to location is not unfounded. Where we live has a deep and abiding effect on how we think and feel, and for migrants that place has shifted radically.

As Rockwell Gray points out, 'Human life is always concretely circumstantial. All experience is *placed* experience. Thought and deed, taste and judgment, occur within the constraints and enabling conditions of highly specific settings.'[46] Migrants can map their placed experience in writing, reflecting on both their emotional and existential location throughout their migration, from when they first arrived to decades later. The personal essay's ability to reflect on the cumulative and long-term effects of distance on a migrant's life gives it the Kierkegaardian dimension, whereby the migrant lives forwards and understands backwards.

Migrants live and negotiate distance in space, time and emotion in relation to people and places they love throughout their lives. This ongoing dynamic ends only when their lives end. Some distances can be overcome, and some cannot. The geographical distance remains permanent and fixed, but how, when and if migrants can bridge it varies. Migrants who make the effort to stay connected with their family and friends by whatever means – letters, phone calls, return visits – keep the distance from becoming any greater than it already is. If friends and family reciprocate, especially if they visit, a migrant's life achieves a deeper meaning and resonance for having been seen in that new place – something felt by both parties.

For some migrants, the effect of distance abates as the ties to the host country become deeper, stronger, more lasting. If their children and grandchildren are born and raised in New Zealand, and as their own narratives become interwoven with those of others, whether through work, community, friendship or the deeply familiar, much of what grounds and connects migrants becomes present in New Zealand and not just in the place they left behind. They have another place to stand. Migrants can similarly find a place to stand in the personal essay as they ground distance in narrative, bridging their past and present selves, and bringing us near to what it feels like to live so far from what was most their own.

Realigning the inner compass

I kept crossing the ocean, first to grow up in Belgium, then to study in
Ireland, then to marry the man who first pulled me to Sweden, and finally
to migrate with our two children to New Zealand, a different ocean,
wider, farther, another hemisphere, where the Pacific and Indo-Australian
plates meet and push up these isolated and beautiful islands. Those
tectonic plates sheared apart and collided to send us back to Sweden
where the distance was cool, measured and unbearable. When I stood
on the rocky shore and looked at the slate-cold arm of the North Sea, I
imagined the blue-green waters of New Zealand. This was not the same
water – it wasn't even an ocean. 'Distance looks our way', but not here,
I thought.[47] No distance looks here. No one sees us here. We have come
too far. We've come to where there's not enough to hold us or make us
want to put down roots in the stony soil. Not language, not culture, not
the Southern Cross, not sharing a cup of tea. Instead, distance looked our
way and called to us.

On our return to New Zealand from Sweden, our route took us over
the Indian Ocean to Singapore. We could not see the ocean but it was
there, thousands of metres below. I had always flown west, never east, and
I could feel the invisible ocean realigning my inner compass to see what I
missed the first time I lived in New Zealand. That realignment held. And
now, with my family settled back in Aotearoa, I see what is here, not what
is missing.

Now I feel very close to the world again: the shops in Newtown
where I walk to buy groceries; Cook Strait just over the hill, where the
weather whips through and the clouds scud by as I write about distance.
My daughter's school is a block away, my son rides the bus for a mere 10
minutes to get to his, and my husband cycles up the Wellington hills to
campus because that is the sort of madman he is – the man who, time
and again, has drawn me across oceans for him and with him. But now
we are in New Zealand, our chosen home, and somehow everything and
everyone that once felt so far away the first time we lived here, no longer
does. We have closed the invisible distance between what we love and
where we are in the world.

Chapter 4

The Second Cup of Tea – On Belonging

'Where you are understood, you are at home.'

—JOHN O'DONOHUE, *Anam Ċara*

The poppies are deep pink with lavender centres, *Papaver somniferum*, opium poppies, gorgeous transient flowers waving on silvery-green foliage. A friend in the United States gave me the seeds when I admired these tall poppies in her garden. The original seeds came from her Danish mother-in-law, who had brought them from the old country. I was thrilled the first year they flowered in my American garden, their beautiful pink petals and green leaves harmonised with everything in bloom – the orange and yellow calendula, the English roses, the purple, mauve and white cosmos, the deep indigo delphinium, the sky-blue flax. They made me so happy, those pink poppies, and even though they were short-lived, I knew they would come back season after season, seeding themselves all over the terraced garden. So prolific were they, I gathered dozens of seed heads that autumn and let the stalks dry in several vases around the house. Inside the pods, thousands of seeds rattled like tiny rain as they shook dry.

And then we moved from the United States to New Zealand in January of 2007. Our garden lay under a foot of snow. Two men came and packed everything up, including the dry poppy stalks – accidental stowaways in their Swedish crystal vases. The seeds came unaware, as seeds often do, migrating by whatever means, from place to place. When the shipping container arrived we unloaded it, wading through the chaos and unpacking endless boxes for what felt like a month. I still cannot fathom how Matt, the lead packer, managed to pack the entire kitchen in a day when it took me a week to put it away.

One afternoon in late February, antipodean August, the sunlight so sparkling it looked rinsed, I unwrapped the seed stalks to find dozens of tiny poppy seeds had shaken free into the paper. I sprinkled them around our rental garden in Christchurch that afternoon. They did not come up the following spring. No permanent residency permit for these migrants. Maybe they knew they came into the country illicitly, although I had completely forgotten about that when I scattered them on the garden. Still in the throes of my resistance to living in New Zealand, I took their failure to germinate as a sign that they were not meant to be here, any more than I was.

As happens for many migrants, working that first year proved difficult because my skills went unrecognised. I worked at one temporary job after another around the university where I had hoped to be teaching, as I had done for years in both Europe and the United States. I was missing something that had defined me: 'Work provides a sense of agency, purpose, and worth that is gratifying on deeper levels of the psyche.'[1] My husband had all that plus a social milieu through work, as did my children with school, while I, freezing in an uninsulated, single-glazed house, was becoming ever more depressed. The house, sunlit and lovely in summer, verged on uninhabitable in winter. 'Your house is like a tomb,' Marcela my Chilean friend and future student told me. 'It makes you feel *entumicida*,' and she made the gesture of hugging herself for warmth. She went on to explain *entumicida* meant numb, not only physically but also emotionally, and likened it to 'a mild hypothermia of the soul'.

What I was feeling was not just physical cold, which was real enough in that arctic house, but also a profound sense of displacement and loss that ensues when one migrates: loss of home, loss of culture, loss of identity, loss of the deep familiarity that comes with time in one place. Five years and two major earthquakes later, having migrated to Sweden I re-experienced all of this with an added and more crucial loss: the loss of language. For the migrant, 'above all there is the problem of language, the most powerful cultural intermediary, vehicle for thought and symbol, principal entrance portal to social relations'.[2] Nothing prepared me for how painful and integral the loss of language would be in my daily world: something as simple as phoning the school to report my daughter was sick, reading instructions, filling out forms or understanding what the checkout clerk said to me became difficult, if not impossible. I had lost my voice.

Full migrant

In retrospect, I realise that migrating to New Zealand where I share the language made my transition far easier than that which non-native speakers experience. I had no idea until I migrated to Sweden how language permeates everything: spoken, written, heard. In New Zealand I was not what Salman Rushdie calls 'a full migrant', someone who suffers 'a triple disruption: he loses his place, he enters into an alien language, and he finds himself surrounded by people whose social behavior and codes are very unlike, and sometimes even offensive to, his own'.[3] Migrants themselves distinguish between being 'a full migrant' or not, as I discovered. On the first day of my class, Cathrine, the Danish migrant, said to her fellow Scottish participant, whom she knew: 'But you're not a migrant!'

'Yes, I am,' Dorothy replied. 'I came from Scotland fifty years ago.'

'But you speak English.'

In the eyes of non-native speakers, if one shares the language of the host country, somehow one is 'not a migrant'. In Sweden, as a bona fide 'full migrant', I empathised with an enormous part of the migration experience hitherto missing: language.

Twenty of the 37 migrant writers featured in this book are non-native speakers. I felt that if they could learn another language, then so could I. These 20 individuals come from many parts of the world: Croatia, Thailand, Russia, India, Switzerland, Denmark, China, the Netherlands, Malaysia, Kiribati, Slovakia, Germany, Chile, Korea and even Sweden. They wrote about their migration experience in a second or third language, and as such were 'the voices of the transplanted and translated subjects'.[4] Even so, their willingness and ability to write personal essays in another language revealed an adaptation to their chosen environment, both on the page and in New Zealand. They are the migrant seeds that took and flourished. And, like poppy seeds that lie dormant, they must be disturbed if they're to germinate: migration is, if anything, a disturbance, an unsettlement. As Mary, the Scottish psychotherapist, found, becoming settled requires effort: 'Fresh off the boat or plane, the basics of daily living absorb an enormous amount of mental and physical energy. Unfamiliarity in a new country robs us, momentarily, of an anchor in society and is disorienting.'

To be without the anchor of language is to be adrift in the world. I experienced this literally and metaphorically when I lost my keys in a grocery store in Sweden. I knew the Swedish word for keys but not the word for lost, and that experience seemed to me emblematic of what it means to migrate: you lose your keys. This loss of language as key echoes what Hélène Cixous believes is the origin of writing: 'The origin of the gesture of writing is linked to the experience of a disappearance, to the feeling of having lost the key to the world, of having been thrown outside.'⁵ In Sweden I was thrown outside because I had lost language, the key to the world. The primacy of language would never have been so blindingly apparent to me had we not migrated to Sweden. Language, more than any other key, grants us access to a new country.

When out in public in Sweden I felt the intense isolation that comes from not understanding much of what is being said. The question I heard over and over as I struggled to make myself understood was '*Vad sa du?*' What did you say? I could have replied, if I had known the words: I've lost my keys, the keys of language. In Sweden my own native language kept me company in a way I had never experienced before. It was as though English was consoling me for its absence in my dailiness. I felt English lap around my head like water. All day while my two children attended school, immersed in Swedish, thrown into the deep end where I could not help them swim, and my husband was at work, semi-fluent in Swedish having been married to a Swede years before, I was alone with my language, trying to express how migrants connect to their new environment.

The irony of being a vulnerable participant in my own research was ever present, always informing my writing. I thought of what the exiled Polish poet and Nobel laureate Czeslaw Milosz said: 'Language is our only homeland.'[6] How true that is, and how bereft I felt of my homeland, which I realised was not just language but all the senses of connection I had with and through language, to people, to places, to every aspect of my life. I realised I was pining as much for New Zealand as for my own language, and the fact that we didn't have a landline with which to phone friends or family in the States or New Zealand intensified my sense of being cut off.

One day I stood on the shore of our local beach and named all the things I could in Swedish: *sten, hav, himmel, sol, jord, träd, snö*. Stone, sea, sky, sun, earth, tree, snow. I was reminded of what my student Anton, the Russian navigator who had washed up in New Zealand when his company went bankrupt, wrote in his essay, 'with no language in my heart but hope'. I had to hope I would learn the language, for how else could I connect with Sweden? But how could I, when the truth was much simpler: I did not want to connect with Sweden. Nor, in turn, did the country or its inhabitants want to connect with me, or my children, or my husband. And so, when I stood on that shore naming the things I could, in those strange vowels spoken at the front of the mouth, the lips rounded like a fish if it could speak, I was trying to summon the world back: *sten, hav, himmel, sol, jord, träd, snö*. Stone, sea, sky, sun, earth, tree, snow. But this was not my world. My world could not be called back. My world was on the other side of the earth, in New Zealand, 12 time zones and two seasons away, where it was summer.

For migrants, the key is to find what makes them feel at home in the new country, what gives them a sense of place, of belonging, of attachment. Having had the good fortune to return to New Zealand, I now fully understand the enduring importance of our need to belong, to feel connected and to be at home in the world. Salman Rushdie, himself a migrant, argues that the triple loss the migrant experiences is significant 'because roots, language and social norms have been three of the most important parts of the definition of what it is to be a human being.

The migrant, denied all three, is obliged to find new ways of describing himself, new ways of being human.'[7]

How migrants find new ways to describe themselves and be human fits well with the exploratory nature of the personal essay, informed as it is by philosopher Michel de Montaigne's motto *'Que sais-je?'* – What do I know? – a question that conjures up every thought and emotion from bafflement to wonder to scepticism to knowledge. Migrant experience has a powerful parallel with the personal essay, a 'mode of writing that is literally a self-trying-out ... a testing ("assay") of one's own intellectual, emotional, and physiological responses to a given topic'.[8] Migration is a dynamic process of 'a self-trying-out' and a testing of one's 'intellectual, emotional and physiological responses' to living in a different country, culture and perhaps language. That connection between the migrant and the personal essay brings to mind Ralph Waldo Emerson's words: 'Then I dare: I will also essay to be.'[9]

As migrants 'essay to be' in the host country, their essays provide a perspective that is informed and inquiring. The vantage points of outsider and insider, at home and not, belonging and not belonging, highlight the dialectical tension inherent in both the migrant and the genre. More than other genres, 'the essay enacts the process of accommodation between the world and the "I", and thus it is consciousness real-izing itself'.[10] This protean form has the capacity to reveal how migrants learn to adapt and accommodate themselves to their new country, or fail to. Or, as with many migrants, find themselves somewhere in between. The process of accommodation between the world and 'I' exists both between the migrant and the host country in all its myriad layers – linguistic, social, physical, existential – and the migrant and the text. They are parallel, analogous processes: the migrant must find a way in the new country, and the writer must find a way in the essay, sharing the voyage of trial and error, discovery and understanding. As the philosopher and essayist William Gass points out, 'the hero of the essay is its author in the act of thinking things out. Feeling and finding a way.'[11]

While the heroic identification with the essayist may seem exaggerated, migrant and writer are nevertheless engaged in the process 'of thinking things out', of '[f]eeling and finding a way'. Susan, the American who escaped to Antarctica and later married a New Zealander, provided an apt analogy for this process of acclimation:

> Moving to a new country is like having your dog hide your comfortable pair of shoes daily. Each day you get up and you have to search for them. If you can't find them you have to wear substitutes until they are found. The risk then is that each different pair of shoes may not be quite as comfortable. This is just like trying to find your place of belonging in your new home. I have tried on lots of shoes since moving here, and I'm still trying them on.

All of us know what a comfortable pair of shoes feels like. What we might not have experienced is losing the ordinary sense of comfort as it applies to where one lives. Susan not only lost this sense of comfort daily and had to search for it anew but, failing that, had to try substitutes. This search for what fits, for what is comfortable, 'is just like trying to find your place of belonging in your new home'. As a migrant, she is still looking for what will give her this 'place of belonging', and her extended metaphor describes this process of accommodation between the world and 'I'. Even though Susan has lived and worked in New Zealand for over a decade, is married to a New Zealander and is a native speaker, she has yet to find what fits: 'I have tried on lots of shoes since moving here, and I'm still trying them on.' William Gass's 'feeling and finding a way' is an ongoing process, not just in the essay, but in the migrant's life too.

How migrants find a sense of belonging, if indeed they do, is, to borrow from Montaigne, *'ondoyant et divers'* (undulating and diverse), like the flow of individual rivers. The desire to belong is central to humans, and however we define belonging, we know it when we experience it and when we do not. Like the word 'home', a concept often associated with belonging, the feeling of belonging sets up a resonance within us that we recognise as much by its absence as by its presence. Belonging is the resonance between the self and the world.

Individuals do not, of course, belong in just any place in the world, as we found from our year and a half in Sweden. As with any abstraction that is difficult to define, impossible to quantify and highly individual, belonging seems to operate on a spectrum or continuum for each migrant. Some migrants feel, free of doubt, that they belong in their new country. Others may never feel this, no matter how long they live there, while yet others fall somewhere in between, continuing to search for and discover the resonance between themselves and their world.

Contrapuntal awareness

The personal essays discussed in this book, written by men and women, both native and non-native speakers of English, cover a span of 60 years and represent an array of ages and countries of origin. They therefore reveal a richness of expression and perception about what it means to belong. Greg Madison, a Canadian migrant who studies the existential and psychological aspects of migration, notes that 'the lived experience of migration has been largely neglected', and that the literature which does exist tends to focus on those forced into exile or who are pressed to migrate rather than choose to do so.[12] This emphasis makes the personal essays of voluntary migrants even more vital to explore, because these capture 'the lived experience of migration'. Phillip Lopate would agree: 'The personal essay', he writes, 'turns out to be one of the most useful instruments with which outsiders can reach the dominant culture quickly and forcefully and testify to the precise ambiguities of their situation as individuals and group members.'[13] As outsiders, as strangers who have come to town, migrants can help us understand one of our deepest human concerns: what it means to belong and to feel at home in the world.

Migrants' personal essays challenge the idea that 'When we are home, we don't need to talk about it.'[14] Perhaps those who have been uprooted, even by choice, have a greater need to talk and write about home than those who've never left. Migrants face a dilemma which those who remain at home may never experience, something David, the American who came to New Zealand in his forties with his family, realised: 'A person who leaves home and finds a new place that feels like home has created a lifelong dilemma. In truth, that person will never be completely "home" again. The longing for the other "home" will never end and it is nothing if it is not emotional.'[15] For many migrants, this dilemma both creates and informs a dialogical discourse in the personal essay, for underneath the braided river of their lives is another, older, deeper current – the current of belonging somewhere else.

Few concepts can be more charged than belonging and home, because unlike those who rarely if ever leave home, migrants know what it means to live elsewhere. 'Most people,' wrote the late Palestinian-American writer and academic Edward Said, 'are principally aware of one culture, one setting, one home; exiles [and I would argue migrants] are aware of at least two, and this plurality of vision gives rise to an awareness of simultaneous dimensions, an awareness – to borrow a phrase from music – that is *contrapuntal*.'[16] The migrant 'plurality of vision' is informed by a frame of reference that is linguistic, cultural and environmental but then becomes overlaid with a new frame of reference. Those simultaneous dimensions – one absent, one present – and that contrapuntal awareness are what make migrant experience challenging. How migrants negotiate that awareness while living in their new country determines whether they feel discord, harmony or something in between.

Anna, who came as a bride from Switzerland to New Zealand in 1968, describes this contrapuntal awareness beautifully. The lack of resonance between herself and the new environment was immediately apparent to her:

> The strangest thing was the nearness of those far away, and the distance of those present. The people I had lost seemed almost part of myself, while the people I was with seemed as remote as the moon. They spoke differently, dressed differently, behaved differently, cooked differently, spent their time differently, and treated me differently. I was a stranger, an intruder who had stolen an only son. As far as they were concerned I need not have come here, but since I was here, I had better do as they said. Even my husband was different. This was home for him and he settled comfortably back into his routine. Several times a day, it seemed, I did something wrong. I should have said that, or not said that, or done that, or not done that, or even not seen that. I tried hard to conform. I could not bear the isolation. I needed to be accepted, and seemingly, the only way to acceptance was complete integration.

This is an eloquent and painful account of one migrant who has lost
roots, her native language (Swiss is a spoken language only) and social
norms but must find a way to adapt. Anna's contrapuntal awareness
is both distilled and embodied: 'The people I had lost seemed almost
part of myself, while the people I was with seemed as remote as the
moon.' Presence and absence reverse themselves. What is distant
becomes present, and what is present becomes, if not absent, far away.
She describes the people she had known in Switzerland as 'lost', not left
behind, yet she internalises them to the extent that they are 'almost part
of myself'. The people she encounters in New Zealand are alien and
distant. They do not welcome Anna as a new bride: she is the stranger
in their midst, and her introduction to the new country is consequently
fraught: 'I was a stranger, an intruder who had stolen an only son.'

Her contrapuntal awareness reveals that every aspect of her in-laws'
lives differs from hers: their speech, dress, behaviour, food, leisure
time, and their treatment of her as a new family member. She is clearly
unwelcome: 'As far as they were concerned I need not have come here.'
But as the daughter-in-law she is forced to accept that 'I had better do as
they said,' a statement that is parental and disciplinary. And if that were
not enough, her one point of contact and familiarity, her new husband,
is also different. She has had to adapt not only to a new country, culture
and family, but also to a partner who has reverted to his home-based
persona: 'Even my husband was different. This was home for him and
he settled comfortably back into his routine.' What is home for him is
displacement for her.

Anna's husband was literally and figuratively back home, fluent in
the language, the social codes, the innumerable little things that enabled
settling 'comfortably back into his routine'. Anna, not at home in the
language, culture or setting, felt that no one around her, not even her
husband, tried to make her feel at home. Instead, she experienced a
daily stream of criticism: 'Several times a day, it seemed, I did something
wrong. I should have said that, or not said that, or done that, or not
done that, or even not seen that.' Also, as is common with migrants, she
shielded her own family from her suffering: 'I never told my parents

about these difficult early years, and how miserable I had been. I did not want to worry them. All I could do was keep trying to survive in this foreign environment, which was so unlike the one I had come from.'

Anna's silence must have intensified her sense of being alone, cut off. Not one person knew she was suffering, including her husband, apparently. Small wonder she wrote: 'I could not bear the isolation.' Her adaptive response was: 'I tried hard to conform. I needed to be accepted, and seemingly, the only way to acceptance was complete integration.' What her essay addresses directly – the need for acceptance – is grounded in the fact that 'human beings are fundamentally and pervasively motivated by the need to belong, that is, a strong desire to form and maintain enduring interpersonal relationships'.[17] Newly married and far from 'the people [she] had lost', her need to form 'enduring personal relationships' with her new family and country would have been crucial.

For migrants, separation from what previously constituted belonging – family, friends, community, sense of place, language – intensifies the need to belong. Those who have been uprooted seek to be regrounded, to regain that sense of belonging. Separated from roots, language and family, Anna's need to forge an accommodation between the world she now lived in and her identity in Switzerland meant 'the only way to acceptance was complete integration'. Integration has many levels, and for her, as the foreign partner, 'this initiation, and the need to commit almost from day one to life as a migrant, is another important factor in the "extreme" assimilation process'.[18] Not sharing the same language or cultural background with her husband, Anna found herself internally and externally dislocated: 'Not only was I between two countries, in a place I could not call home, and between two families, one I had lost and one I did not yet belong to, but now I was also between two languages, neither of which I could manage efficiently.'

To be between languages is a transitional, liminal state, a place without words or means of connection to either one's present situation or one's past. Professor of comparative literature Azade Seyhan argues that diasporic texts address 'spaces of untranslatability between languages, cultures, and texts, that these spaces define and mark the silences and pathos of exile'.[19] With the notable exception of perhaps being able to return to their country of origin, migrants, unlike some exiles, share these spaces of untranslatability marked by 'silences and pathos'. Anna experienced this silence quite literally in 'that horrifying moment when I met another Swiss and discovered that I could no longer converse in Swiss'. The silence extended to her inability to share her language and cultural memory with her New Zealand husband. She laments that if she had been married to someone Swiss, 'We would have spoken the same language. I would not have lacked the vocabulary to express how I felt. Above all, we would have had shared memories and been able to reminisce together.' Not being able to communicate so much of who she was and how she felt intensified her isolation. As Anton, the Russian migrant, observed: 'Not having language keeps everything inside you.' He too married a New Zealander who did not share his language.

The binary for many migrants is therefore loss/belonging, and Anna articulates exactly the plight of the full migrant who has lost roots and language and is living among people with a different social code. She was between countries 'in a place I could not call home', which is all the more painful when she realised her mother tongue 'was slipping away'. Her home had disappeared, both literally and linguistically. She had no place, neither Switzerland nor New Zealand, and her family was lost. The word 'lost' recurs in her writing, and its repetition is not accidental, polarised as she was by a family 'I did not yet belong to'. Despite her feelings of loss, Anna was willing to adapt and to accept her husband's family, but they had yet to reciprocate that acceptance.

Anna's loss of connection in New Zealand was further aggravated when she learned she could not practise as a midwife, which she had done for three years in Switzerland. During that time she had delivered over 600 babies. In New Zealand she could only work as a student, sidelined in terms of both responsibility and salary. Here we see her contrapuntal awareness applied to the workplace: 'I found it incredibly frustrating not being able to deliver babies anymore. I had much more experience in midwifery than the average GP here, and they often did things that horrified me. That did not exactly help me with my settling in this country.' Not being able to practise as a midwife further compromised her ability to settle: 'If the vocational shift is sharply downward, the resulting psychic turmoil can be great indeed.'[20] Stripped of so many contexts for connection and belonging it is no wonder she felt complete integration was her only choice.

In another of her essays, written 40 years after her arrival in New Zealand, Anna revealed that her sense of self was not completely subsumed by the family and culture she joined. As she became more familiar with her environment, able to negotiate between herself and this new world, she discovered something small but remarkable:

> Years later I realised that I had not, as I thought, adjusted to New Zealand customs, but to the customs of my in-law-family. I had no means of telling the difference. All I knew was what they told me. These were often quite trivial things, but in my endeavour to get it right, I accepted them as the New Zealand way. I remember the astonishment I felt one day, to find that in other New Zealand families you did not have to wait till everyone had finished their first cup of tea before you were given a second one.

Intent on adapting to her new family, in an effort to belong she accepted what they told her was 'the New Zealand way'. What a revelation that second cup of tea must have been, casting all those earlier and future cups of tea in a new light. Here we see how the essay 'can present its story *and* consider the meaning of the story.'[21] Her writing delivers this moment of understanding that transformed how she saw New Zealand. The personal essay allowed her to look back and discover the river under the river, thereby revealing that the surface of her daily life in her new family was not actually the cultural truth. Thanks to the reflective power of the genre, she could understand in the present what she could not in the past.

What fosters a sense of belonging is understanding – being understood on multiple levels: linguistic, existential, emotional and cultural. As the philosopher and poet John O'Donohue reminds us: 'Understanding nourishes belonging.'[22] Migrants may not initially understand that they can have a second cup of tea, or any of the myriad ways of navigating custom, landscape or language. That process takes time, even years, a fact Anna verified when she concluded: 'I now feel thoroughly at home in this country. My language problems have sorted themselves out too and I can switch easily from one to the other.' Her eloquent personal essays reveal how deeply at home she now is in a language she once could not 'manage efficiently'.

Grounding the unsayable

The personal essay offers the second cup of tea, a recognition of something that was not realised until later, which is akin to how migrants learn to live in their new country. Just as the world offers ongoing lessons to the migrant, 'the essay is trying to teach you something about how to live your life'.[23] The migrant writer only realises this by being attentive to both the world and the page. That nexus between migrant and world and migrant and text is what makes the personal essay such a rewarding form to write and to read: '… the essay's payoff is recognition, which is different from knowledge or mere understanding in that it arises in felt or shared experience. To recognize something is to be affected by what we already know but didn't realize, an insight that leads us back to what is both familiar and strange.'[24]

Once again we can see the Kierkegaardian orientation of the genre, of the essayist living forwards but understanding backwards, recognising only in the present that which could not be recognised in the past. The essay, like the braided river, reveals far more over the course of its flow than the mere surface facts of a migration narrative. More than any other genre, the essay has this ability to flow forwards into recognition in the present through the backwards look into the past:

> The essayist thoughtfully scrutinizes the world, drawing out significances which until then may have never been clearly seen or fully understood, creating and explaining new artifacts of intelligence through the alchemy of mind and words. Essays wander, wonder, and make connections; they meander among and sift through the bewildering array of the world's physical, social, and cultural phenomena, creating meaning and structure in life which may never have been evident before.[25]

The personal essay, moreover, makes evident the meaning and structure in an individual's life, not only for the writer but also for those who read their work; the recognition therefore is twofold.

The migrant writers in each class I taught shared frissons of recognition. Time and again they were struck by one another's narratives, both in life and on the page, as they 'essayed to be'. They recognised in their classmates' prose something both 'familiar and strange'[26] but unique to each individual, which Adriana Cavarero argues is the relational nature of narrative: 'This ethic desires a you that is truly an other, in her uniqueness and distinction. No matter how much you are similar and consonant, says this ethic, your story is never my story … [and] your uniqueness is exposed to my gaze and consists in an unrepeatable story whose tale you desire.'[27] Because migrants are often perceived as other, they recognise and value this quality, where the familiar and the strange coincide, a happenstance that echoes their own contrapuntal awareness. They intuitively understand that a relational dynamic is always in play in the contact zone where self meets other.

The recognition of being 'other' informed all the migrant classes. From the moment class members saw the course title, 'Writing the Personal Essay: Migration and identity', they were making a choice based on that link between 'migration' and 'identity' and their desire to write about it. Even if they knew nothing about the genre, they had an inkling as to what the word 'personal' means. Underpinning the course design was the idea that 'other migrants are already known as not known; they are already assigned a place as strangers before the identifications can take place. In other words, it is through an uncommon estrangement that the possibility of such a migrant community comes to be lived.'[28] I wanted to address the concept of 'known as not known', albeit while recognising that migrants themselves understand this idea first-hand. As the stranger who comes to town, they are well acquainted with being 'assigned a place as strangers'. But what if that 'place' was acknowledged in writing? In their essays, the migrant writers in my class were free to explore questions relating to migration and identity however they chose, each of them driven by their own concerns and narratives, each of them, one way or another, wrestling with a central question:

> Can the events and accidents of life add up to a coherent story? That is every migrant's question. And since these events and accidents are beyond an uprooted person's control, the unity of a life-story has to reside in the person telling it; unity, we would say, lies in the quality of the narrator's voice. The narrator, following Pico [della Mirandola's] precept, must learn how to tell about disorder and displacement in his or her own life in such a way that he or she does not become confused or deranged by the telling.[29]

In five different classes, two of them disrupted for multiple weeks by major earthquakes, the migrant writers met to write and talk about their personal essays. The richness of that exchange, the combined elements of risk and trust disclosed in their writing, the moments of recognition and vulnerability from 'an uncommon estrangement', created a migrant community of writers. Both their essays and the class provided a space where they could voice what it means to belong or not. They developed and shared an understanding, a space that sometimes even those closest to them had been unable to provide. Livingston, the Scottish doctor, acknowledged this in his final essay: 'So I think, where do I turn? Why not to this happy band of ex-pats who have been brave enough to bare their souls to me and have indulged me in the same?'

Regardless of age, gender, language or point of origin, migrants share one thing: they all left their home country. Home. The word alone implies a range of emotion, meaning and resonance, as personal as it is universal, as abstract as it is visceral. Home is where we connect to what matters most to us, however that is defined: 'One's conception of home is simultaneously imagined and real, nostalgic and concrete, clear, yet contradictory. Its perception is influenced by personal emotions as well as social-cultural memories, symbols, and traditions. It is not one clearly defined spatial or emotional notion but a multiple construct in individuals' lives.'[30] For the migrant, the concept of home is particularly freighted and ineluctable, as much by absence as presence. We know what home is even if it remains rooted in what remains unsayable, as the poet Rainer Maria Rilke recognised: 'Things are not nearly so comprehensible and sayable as we are generally made to believe. Most experiences are unsayable; they come to fullness in a realm that words do not inhabit.'[31] Of course the challenge for the writer and for the migrant is to ground that unsayable experience of home in their lives and in their texts.

In Suk, who left Korea in her forties, grasped this unsayable quality of home: 'The taste of our homeland life is alive all the time in our minds. It transcends time and space which impacts nostalgia. It is difficult to ensure a deep inner satisfaction with life in this country. Happiness will in part create a home where one is planted, but our roots are always deep within the motherland.' Here we see how disembodied and yet pervasive the concept of home is: 'The taste of our homeland life is alive all the time in our minds.' She signals this 'taste' as universal to all migrants and 'alive all the time in our minds', and states that 'It transcends time and space.' This presence/absence of home in the mind makes it 'difficult to ensure a deep inner satisfaction with life in this country'. Home remains on the level of abstraction and happiness, which 'will in part create a home where one is planted'. The distancing effect of 'one' and the I absorbed into the collective 'our' indicates just how ungrounded In Suk still felt, not only in the text but also 'in this country', perhaps because 'our roots are always deep within the motherland'.

Migrants leave their roots, their social norms and perhaps their language when they come to a new country. When In Suk migrated in 1994 with her nine-year-old daughter, she knew no one; she had neither a place to live nor a job, and she scarcely knew English. Yet she recognised what was required of her to make this transition successful: 'I started to see this new life as different, as a beginning, as a time requiring profound change.' She embraced this change from the start: 'Looking back to the beginning of my migrant life I found myself utterly captivated by the Kiwis, Māoris and Polynesians I met. I have chosen New Zealand, the small islands, as my second home and love the people.' Critical to In Suk's sense of belonging was her acceptance of those she met and her active choice of New Zealand as her 'second home'.

That In Suk was 'utterly captivated by the Kiwis, Māoris and
Polynesians' dovetails with what essayist, traveller and serial migrant
Pico Iyer advises: 'My first rule is to look for the distinctive good in
any place and try to learn from it.'[32] Yet despite In Suk embracing
New Zealand as her 'second home', the experience has been neither
straightforward nor easy for her because acceptance must be reciprocal,
a point she made in an essay with the revealing title, 'Where Is My Real
Home?'

> I felt like I wanted to be born again into this country. Physically I knew
> beyond a shadow of a doubt that I was accepted here, but there were still
> many others who treated us as gentile intruders. To venture out into the
> new environment, I have learnt English and taken new cultural norms. I
> didn't isolate myself, but I was often pushed into isolation.

In Suk is a devout Christian, so it's not surprising she invoked the
metaphor of wanting 'to be born again into this country'. But this desire
for a rebirth was not without complications. Her statement, 'Physically I
knew beyond a shadow of a doubt I was accepted here,' reflects her status
as a legal migrant, but it is offset by her experience of 'many others who
treat us as gentile intruders'. The religious analogy of 'gentile intruders'
underscores her sense that she at times felt both other and unwelcome in
her new country.

At the time In Suk immigrated in 1994, migration from Asian
countries had increased. A significant change in New Zealand's
immigration policy in 1986 meant the country no longer focused on
ethnicity alone.[33] Anti-Asian sentiment became rife, something In Suk
personally experienced: 'A few naughty youths, "Go back to your land,
yellow Asians," bawled to us behind our backs. They even threw some
eggs onto my car when I got out of my car in town.' Despite her effort
to adapt to New Zealand by learning English and adopting new cultural
norms, results were not necessarily forthcoming: 'I didn't isolate myself,
but I was often pushed into isolation.' In this balanced sentence, meaning
pivots on the comma: what she strives to avoid – 'I didn't isolate myself'
– meets with a negative response, 'but I was often pushed into isolation'.
The verb becomes the noun in a rather telling enactment of how some

people in the host country thwart integration. No matter how willing a migrant is to adapt, unless members of the host country help facilitate integration, that person may never feel at home.

Fortunately, In Suk also met New Zealanders who helped her feel accepted in her chosen 'second home'. Their acceptance was particularly important given some members of the Korean community shunned her because she was a divorced mother. This situation counters our likely expectation that 'Within the familiar surroundings of the ethnic group, the immigrant or minority group member will usually find acceptance, common interests, opportunities to give and receive and a sense of belonging.'[34] For In Suk, the stigma against divorce was so strong in the Korean community, both natively and locally, that she didn't necessarily find that acceptance: 'Whereas in NZ, most people here have accepted me as who I am. I could get out of this Korean snail shell with the support of Kiwi friends.' In Suk is a very shy and modest woman, and 'this Korean snail shell' circumscribed her existence in her own country and in the Korean community in New Zealand. It was her Kiwi friends who coaxed her out of that shell.

In her final essay, in which she weighed the pros and cons of her migration, In Suk wrote: 'With regard to different societal values and norms, I have encountered a new world, in some ways this is freeing, but also daunting. There was an inner conflict between the host country and the home country, but I seem to be set free from the chains of my cultural and religious practices.' Again, we see her experiencing the polarisation between the countries and their cultures, but this time as an inner conflict, a contrapuntal awareness. But then that conflict is resolved when she frees herself from 'the chains of my cultural and religious practices'. The 'new world' sees her shed confinement and constriction, snail shells and chains.

Perhaps it is not surprising that a woman who continually weighs matters and appears to be both open and fair-minded now works as a justice of the peace: 'I challenge each situation from my experience. My diplomacy has yielded good results within the community. That means, I continue to pass *Jung* onto Kiwis with a big smile and explain that is a Korean way. It then becomes the reciprocal relationship.' *Jung* represents one of the most important attributes of Korean culture, and In Suk translates it as affection, humanity, warm-heartedness, paternal love, friendship, becoming attached and enjoying thoughts of one's beloved homeland. *Jung* also exists in its negative form, the absence of all the aforementioned traits. Clearly, for Koreans, *Jung* underpins what it means to belong. In Suk's delight in sharing the concept of *Jung* with New Zealanders shows how migrants can enrich the host country when the relationship between the two becomes reciprocal.

The contact zone

Reciprocity, the act of sharing that helps one gain a sense of attachment and belonging, is vital in helping migrants offset the losses experienced on leaving their home countries. They must reconnect with a community, the very thing that migration ruptures: '… immigration forced or unforced, is accompanied by factors such as the severing of community ties, the loss of social networks and familiar bonds, and the loss of resources and meaning systems. One of the ways in which immigrants cope with these losses is through adaptation to their new experiences, through a process called community making.'[35]

Some migrants find community through work, school or church, through neighbours, their children or volunteering, or through sports or joining groups that interest them. Other migrants may be welcomed outright if they fulfil a vital community role, as happened to Gareth, the Welsh doctor, who became the local GP: 'They were excited on our arrival and wanted us to feel wanted and at home. If anything they tried, at times, too hard. Our celebrity had spread through the district and wherever we went men and women asked how we were settling in and what did we think of New Zealand.' Still other migrants actively seek out community, which is what Elizabeth, the Englishwoman whose marriage became a casualty of migration, did.

Elizabeth's experience could well serve as a textbook example for single parents endeavouring to find and build community:

With no family or local friends, I made a real effort to become a member of the community. However flat or lacking in confidence I felt, I made a daily effort to embrace the life here. I went to church and suspended my agnosticism to enjoy the truly uplifting and friendly sermons. I took Poppy to the Monday playgroup, the Tuesday and Friday toddler music classes, and started my own single mothers' coffee group. This is now a thriving Thursday morning salon of 10 delightful, intelligent Sumner mums and their little ones.

Elizabeth not only joined in everywhere – church, playgroups, toddler music classes – she also created a group for single mothers like herself who were juggling work and family. The idea of suspending agnosticism to enjoy something one otherwise might not seems instructive. If the migrant neither believes nor disbelieves in community but instead decides to participate in it, other possibilities and opportunities arise.

The embrace of community must be mutual, however, and in this respect Elizabeth was fortunate in where she chose to live: 'I was astonished at how friendly and open the people were after my experience of living in Southshore, renowned among the locals for being a backstabbing unfriendly commune of unwilling neighbours.' On comparing the two different neighbourhoods in which she had lived, she realised the second one's friendly and open acceptance of her was what made the difference.

Both mutual respect and understanding are at stake for migrants and their host country. Willingness and the ability to adapt are no guarantee that the people migrants live among will accept them: 'The relational nature of belonging is important here. Belonging is about the formal and informal *experience* of belonging.'[36] Migrants may be formally accepted with permanent residency, even citizenship, and still not feel they belong. Belonging, the experience of being accepted or rejected, works both ways, and that resonance between self and world must reach some degree of accord. Both migrants and hosts can accept or reject the other. Thus, belonging occurs literally and figuratively in a contact zone, in 'social spaces where cultures meet, grasp, and grapple with each other, often in highly asymmetrical relations of power.'[37] These 'asymmetrical relations of power' may be based on roots in the community, language or familiarity with social codes, the keys that give access to feeling at home.

Migrants who learn to adapt to the new culture find the process an ongoing one worked out and through the contact zone. Although these asymmetrical relations of power abate as migrants become more conversant with the new country, some of them continue to be in place or in play, particularly with regard to belonging. In an essay exploring familiarity and sense of place, tellingly entitled 'Lost in a Twilight Zone', Theresa, the Indian nurse, illustrated this potential tension in the contact zone:

> When your social system has a way of looking at its citizens differently you are not eligible to criticize a country that at least legally tries to treat its citizens equally. New Zealand is a country of my imaginations. People really try to make you feel at home. (Don't count the small minority.) Friends make you feel welcomed, forget about the few who ask you why did you come here? Love the landscapes (keeping in mind some part of India has great landscapes, which no one finds time to enjoy).

Aware of the inequality of the Indian caste system, Theresa feels she is not 'eligible to criticise a country that at least legally tries to treat its citizens equally'. Her disenfranchisement is not offset by the fact that her skilled profession grants her permanent residency, nor by her fluency in English. Her claim that she has no right to criticise New Zealand exemplifies the asymmetrical balance of power migrants can feel in their chosen country. Migrants can never have prior claim on the host country, and in this regard they are like those descendants of Pākehā settlers who 'are aware that not being tangata whenua means that [they] don't have a natural, or prior, claim on this country, and so there can be an obstacle between emotion and language'.[38]

The absence of the pronoun 'I' throughout Theresa's passage underscores her lack of voice and individual agency. Instead, she identifies with the universal and migrant 'you' who is not eligible to offer criticism of the adopted country. However, this 'you' voices a critique in writing of what occurs in the contact zone and might otherwise be silenced. While New Zealand 'at least legally tries to treat its citizens equally', the implication that what is mandated by law may not be concurrent with reality is further substantiated by her next sentence:

'New Zealand is a country of my imaginations.' Whether 'imaginations' is a typo or deliberate, New Zealand becomes fictive. The one slip into first person occurs here – 'my imaginations'. But even here, it is not tied to reality.

The reality for Theresa at the time she wrote her essays was that she had lived in New Zealand for over seven years with her husband and two daughters. What follows is the argument she presented in her writing as to what makes for a sense of belonging and what undermines it in the contact zone. Although Theresa wrote, 'People really try to make you feel at home,' the telling parenthesis that follows inscribes the minority who do not: '(Don't count the small minority.)' From generic 'people', the relationship moves to friends, and again we see the experience of belonging being undercut: 'Friends make you feel welcomed, forget about the few who ask you why did you come here?' Here the counter argument is spliced together with a comma, showing an even closer connection in the contact zone. The tension between a sense of belonging or not hinges on that one comma, with the supposed welcome made questionable by 'the few who ask you why did you come here?' The imperative 'Forget about the few who ask' is paradoxically denied even while it is enjoined. Finally, the most truncated of points, 'Love the landscapes', is immediately followed by an embedded parenthesis: '(keeping in mind some part of India has great landscapes, which no one finds time to enjoy)'. Here the argument is thrown back, perhaps on the very people, including friends, who might not realise that India, like New Zealand, has beautiful landscapes, however with a distinct difference: 'which no one finds time to enjoy'.

The contact zone need not be negatively charged or contentious. The point where people meet and connect – migrant meeting local – can be positively valorised if it includes 'identifying with the ideas, interests, histories and attitudes of others' and allows for 'communication across lines of difference and hierarchy that go beyond politeness but maintain mutual respect'.[39] Theresa addresses the issue of mutual respect. She does not shy away from use of the first person but speaks directly from it: 'Many a time I tried to explain to people that there is nothing I can compare in New Zealand with India. It is unique. I was brought up in that culture but [was] prepared to accept and respect the values and customs of my new adopted country. And I do hope that I wasn't a complete failure in that.' She engages in dialogue within the contact zone, trying to explain why the two countries cannot be compared – they are too dissimilar. Yet she is prepared to accept and respect the culture of her adopted country.

However, such effort will never be fully rewarded if it is not met with reciprocal acceptance and respect. Also, as Theresa noted at the opening of her essay, 'a complete merging was impossible due to the physical differences'. In New Zealand the physical and linguistic aspects of her ethnicity remained an issue for some. Her New Zealand co-workers frequently told her to 'speak English' because they were unwilling to try to understand her accent: 'The language or so-called accent was my main or rather only hurdle. There are still times I find it hard after nearly seven years. I was always proud of my English and was the only one who could speak fluent English when I worked in Saudi Arabia. But here I felt like a zero.' Her essay illustrates a common experience for migrants wherein their 'accent might call attention, rendering … [them] vulnerable to undue self-consciousness and shame'.[40] By virtue of how she speaks and looks, Theresa remains outside the dominant culture, no matter how hard she tries.

When citizens of the host country perceive migrants as other, 'a strong sense of *difference* is the most notable aspect found in the narratives in relation to "belongingness" references. This is generally not accompanied by a strong sense of identity if that is seen as a coherent notion of who and where a person belongs.'[41] The wistfulness and longing behind Theresa's efforts to belong are captured in her aside: 'And I do hope that I wasn't a complete failure in that.' 'And', one tiny word at the beginning of the sentence, yet all that has been said turns on it – migrant *and* native, self *and* other. She has tried to connect, made herself vulnerable and open to becoming part of the New Zealand culture, yet she has been, if not rebuffed, only partially accepted. In short, efforts to be part of a culture will not necessarily lead to acceptance within the contact zone.

Theresa addresses the reasons she might have failed in her endeavour to belong:

> Too keen to establish in the new chosen society, didn't care much about the troubles. Made myself believe that everything is for good and all are good. Worked well for a period of time. When we slowed down, recent chain of thoughts always leads to the same old question. Where do I belong? I neither belong here nor there, as a case of lost identity. So we are somewhere in between?

She realises that being 'Too keen to establish [herself] in the new chosen society' has not worked. Even if she initially didn't care about 'the troubles', the troubles were still present. She can no longer make herself believe 'that everything is good and all are good'. Nor can she maintain the concept of New Zealand as 'a country of my imaginations'.

Non-existent in all these sentences is 'I', which she subsumes while narrating the experience of trying to establish herself. When she does bring in first person, it is 'we', and then only briefly, in just one clause that prompts a 'recent chain of thoughts [that] always leads to the same old question'. Confronting what she has been seeking and not finding, she poses the most pressing and fundamental question a migrant can ask: 'Where do I belong?' The answer is unsettling, as it is for many migrants: 'I neither belong here nor there, as a case of lost identity.' Now the missing I is accounted for. It is the I that belongs in neither India nor New Zealand, and Theresa elaborates why: 'Love the food, made many great friends around, comfortable job but something vital is missing. Tried to pretend not but didn't work.' Again we see the eclipsed I and her attempt to pretend 'something vital' is not missing. She does not detail what 'something vital' is. It, too, like the I, is missing from the text, but its absence is enough to disrupt both her identity and her sense of belonging.

Identity and belonging are the resonance between self and world that cannot be forced or imagined. Theresa finally admitted to a lack of resonance in the conclusion to her essay: 'Life is not what it was all hoped to be. In other words despite all the struggles to get along we don't belong here … or can never belong here.' Now we see the fallout from the contact zone, and any pretence that it was otherwise – 'In other words' – drops away. She acknowledges what has happened: 'despite all the struggles to get along we don't belong here … or can never belong here.' The first clause, where the cultures meet, grasp and grapple with each other in the contact zone, leads into 'we don't belong here', a conclusion acknowledged by both parties. The ellipsis shows the charged place where she recasts and clarifies that idea. Which is it: 'we don't belong here … or can never belong here'? Her answer in the next sentence only reframes this conflict as another question: 'So we are somewhere in between?'

Caught in the ellipsis, the dots that mark the omission, the space between belonging and not, is where some migrants remain, occupying a place of ambiguity that Theresa explored in her essay with all its tensions and hopes. Her experience supports the fact that 'Migrant stories are linked with the experiences of adjustment, settlement, nostalgia, a shattered sense of belonging, renewal, loss, discrimination, abrupt endings, new beginnings and new opportunities – all potent sources of emotions.'[42] Speaking as an outsider within the dominant culture, Theresa has experienced discrimination and 'a shattered sense of belonging'. Her closing sentence is especially poignant because she knows she does not feel fully welcome in New Zealand: 'As time goes it gets better or worse, hope for the best …' The ellipsis trails off in longing.

Migrant personal essays make it possible to address what makes the contact zone productive. The writer can speak as an outsider to the dominant culture, yet observe that beyond the cultural and linguistic differences people are, in core aspects, similar. Cathrine, the 80-year-old Danish migrant looking back over the 60 years since her arrival in New Zealand, wrote: 'But there was no distance between the people in outlook, interests, humour and all the other qualities that bring people close. The distance between countries and customs does not mean distance between people. It may in fact have brought us nearer to each other.' Mary, the Scottish psychotherapist, concurred: 'I lived in Brazil for a few years. The culture, language, food, climate and geography were nothing like I'd encountered before. People are people the world over, however. We laugh and cry and strive for the same things.' Recognising our common humanity is central to acceptance despite perceived differences, or, as the Māori proverb holds: 'He aha te mea nui o te ao? He tāngata, he tāngata, he tāngata.' What is the most important thing in the world? It is people, it is people, it is people.

Celebrating and honouring difference can be an adaptive strategy for migrants. Barbara, who became a refugee in her native Germany during World War II when communists threw her family off their farm, has been a migrant in four different countries – England, Canada, the United States and New Zealand. Now in her seventies, Barbara teaches English to migrants in New Zealand and acknowledges that her experiences have aided this endeavour:

> I gradually began to see my 'being different' as an asset not only for myself but possibly for people who were surprised or troubled by it. By presenting my own case, I could help with integration. I could show that a willingness to be seen and assessed as being different coupled with a positive attitude could be an asset to this new country which after all was actually made up of immigrants, going all the way back to the Māori people.

The utility of Barbara's decision to draw on her own life speaks for itself in her writing. Her 'willingness to be seen and assessed as being different' becomes a positive attribute, a means to connect rather than separate. The essayist Scott Russell Sanders holds that 'writing essays allows me to gather what is essential in my life, and by pondering these things perhaps to discover something essential to the lives of others.'[43] By reflecting on her difference from others and identifying it is an asset rather than a hindrance to integration, Barbara was able, in her essay, to present a way forward for migrants and for the globalised world as well.

'I can never be a Kiwi'

The extent to which migrants form a connection to the people they live among is fundamental to their sense of belonging, well-being and home (assuming they feel any of those things), for as Avril Bell notes, 'all belonging is understood as conditional.'[44] Beth, from South Africa, showed just how conditional belonging can be: 'I realise that my connections to New Zealand all take place through people – my husband, my friends and colleagues, visitors, students and customers – all wonderful people. If I was a plant, in New Zealand I would be an epiphyte, lifted heavenwards by other plants and feebly flapping my aerial roots in the breeze.' Despite her many attachments to people in New Zealand, she remains an epiphyte, 'feebly flapping ... aerial roots in the breeze'.

For Beth, the image of the epiphyte is apt: her roots will always be up in the air while she lives in New Zealand because she longs to be in South Africa, her home for five decades. Yet now, having lived in New Zealand for over 10 years, she also longs to be with those she loves in her adopted country, and that dichotomy means she cannot reconcile the two places: 'When I am in New Zealand, I yearn for South Africa. When I am in South Africa, I long for my husband, my little Scotty dog, my friends and my home, but not New Zealand – yet.' The place name South Africa stands for everything she yearns for, whereas what she longs for in New Zealand is quite specific, 'my husband, my little Scotty dog, my friends and my home', and does not include 'New Zealand – yet'. While those very real things may be in New Zealand, she does not equate them with New Zealand itself.

Our attachment to place is seminal, and for migrants that place has changed. 'The sense of place,' writes Yi-Fu Tuan, 'is perhaps never more acute than when one is homesick.'[45] Because those migrants who come to their new country relatively late in life have frames of reference that are generally strongly placed and marked, their contrapuntal awareness can set up a dissonance. Beth migrated to New Zealand in her fifties, and her awareness of this discord is evident in her descriptions of the landscapes of her home country and her host country:

> It's really not New Zealand's fault and in my heart of hearts I know this. How could it help being too small? There are still seagulls in the sky when you are in the middle of the country for heaven's sake. How can it help being so beautiful? Like a Swiss chocolate box lid, when what I yearn for is great swathes of Karoo bush and colours that are warm and dry. It certainly can't help being this isolated: 'The Gateway to Antarctica' the sign at the airport reads. I could weep.

Beth recognises from the beginning that she can't hold New Zealand at fault for not measuring up to her preferred and dominant frame of reference, South Africa. She sets up the comparison with a series of rhetorical questions and her answers to them. The first one is New Zealand's small size, which she dismisses handily: 'There are still seagulls in the sky when you are in the middle of the country for heaven's sake.' Should there be any doubt how she feels about seagulls in the middle of the country, her 'for heaven's sake' gives it away. She renders the country she deems 'too small' geographically even smaller, if not trivial, by likening its beauty to 'a Swiss chocolate box lid', something portable, decorative, with the connotation of tourism. And, then, how easily New Zealand becomes diminished and shrinks when compared to 'great swathes of Karoo bush and colours that are warm and dry'. The vast South African bush overwhelms the New Zealand landscape, and even when that landscape does resonate with her, she yearns for somewhere else.

Finally, the country's isolation, admittedly another factor 'it certainly can't help', is driven home by the sign at the airport reading, 'The Gateway to Antarctica'. Not only is New Zealand isolated, it boasts its proximity to a continent that is scarcely habitable. Her response is 'I could weep', as might any migrant who longs to be somewhere else. After living 50 years in the South African landscape, Beth has formed 'a lifelong, bone-deep attachment to place' that is not easily supplanted.[46]

As a migrant Beth is well aware of the lack of accord between herself and New Zealand, which she characterises in terms of music: 'In New Zealand I am annoyingly just slightly out of step. I move through this country to the beat of a drum so subtly different that at times it almost looks as if I belong. My Scottish roots, my English language and my education – ever a great leveller, all conspire to make it appear as if I fit.' She looks at herself from a detached, abstracted viewpoint, one that is not a scene so much as it is an existential condition because she is 'annoyingly just slightly out of step'. But annoyed in whose eyes? Her own or others'? She describes her almost near resonance: 'I move through this country to the beat of a drum so subtly different that at times it almost looks as if I belong.' All that should help her harmonise – roots, language and education – 'conspire to make it appear as if I fit'.

Yet appearance is just that: appearance. Despite what 'appears', 'looks' and 'conspires' to make Beth fit, belonging may also be determined by the individual, as her essay reveals: 'But at some almost chromosomal level, I can never be a Kiwi. I can never use pronouns like "we" and "us" to mean New Zealander. I can never relinquish my South African passport even though I gritted my teeth through the New Zealand citizenship ceremony.' She refutes her ability to 'be a Kiwi' first on 'some almost chromosomal level', arguing it is hereditary, innate and unchanging, and therefore predetermined. Next, she moves up to the pronominal level: 'I can never use pronouns like "we" and "us" to mean New Zealander.' She is adamant she will not ally herself, even through language, with the host population. Beth's resistance corresponds with the relational aspect of narrative that recognises the distinctiveness of the individual existence Adriana Cavarero stresses: 'No matter how much the larger traits of our life-stories are similar, I still do not recognize myself *in* you, and, even less, in the collective *we*. I do not dissolve both into a common identity, nor do I digest your tale in order to construct the meaning of mine.'[47]

Beth ultimately moves to the level of citizenship, declaring with respect to national allegiance, 'I can never relinquish my South African passport'. And although she becomes a New Zealand citizen, she gritted her teeth throughout the ceremony. The emphatic repetition of 'I can never' emphasises that she will never undertake the effort to belong because she doesn't want to – on the cellular, linguistic or national level. Perhaps it is this very opinionated and refreshing frankness that keeps her from being 'a Kiwi'.

Apparent in Beth's migration narrative is her strong sense of self-awareness, related in a voice that is direct, abrasive, witty, uncompromising. Voice is one of the hallmarks of the personal essay, and it gives each of the migrant narratives a distinct flavour, 'a palpable sense of *a particular person, with a distinctive voice*'.[48] All of the migrant essays are marked by a distinctive voice, a presentation and sense of self that cannot be exchanged for another. And it is this singular first person that the personal essay celebrates because it 'is a haven for the private, idiosyncratic voice in an era of anonymous babble'.[49]

Not wanting to be identified with the anonymous babble or, in her case, New Zealand, Beth nevertheless can laugh at herself, evident in her description of waiting to board the plane to New Zealand from Australia:

> I yearn to be getting on any other flight. I feel sorry for all the people waiting to board the plane to Christchurch. On my really bad days those people look dull, badly dressed and ugly; all the women look fat and have dyed their hair the same red brown. I want to take tourists aside and say 'Don't Go There'. In short I am temporarily nuts. They shouldn't even let me into the country. But they do, without any problem at all. It is only when my suitcases trundle into sight, the only ones incarcerated in plastic wrap to foil theft and sporting snap-lock belts in the colours of the South African flag that I become marked as not quite belonging.

Even as Beth makes disparaging, albeit humorous, comments about her fellow travellers, she applies the same scrutiny to herself, winning the reader's trust with the refreshing candour of her prose. As E.B. White, a brilliant essayist himself, warned: '... there is one thing the essayist cannot do, though – he cannot indulge himself in deceit or in concealment, for he will be found out in no time'; candour is thus 'the basic ingredient' in the essay.[50] Beth is disarmingly candid about her fellow travellers: 'On my really bad days those people look dull, badly dressed and ugly.' She is equally unsparing with herself: 'I am temporarily nuts. They shouldn't even allow me into the country.' She maintains that the authorities should not let anyone who is as uncharitable and unkind in their thoughts about both New Zealand and its inhabitants as she is into the country, a self-aspersion that is both funny and telling.

Equally telling is Beth's description of her luggage, which literally signals her sense of difference: 'It is only when my suitcases trundle into sight, the only ones incarcerated in plastic wrap to foil theft and sporting snap-lock belts in the colours of the South African flag that I become marked as not quite belonging.' In keeping with her acknowledgement that she is somewhat out of step with the rest of the country, her luggage sets her apart: 'I become marked as not quite belonging.' Like her suitcases, Beth has actively chosen a means of self-identification to prevent theft, on both literal and figurative levels. She is South African, first and foremost, in a classic example of 'how an individual reinforces his or her self-identity in a physical environment to represent that part of their identity that is not shared with others'.[51] Even in transit she marks herself with the 'snap-lock belts in the colours of the South African flag'. What is remarkable about this image is the transparency and accuracy of it. She herself becomes 'incarcerated' in plastic wrap to foil theft, held together by the snap-lock belts of her native flag, and portable (migratory?) like a piece of luggage. Her essays, like her baggage, both literal and existential, make it clear she does not quite belong in New Zealand because her attachment to South Africa overrides it.

The topos *of memory*

Migrants who come to the host country in the later years of their lives will be more deeply marked by where they have lived and 'the steady accretion of sentiment over the years'.[52] As a consequence, they may be less able to form attachments to their new country than those who come earlier. They may feel displaced, which is what Livingston, the Scottish doctor who came with his second family at age 60, experienced: '... the truth is that my displacement here is total because I am not from here and I came here late in life full of somewhere else'. He recognises his state of being other, 'I am not from here', which is true of most migrants. He also acknowledges that those who are 'from' a place may have a prior, stronger claim upon it. As with many older migrants, Livingston left behind longstanding ties to his homeland, including his aging father, grown children from his first marriage, siblings, lifelong friendships and the medical practice he had established over decades. Having come to New Zealand 'late in life', he is indeed 'full of somewhere else'.

Many migrants also have attachments to things that are inanimate yet equally charged with meaning. Livingston witnessed the disappearance of some of these as his plane departed from England: 'I peered through the little window in the emergency door. The Thames curled out to sea flanked by the lights of Kent and Essex. Colchester oysters, Estuary English, chavs, oast houses, Cox's Orange Pippins, Magwitch's marshes all floating away and, seemingly, out of my life.' He maps his familiar world from above in terms of landscape, food, dialect, culture, architecture and literature, seeing these receding landmarks, both real and abstract, flowing like the Thames out to sea.

Migrants leave behind an entire matrix of identifications that gave their lives meaning, as evident in Livingston's comment: 'I have jettisoned my own for the here and now and that is good.' He may have seen 'jettisoning' as an appropriate and determined action prior to New Zealand, but his essay shows how clearly he remembers all that constitutes 'my own', anchoring it in vivid, concrete detail. Essayist and editor Robert Root suggests, 'association and accumulation have always been major ways of knowing in the personal essay'.[53] Perhaps for migrants who arrive 'late in life full of somewhere else', the personal essay offers not only a way to capture those rich associations and accumulations which informed that life, but also the means to re-home them in language and to save them from erasure.

Livingston concedes, 'there is bound to be a sense of displacement in moving away from things imbued in you'. This feeling of being imbued echoes the idea that 'the home as skin suggests the boundary between self and home is permeable'.[54] Many of the migrant essays confirmed how permeable that boundary can be, even if what their writers experienced was quite intangible, as is evident in an essay by Korean migrant In Suk: 'The smell and taste of the origin soil is the ingredient which is absent in the minds of migrants rather than food itself. Climate differs in each country. Therefore, the familiar taste, texture and smell are as varied as weather [which] causes the nostalgia for our homeland life.' The origin soil, as she aptly calls it, where she was rooted in Korea for over 40 years, has left an indelible trace. Migrants all over the world can taste what she is saying in their own mind – the flavour of what is missing.

What is missing resonates against what is present for migrants in the ongoing comparison between here and there, then and now. As Gareth, the Welsh doctor, so eloquently put it: '… living on a plain cannot replace the feelings and emotions of the mountains of your homeland; fresh air cannot bring back the memories and thoughts associated with the tang of industrial pollution; a Christchurch street does not evoke the feelings of a bus ride along narrow country lanes to visit an aunt.' Migrants remember landscapes, smells, the feel of the familiar route unwinding, even if only in memory. For some, the longing for what is left behind may be so strong that they cannot in part or fully appreciate where they now live. Moreover, the memory of that place and time may be unreliable, as Livingston, who pines for Britain, attested:

> My feelings of communion with Britain in the hills of the Lake District, the cloisters of Lincoln Cathedral or the conviviality of The Morning Star are profound. Arriving to the surly disorder of Heathrow engenders in me a feeling of being at home I shall never experience in the arrival hall at Christchurch.

> But the memory of these things British is unreliable. It gilds the remembered with a kind of unreality. It can never be as intense as the actuality but it can be more intense for the longing. And longing, perhaps, should be the eighth deadly sin – a ruinous and imperfect desire for something you do not have. Neither lust nor envy, it hangs in between, gnawing at the present with its tenacious hold on the past.

Here he evokes what resonates most with him: 'My feelings of communion with Britain in the hills of the Lake District, the cloisters of Lincoln Cathedral or the conviviality of The Morning Star are profound.' He juxtaposes those places with how he feels in two different airports, one in England, one in New Zealand, the literal threshold, the transit place between the two locations: 'Arriving to the surly disorder of Heathrow engenders in me a feeling of being at home I shall never experience in the arrival hall at Christchurch.' The sentence declares where he feels at home upon arrival, and it is not New Zealand.

Memory is problematic for all migrants, because memory migrates in its own fashion and therefore colours what migrants remember: '… migration has an effect on how and what we remember and that displacement intensifies our investments in memory, illuminating the *topos* of memory itself'.[55] Livingston questions his memory 'of these things British', claiming memory is unreliable and 'gilds the remembered with a kind of unreality'. Thus, his nostalgia affects what he recalls. Ha Jin argues that his fellow migrant writer Milan Kundera 'believes nostalgia actually impairs one's memory'.[56] Livingston recognises that even if his memory is unreliable and 'can never be as intense as the actuality', memory can be more intense for the longing.

His words identify the crux of the matter – longing affects both the past and the present for the migrant: 'And longing, perhaps, should be the eighth deadly sin – a ruinous and imperfect desire for something you do not have. Neither lust nor envy, it hangs in between, gnawing at the present with its tenacious hold on the past.' The religious imagery that began with feelings of communion for Britain invoked by the cloisters of Lincoln Cathedral now reaches the arresting conclusion where longing becomes the eighth deadly sin, hanging between lust and envy. The very things Livingston misses provoke 'a ruinous and imperfect desire for something you cannot have'. The extent to which longing, 'gnawing at the present with its tenacious hold on the past', impairs the migrant's ability to belong or bear life in the present is open to question. Livingston raised this idea in the closing sentence of his essay: 'What will be interesting will be to see if, when I am really old, I shall miss too much the stuff of home.' He may claim, 'I have jettisoned my own for the here and now', but like the native Colchester oysters he visualised as he left England, they taste of the water from where they came. Those migrants whose original home resonates most deeply may always 'miss too much the stuff of home' and therefore be unable to truly settle in the new country.

Some migrants miss the stuff of home long before they reach their later years. Unable to establish a resonance between themselves and the new country, they return home. Marcela, who migrated from Chile in 1996, states in her essay that all of the cohort of fellow migrants who left Chile with their partners when she did 'went back, not forward to the departure point. There were those invisible links calling them back that they could not resist: the warmth of the familiar embrace, the whisper of the known music, the comfort of the narrow taste and the smell of their cherished segment of the world.' She defines 'those invisible links' that bind one to a place – touch, sound, taste, smell, which embody 'warmth', 'comfort' and are 'known' – but the text judges those who return to the 'familiar embrace'. The taste is 'narrow' and the smell but a 'cherished segment', while she 'dared to stay away in an alien environment without the support of the obvious sameness'.

Marcela sees the contact zone as combative: 'I was going to be hurt in many blind battles but feel victorious at the end of the war. That was it; I believed it was never going to be easy; I had to find the strength to fight one battle at the time, go for the unknown.' She knows that she does not wholly belong: 'It worked out being a mismatch, like trying to like smaller shoes that I had to fit in. In the long term the shoes wear off and your toes or heels show up how they really are or what they have become.' Indeed. If our metaphorical shoes are not a good fit, they will wear away, at which point who we are and what we've become in the new country will become manifest. We don't necessarily need to fit in to belong.

When I told Marcela about my children being friendless in their Swedish school, she wrote: 'We cannot change the fact that we are outsiders so let's use it to our advantage. Everyone has to do their homework and discover the advantages that best suit them. Lastly, when we find people who really accept us as outsiders, we have found a real friend.' Marcela addressed something essential about how we felt in New Zealand: we were accepted as outsiders and had made real friends, both with fellow migrants and New Zealanders. The acceptance of difference is what makes migrants feel welcome in their new country, but in deeply conforming Sweden this acceptance was neither forthcoming nor likely to occur. Without acceptance, we would never feel we belonged, no matter how long we lived there or how fluent our Swedish became. We would remain strangers who came to town.

When migrants move away from the people and places they love, memory may be the form of consolation for what is absent, the imaginative present. This process is seen when migrants write about their experience of migration. They explore what is absent, missing and unaddressed; the things they may not have known or felt find expression and are shared on the page. The connection they feel to everything they leave behind – people, places, culture – perhaps resonates most powerfully when shared and acknowledged by others in their personal essays: 'an essay … gives back to the reader a thought, a memory, an emotion made richer by the experience of another … and in glorious, mysterious ways that the author cannot control, it begins to belong to the reader.'[57]

For migrants who have given up so much and in turn had to recreate so much, memory informs their writing and their lives. If the desire to connect is at the heart of the desire to write, such connection with readers will have to be forged through memories, both true and unreliable, of what has been lost and what has been found. According to Gareth, the Welsh doctor, 'Without memory there is no nostalgia, no regret, no sense of loss, no sense of achievement, no happiness and no mourning. Memory may not always be truthful, but it is all we have to link our present to the past and even those memories which distort and disguise help us understand what and why we are.' The tone is more one of melancholy than not, perhaps because Gareth, now in his seventies, has most of the span of his life to look back upon. But he's right, memory does help us understand 'what and why we are', just as writing the personal essay does, driven always by Michel de Montaigne's motto, '*Que sais-je?*' Migrants' ability 'to link our present to our past' is thus essential to how they reground themselves in their new country.

The sense of belonging

Sometimes what forms the link between the past and the present is inexplicable, and yet the migrant recognises it from the outset, as Sabina, who came from the Netherlands, claimed: 'Although the country looks so different from my homeland there must have been something familiar, it felt good, so good that when going home I was homesick for New Zealand.' She liked the ring English had to it in New Zealand, 'no stiff upper lip here', and was homesick enough to make a country she had only visited home. The fact that she carefully planned her migration for three years shows her level of commitment was high, which factored into how eager she was to settle:

I was so happy with the household effects container because all the things felt like home. I could start to root here. My own things are familiar and I needed that at that point so much. With no family or friends here, with a totally different job and with the realisation that my residence was going to be granted a permanent status I suddenly wanted to feel at home, be rooted and be familiar with this new life. The cupboards with my books, the photos and the paintings on the wall gave me just enough familiarity to start to enjoy this unfamiliar land and its people.

The shipping container arrived, was unpacked, and 'all the things felt like home'.

'An entire past comes to dwell in a new house,' said French philosopher Gaston Bachelard; 'we bring our *lares* with us.'[58] Nothing proved that so much to Sabina as the familiarity of having 'her own things'. Like the household gods of protection in ancient Rome, the *lares*, her possessions helped her to feel grounded in a country where she had neither family nor friends. Realising she had been granted permanent residency, she 'suddenly wanted to feel at home, be rooted and be familiar with this new life'. The dear familiar, her books, photos and paintings, gave her 'just enough familiarity to start to enjoy this unfamiliar land and its people'. That familiarity, which enabled her to explore the new country, has parallels in the essay: the writer moves from the known and begins 'to see the essay as a way of discovery ... to take risks on the page, to venture out from familiar territory into the blank places on their maps'.[59]

For migrants, learning to become familiar in a new country takes time as they venture into the blank places on their maps. The process is one that never really ends. Daisy, the Irish nurse who came to New Zealand in 1974, addressed this point: '... the more one becomes bedded down in a place, the more one deals with the nitty gritty, the more there is to learn and to adjust to. The nuances of Kiwi English even after all these years still catch me out.' Perhaps an awareness of difference encourages migrants, even decades later, to deepen their learning, to not be caught up in superficial differences but to deal with 'the nitty gritty'.

With increased understanding comes increased awareness of nuance, in culture and language, an idea the Polish migrant writer Eva Hoffman explains:

I think every immigrant becomes a kind of amateur anthropologist – you do notice things about the culture or the world that you come into that people who grow up in it, who are very embedded in it, simply don't notice. And at first you notice the surface things, the surface differences. And gradually you start noticing the deeper differences. And very gradually you start with understanding the inner life of the culture, the life of those both large and very intimate values. It was a surprisingly long process.[60]

Migrants never cease being amateur anthropologists. Their awareness of difference continues to operate decades later, as Dorothy, the Scot who has lived in New Zealand for 50 years, verified in one of her essays: 'Sometimes I still feel an outsider and I am aware that I am the only non-New Zealand born person among my family. But this has a positivity as I can bring a differing perspective to them. So, most of the time I feel I belong.' Although Dorothy feels she belongs 'most of the time', 50 years has still not been long enough for her to fully lose her sense of being an outsider.

Migrants negotiate between the familiar and the strange, with the known frame of reference resonating against the new and unfamiliar one. Noki, who migrated from the Netherlands in 1974, understands that adjusting to a country is a work in progress:

Becoming familiar was a long, and still ongoing process. Although we 'knew' what to expect on our arrival [they had travelled in New Zealand prior to migrating] it was still a big adjustment to settle … Slowly, but surely we got to know the area and its people. Became part of it, because basically there was no choice. And we loved it. All the picture postcard facilities on our doorstep, a satisfying job, part of the community.

Having spent over half of his life in New Zealand, Noki can confirm that '[b]ecoming familiar was a long, and still ongoing process'. Migrants go on discovering aspects and features of their new country because 'the sense of belonging is a dynamic process continuing throughout a person's lifespan, and not only tied to the individuals' [sic] home of origin'.[61]

Noki mocks the idea that as migrants 'we "knew" what to expect', because now he knows they did not entirely, any more than the writer knows what to expect when writing the essay, with its elements of 'self-discovery, self-exploration, and surprise.'[62] He describes a process of assimilation: 'Slowly, but surely we got to know the area and its people. Became part of it, because basically there was no choice. And we loved it.' The 'we' becomes absorbed literally in 'Became part of it, because basically there was no choice.' Yet on each side of having no choice but to become 'part of it', the collective 'we' gets to know the area and the people and declares, 'And we loved it.'

For Noki, landscape, work and community all came together but still didn't add up to a sense of belonging: 'Do I belong here? I do not know. I feel extremely comfortable here, but I would not call it belonging. My roots are on the other side. The Waitaki valley is a good substitute though. Our children regard it as home. They grew up there and keep fond memories of the area.' He is adamant about where he does not belong: 'Do I belong in Holland? No, definitely not.' He has not returned there since he left in 1974. Yet with respect to New Zealand he still feels his 'roots are on the other side', and while 'extremely comfortable here', he 'would not call it belonging'. Poet Harry Ricketts, who has lived in New Zealand since 1981, echoes this idea: 'The thing about being an immigrant is that you will only ever fit in up to a point. But if the conditions and the people suit you, and you seem to suit them, that can be enough.'[63] Noki considers the Waitaki Valley 'a good substitute', whereas his children regard it as home. Unlike their father, having never migrated his children have no sense of ambivalence about where they belong.

What allows migrants to feel a sense of belonging or home is as varied as they are. Rather than perceiving discord between their landscapes, past and present, or between themselves and New Zealanders, some migrants perceive an accord. Daisy, the Irish nurse, described a feeling of congruence between the New Zealand landscape and that of Donegal in Ireland: 'When I stand on the little hillock there and look out over the native bush and across the broken waters along the shore to the ocean beyond I could be facing the Atlantic and I feel utterly at home.' The two landscapes, thousands of kilometres apart, on two different oceans, and facing in opposite directions, nevertheless contribute to her feeling 'utterly at home'. She admits: 'It took me years to learn to love fair tussock and brown landscape. When at last I did, I think that's when I fell in love with here.'

An active decision to settle may incline migrants to view the country in a more positive light: they see what is there rather than what is not. Daisy comes to 'love fair tussock and brown landscape' and not just the saturated green of her native Ireland. She might have been even more predisposed to love New Zealand because the unrest in Northern Ireland had accelerated: 'So at that time, no longer belonging, it seemed easier to stay away than to go home.' Here might be the real root of deciding to settle – no longer belonging at home. Four years after settling in New Zealand, Daisy experiences a sense of homecoming:

> One time (I can't remember exactly when – perhaps four years after we decided to settle here) I was returning from Ireland and flying back into Auckland alone. Below me the complicated outline of the land was very strongly drawn and around it the water was sparkling. It was a captivating sight and I suddenly thought, 'I'm coming home.' It seems to me that I had no control over this cheerful idea; it just bubbled up on its own.

The sudden thought 'I'm coming home', prompted by the sight of New Zealand from the air, sees her shift into present tense: 'It seems to me that I had no control over this cheerful idea.' Where that sense of homecoming originated remains a mystery even as she writes about it: 'it just bubbled up on its own'. She acknowledges this epiphany is not common to migrants: 'I'm grateful to have had that experience which doesn't seem to come to everyone. For me it had a very settling effect.' To see the new country from above and know you are home is a gift for any migrant.

Migrant poppies

When I was growing up the military moved my family every three years. I believed I was immune to mobility and displacement, vaccinated as I was against typhoid, smallpox and homesickness, and free to cross borders and oceans easily and unthinkingly. Having made four

hemispheric shifts in the past 15 years, I now know this is not true.
I realise my own constant uprooting in childhood and adulthood
colours how I perceive things. I see not fitting in, not feeling at home,
as experiences to be expected when you move often. 'We left everything
behind!' my 11-year-old daughter wailed to me in Sweden, her eyes
full of tears. How that phrase undoes me still and bears repeating. Not
everything, but the very things that make migration painful.

When we left New Zealand for Sweden, we yet again left who and
what we loved behind. Friendships, landscapes, the taste of the world's
best water, the impossible clarity of the southern stars, knowing and
being known. Sammy from Syria at the local Sunday market always
remembering my falafel order, asking, 'And how are you, my dear?'
Where to get free dog bones, what wind brings what weather, and how
long is a piece of string. Language. Kiwi as, but still recognisable. Sitting
with friends having a cup of tea.

We gave all that up when we migrated to Sweden. No wonder we felt
bereft. But that was not the end of the story. The story continues, and it
will continue until we're dead. But where does the story begin? Where
it wants, akin to a seed germinating, in a particular place and time.
One morning back in New Zealand I saw the silvery-green leaves of the
heirloom poppies in the garden making their way among the established
perennials. They had come up, not in the first but in the second spring
we lived there, as though their inner residency permit had been granted
and they had allowed themselves to take root. I was delighted to see them
appear on the other side of the world, in another hemisphere, given they
had come from my garden in the United States. They bloomed among
the roses, freesias and calla lilies, fitting in and then dying back, seeding
themselves. I gathered the first seedpods, dried them, put the seeds in a
bag labelled 'NZ-grown poppy' and forgot about them.

On the other side of the world while writing this chapter on
belonging, I found the seeds in my desk drawer. Autumn, the days
already short, the light shorter. Before winter set its jaws, I scratched
the New Zealand-grown poppy seeds into the Swedish soil in the beds
around the house, the soil more granite than earth. I planted a dozen

tulips named 'Hemisphere', which promised to change colour as they bloomed. My Swedish neighbour warned me the deer would eat them, the only conversation I had with her the entire year and a half we lived there, despite her fluent English and our sharing a long garden boundary.

Spring arrived six weeks late and everything leafed and bloomed at once, unlike the slow unfurling of the season in New Zealand, which lasts and lasts. Two yearling bucks mowed the tulips down when they were barely out of the reluctant ground. Tiny white *vitsippor*, a wood anemone, harbinger of spring and the symbol for the Swedish cancer foundation, waited until May to carpet the forest floor. The forsythia's glowing yellow, usually the first to ignite in the garden, overlapped with the white froth of pear and apple blossom. The trees leafed out overnight into luminous green, hallucinogenic in its intensity, a green more vivid than any I had ever seen – that, or I was winter-starved for colour. The air hadn't lost its edge when our landlady, wearing a sable coat to her ankles, discussed the advent of ants for which the area is famous. The April showers came a month late, and the long daylight accelerated weeds and plants alike. I noticed with alarm that twitch grass was rampant among the perennials, outpacing them even. Between rains I went out to weed, knowing twitch grass is almost hopeless to eradicate by hand because it spreads by forming a mat of rhizomes under the soil and entangling itself in the roots of established plants.

The soil was soft and pliable, perfect for weeding. I checked the beds around the house where I had seeded the pink poppies among the catmint, black-eyed Susans and globe thistle, but saw nothing, not even many weeds, the soil dry with white ant powder dusted along the stone foundation of the house. I walked over to the main perennial bed in the middle of the lawn where the twitch grass waved madly at me, screaming 'Rental house!' Knowing I was leaving Sweden, that this was not my garden, I pulled indiscriminately, yanking out handfuls of twitch that broke off leaving its invasive, snaking root system underneath the soil. And then, suddenly, among the weeds were the silvery-green leaves of the heirloom poppies, newly sprouted. I had forgotten I had seeded them in this bed too. I started to weed more carefully, finding more and more seedlings as I did so. Clever migrant upstarts. They had come all the way around the world to where they had begun decades ago, flowering in a Danish garden just across the Kattegat, the sea that stretches between Sweden and Denmark.

That summer, the long northern summer, the pink poppies bloomed in Swedish soil, far from where they had gone to seed in New Zealand. Migrant annuals thriving amidst old perennials. They would go to seed that autumn, shaking hundreds of seeds all over the garden while we packed and loaded to move back to New Zealand, shedding half a cubic metre of belongings in the process. Maybe the poppies' rogue, irreverent presence would flourish alongside the blue delphiniums and white Shasta daisies, year after year, long after we were living on the far side of the world, or maybe not. For what stirs belonging in anything, in any of us, is at root, a mystery.

Chapter 5
The Migration of Identity

'Our roots can be anywhere and we can survive, because if you think about it, we take our roots with us.'

– GERTRUDE STEIN, 'A Conversation with Gertrude Stein'

My teenage son and I were returning to Sweden from a brief trip to Dublin. What a pleasure to share with him everything I loved about the city from my student days and later visits. The Long Room at Trinity College and the illuminated *Book of Kells*, the Stag's Head pub, the exquisite tiny golden boat in the National Museum, fish and chips in the old fishing village of Howth and, best of all, introducing him to dear friends I'd known for decades. In Hodges Figgis Bookshop my son sighed, 'All the books are in English', his dark eyes shining with joy. I bought him several for his birthday, which we had celebrated the night before. Now we were walking through the deserted Stockholm airport to passport control. I pushed our black and silver New Zealand passports through the slot. The officer opened to the photo page, looking at each of us in turn, and asked in the excellent English of the Swedes, 'How long do you intend to stay in Sweden?'

'We live here.'

She flipped through the pages. 'You don't have a stamp.'

'I didn't know we needed a stamp. We just moved here a few months ago.'

She frowned. I fished in my wallet and showed her my Swedish ID card that had taken weeks and weeks to obtain and had required registering with the tax authorities, followed by registering with the immigration authorities, who finally issued me with the card Swedes use for everything. It is called *identitetskort*, identity card.

'Where is your migration ID card?'

'I didn't know we had to carry that with us.' She frowned some more. Fine, send us back to Ireland.

'What are you doing in Sweden?'

Excellent question. Do I mention earthquakes, job security or fate? 'My husband teaches at Chalmers.' I pronounced it as she would, the *ch* softened to *sh*. The Valkyrie thawed. Drop the right name of the right school. She flicked her blue eyes at me, still not pleased we were travelling without the proper credentials, but she stamped our passports and slid them back through the slot.

As we walked through the gate I realised how easy it is to bar someone's entry, anywhere in the world, for whatever reason, at these checkpoints. My migrant identity is what matters here – that is the snag – and my passport bears no indication of that identity. I appear to be and am a New Zealand citizen. I looked at my son, now taller than his father, and born in Sweden, although not a citizen. He had no idea of what threshold we had just crossed based solely on one official's discretion, or that neutral Sweden along with Switzerland asked Germany to distinguish its Jewish refugees at the beginning of the war to control the flow of immigration. This request led to Jewish passports being stamped with a red letter J from 1939 onward.[1] My son and I were missing a stamp that distinguished us as migrants in our passports, but even without it, a person can be seen as other and unwelcome, as we were, with subtle or terrible consequences. Sweden prides itself on being an egalitarian society, and for the most part it is. I looked at the illuminated sign ahead of us: *Välkommen*, Welcome, *Bienvenido*, 환영, 欢迎, بترحيب. Every major airport in the world bids you welcome in their native language and others, but that welcome is conditional upon permission of entry.

My brief interrogation at passport control encompassed issues of migration, identity and nation – who gets to cross the border, and why. These powerful abstractions have a visceral equivalent: the heat rising in my body, my pulse accelerating, a feeling between anger and humiliation as to whether we were entitled to live in Sweden. More revealing was my immediate desire to return to a country where I spoke the language and felt welcome even though I was not legally entitled to reside there.

The exchange with the immigration officer also encapsulated the disjunction between self-identification and the external identification of others in the modern state, with its 'power to name, to identify, to categorize, to state what is what and who is who'.[2] The state, embodied in the form of the immigration officer, identified us as non-EU citizens with no right to reside in Sweden. However, the officer took me at my word, though even then our admittance was granted because of my husband's employment. No doubt our reception at passport control would have been different had we presented the proper identification proving we had residency. Instead, we were treated as foreign and other, admitted on sufferance. The experience of being treated as other rankled, and when I thought of migrants worldwide being discriminated against because of skin colour, accent or any other reason, I felt a sense of solidarity.

Being other

Migrants are all 'other'. As Salman Rushdie points out, migrants are 'people who have been obliged to define themselves – because they are so defined by others – by their otherness'.[3] Anna, the Swiss migrant, described the literal experience of being identified as other when she was on her way to New Zealand in 1964: 'My husband Nigel and his mother walk through the passport control reserved for the Commonwealth. I have to join a long queue where it says "Others". A week ago I had been special. Not everybody married a New Zealander and followed him to the other side of the world.' As a new bride she was transformed from being special to being 'other', not realising then that what made her special in her own country, marrying a foreigner, would differentiate her for the rest of her life in the new.

Because I, too, am marked visibly and invisibly by this choice to live elsewhere, I exemplify Jacques Derrida's claim: 'All national rootedness … is rooted first of all in the memory or the anxiety of a displaced – or displaceable – population.'[4] I am not a displaced population but an individual, and yet at passport control my own sense of identity was challenged, revealing the power of the nation-state to define me in ways I myself did not, like a scene from Kafka. As Stephen Castles and Alistair Davidson explain in their book on the politics of belonging, 'the nation-state has an inbuilt tendency to create difference and to racialize minorities' and through its 'discursive and material practices create Other, and then take Otherness as a justification for the differential treatment'.[5] For everyone, migrant or not, being defined as other is contingent upon how one is identified and by whom – or, more importantly, how the other is perceived.

The idea of other can be positively valorised, not as a point of discrimination but for illuminating who we are and how we perceive ourselves. Perhaps it's not surprising that Hélène Cixous, a Jew who migrated from Algeria to France and then felt in school as if she had been 'deported right inside the class[room]',[6] would understand how the other constructs our own sense of I:

> The other in all his or her forms gives me *I*. It is on the occasion of the other that *I* catch sight of *me*; or that *I* catch *me* at: reacting, choosing, refusing, accepting. It is the other who makes my portrait. Always. And luckily. The other of all sorts is also of all diverse richness. The more the other is rich, the more I am rich. The other, rich, will make all his or her richness resonate in me and will enrich me. This is what people do not know, in general, and it's too bad.[7]

The other in this instance is perceived not as threatening and unwelcome but as a source of enrichment. Creating the I through the resonance of the encounter with the other echoes Martin Buber: 'Man becomes an I through a You.'[8]

An example of how the other confers and deepens our own self-understanding occurred in an exchange at passport control that differed from mine. Daisy, the Irish nurse, is returning to New Zealand after visiting her aging parents in Ireland: 'Then, after yet another visit, and by this time travelling as a New Zealander, my sense of belonging was greatly boosted when a broadly smiling immigration officer of Polynesian ethnicity looked me in the eye, bang-stamped my Kiwi passport and handing it back to me (the pale, tired, freckled one) said warmly, "Welcome home". Unlike our reception in Sweden, Daisy arrives in a country where she's now a citizen. The text reveals several layers of identification, both internal and external. First, she is 'by this time travelling as a New Zealander', which implies the persona is a recent one and not necessarily how she would identify herself. However, upon presenting her New Zealand passport to the immigration officer, something happens to change 'travelling as a New Zealander' to a 'greatly boosted' 'sense of belonging'.

Daisy describes the actual moment of exchange in the contact zone where 'a broadly smiling immigration officer of Polynesian ethnicity' emphatically stamps her passport and warmly welcomes her home. We see her through the immigration officer's eyes: her passport denotes citizenship, and when he looks her in the eye we see what he literally sees, the parenthetically noted '(pale, tired, freckled one)'. The passport grants Daisy right of admittance, but the immigration officer grants her something deeper and more intangible, 'a sense of belonging', an acknowledgement that in his eyes and now her own, she is home. They both recognise each other's ethnicity, but that is no barrier to his friendliness and warm greeting: the acceptance of the other here is mutual and gives Daisy a stronger sense of who she is because of where she is – home.

What gives anyone a sense of identity is an extremely complicated and often conflicted subject, particularly for migrants. While identity remains an elusive, overburdened and ill-defined concept, it nevertheless 'can suggest ways in which people conceive of themselves and are characterised by others'.[9] Migration affects our identity, externally in terms of how we are categorised and in our own sense of who we are, reaching past national borders to more permeable and existential ones. My own migrant status was what called my identity into question at passport control and whether I 'belonged' in Sweden. The link between migration, belonging and identity is thus fraught because 'migration comes with a vengeance in terms of identity, belonging and homeness, since old identities and memories of the places they come from, or have been told about, or are constantly reminded of by people and institutions in their new homes, stick in their minds and keep (co)defining their sense of belonging.'[10] And just as our sense of belonging may be tied to more than one location, so too may our sense of identity be defined by experiences of what came before. In Sweden I asked my then 11-year-old daughter who she thought she was. She immediately answered, 'A Kiwi,' and then added, 'but I'm American underneath that.'

My daughter's youthful perception revealed something elemental about our sense of identity, that while we might identify and consider ourselves one thing, in her case 'a Kiwi', other identities inform and contribute to that sense of self. Underneath my daughter's self-proclaimed Kiwi identity was another dimension of self that she acknowledged, which was American. The likelihood of this identity not being apparent to others because of her Kiwi accent demonstrates that surface appearance doesn't always reveal who a person believes herself or himself to be.

When I was studying Swedish at the *Folkuniversitetet* (People's University) in Gothenburg, the European students in my class told me I didn't seem American to them. In what way did I not 'seem' to be American, I wondered. My sense of identity, who I am, is more than my name, my language, my nationality – those are signifiers. However, we cannot disregard certain categories either, as interdisciplinary scholar James Clifford cautions: 'I do not accept that anyone is permanently fixed by his or her "identity"; but neither can one shed specific structures of race and class, culture and caste, gender and sexuality, environment and history.'[11] I cannot dismiss the fact that I am female, white, heterosexual, English-speaking, privileged, educated, born in the latter half of the twentieth century. Millions and millions of other people are like me, but what differentiates each of us is our life story – a story that does not fall into specific structures but into narrative.

Adriana Cavarero agrees. For her, what matters with respect to personal identity is the story: 'Personal identity, which – in the gaze of the other or in the momentary encounter – cannot be exchanged for another, thus finds in his or her life-story a temporal extension; or, the continual dynamism of his or her persistence. In other words, the verbal response to *who* someone is always consists in the narration of his or her life-story.'[12] For example, the Swedish immigration official assumed from my New Zealand passport that I was travelling, but the moment I admitted we lived in Sweden everything changed. Suddenly, my migrant identity came into play. Only my narrative and her acceptance of it clarified my personal identity, providing what was missing in the passport: my right to live in the country. Likewise, an entire narrative was assumed between the Polynesian immigration officer and the Irish migrant Daisy when she presented her New Zealand passport and he said: 'Welcome home.' His greeting boosted her sense of belonging, and his recognition mattered more to her self-understanding than the external passport upon which it was based, an acceptance of otherness that fosters the sense of self.

Identities: Narratives of formation

The personal essay has the power to address the gaps between the external identification of migrants and their own self-understanding, and it does so in the migrant's own words, forcing a rethinking of what we mean by identity and belonging. Homi Bhabha recognised the need for self-representation for 'new communities of interest, such as refugees, underclasses, diasporic', when he said: '... their experiences, and their voices must be heard in their own words in order to make us rethink what we understand by nation, national belonging, or national culture: to question nation, to question citizenship, to question community'.[13] The 258 million people who are migrants certainly constitute a community of interest.[14] The personal essay allows us to hear in migrants' own reflective narratives what they think about the complex relationship between identity, nation and belonging. How the migrants wrestled with these abstractions in their essays was wholly up to them, but the importance of their life story to personal identity and belonging was critical.

Audrey, a retired English psychiatrist, was evacuated to New Zealand as a child during World War II. In her final essay she recognised the connection between identity and life story: 'In the whole world families are the most important thing most of us have. And holding it all together is our essential core. Each of us leaves behind our life story. So, at eighty-two I still feel like a global citizen.' Writing from the long view of eight decades and over 40 years as a practising psychiatrist, she can state with some authority what constitutes identity: 'And holding it all together is our essential core,' followed immediately by what gives a sense of personal identity: 'Each of us leaves behind our life story.' These comments correspond with Cavarero's emphasis on the connection between identity and narrative, 'the verbal response to *who* someone is always consists in the narration of his or her life-story'.[15] Audrey ended her account by meshing the internal and external identifications, the past and present selves: 'So, at eighty-two I still feel like a global citizen.' Here she acknowledges the continuity of identity from the 11-year-old sent halfway across the world to New Zealand to her 82-year-old self. And because this sentence is her final one in her final essay, it sums up who she still feels she is: a global citizen. She identifies herself not with the nation-state but with the global community.

The personal essay is an ideal method of inquiry with respect to identity, again because it always asks the writer to address the question: '*Que sais-je?*' What do I know? Who better to explore migrant identity than migrants themselves, a rhetorical question in sympathy with Henry David Thoreau's 'I should not talk so much about myself if there were anyone else whom I knew as well.'[16] The personal essay's inquiry into identity offers insights that are rich, idiosyncratic and various, the very things not captured in the census categories or immigration statistics. Individuality distinguishes the essay because 'Every essayist deals with the same general ingredients – self and experience and idea – but everyone deals with them differently'.[17]

All the migrants in my classes shared one thing: their coming to New Zealand. However, that experience and its impact on how they perceived themselves or how others perceived them varied considerably, as did its expression in their personal essays. Part of our sense of identity is based on self-understanding: 'one's sense of who one is, of one's social location, and of how (given the first two) one is prepared to act'.[18] The interaction between the self and the world, between the writer and the page, provides the place for recognition, exchange and resonance, and the essay becomes the matrix.

Migrants mine personal experience, as well as anything else that strikes them. Phillip Lopate stresses that 'the essayist must be a good storyteller' even while 'the glory of the essayist is to tell, once and for all, everything that he or she thinks, knows, or understands'.[19] The combination of narrative and reflection makes the essay well suited to exploring questions of identity because few genres are as devoted to self-examination, which has been its hallmark since Michel de Montaigne retired to his estate in 1571 to write and, of course, invent the genre. Prefacing his intention in the second edition of his essays in 1580, he wrote: 'I want to be seen here in my simple, ordinary fashion, without straining or artifice; for it is myself that I portray.' And, in case there's any doubt as to the subject matter: 'I am myself the matter of my book'.[20]

Clearly, questions of identity – who we are – have been central to the essay since its inception. Centuries later Virginia Woolf claimed the same ground for the essay as Montaigne: 'what we take to be the chief stock-in-trade of the essayist – himself'.[21] Given the self as subject, the personal essay often deals directly with the problem of identity, particularly as it's expressed through narrative. Adriana Cavarero likewise argues that our unique and unrepeatable existence is best captured in story: 'the identity of a unique being has its only tangible unity – the *unity* that he/she seeks because it is *unique* – in the tale of his/her story'.[22] As the poet Galway Kinnell reminds us, 'an incarnation is in particular flesh'.[23]

Thus are identities and understanding entwined and exchanged through stories, through the 'particular flesh' of individual narratives. Echoing Cavarero and the relational quality of narrative and identity, Susan Stanford Friedman maintains that 'identity is literally unthinkable without narrative. People know who they are through the stories they tell about themselves and others … [I]dentities themselves are narratives of formation, sequences moving through space and time as they undergo development, evolution, and revolution'.[24] For migrants, the awareness of who they are occurs in part because of where they are – what country, culture and sometimes language they inhabit. Migrants are constantly asked: 'Where are you from?' In response, a narrative unfolds.

When answering this question, Damira, the Croatian migrant who is a lawyer for Immigration New Zealand, replies in her Slavic accent, 'Wellington', the W pronounced as a V. Her answer trumps the assumption that migrants self-identify with their country of origin, even while her accent anticipates further questions. To understand 'Vellington', we must spool back to the Yugoslav Wars, her migration while pregnant to New Zealand, her husband's return to Croatia two years later, her single parenthood – an entire narrative leading to this particular city 20 years and many stories later, in fact.

My own narrative intersects with Damira's, first coincidentally and then familiarly. As mentioned earlier, quite by chance she signed our immigration paperwork and later became my student, writing extraordinary prose in a second language: 'I have no name for my baby. There is no sound, no recognition, it is nameless and safe as it cannot be called upon. With a name it will belong to everyone who calls, without it, it belongs to me only.' Having come from a war-torn country she sees the act of naming as dangerous, since how one is identified and by whom has consequences in wartime. She deliberately gave her daughter a straightforward English first name, Sara, to go with her Croatian surname, Novak, and that blended identification is itself a narrative of formation.

We see identity form on the page of the essay as well, for essayists discover who they are and what they know in the process of writing. The essay becomes a narrative of formation and an epistemology because it is 'a particularly interrogatory form. We write in order to see what we think: our own thoughts are revealed to us as we write.'[25] Identity's narrative embodiment has particular relevance when those narratives are personal essays with an ethos to explore what one knows and how and why one understands. Gareth, the Welsh doctor, described his work as essayist well: 'They are personal essays in that they are written from my point of view with little or no regard for the views of others. They then become a strange collection and at times the mixture of truth, family myth, imagination, memory and even lies is hard to disentangle; or perhaps they are all just my truth.' Everything becomes grist for him as an essayist, to make of what he will, but Gareth recognises that his truth is subjective.

Joseph Epstein, one of the personal essay's great champions and practitioners, considers the essay 'an invention for discovery', and that 'what the essayist seeks to discover is himself'.[26] Lest this genre seems wholly solipsistic, the essay's method is reciprocal, allowing us to study both self and world and to explore the ongoing interaction between them. As philosopher Theodor Adorno wrote in his treatise on the essay: 'All levels of the mediated are immediate to the essay, before its reflection begins'.[27] This process of reciprocity and mediation within the essay has clear parallels with migrant identity construction, whereby the contact zone exists not only in the text but also in the world.

Tūrangawaewae

Migrant narratives provide vital insight into how migrants understand and identify themselves. We see migrants mediate between the world and their text through their essays because 'Personal testimony speaks precisely to how im/migrant subjects constantly build, reinvent, synthesize, or even collage identities from multiple sources and resources'.[28] Consider Gareth, the Welsh doctor: first name (male) followed by nationality and profession; several identifications can be based on that appellation, and indeed Gareth himself strongly identifies with at least two of them – his nationality and his profession.

Gareth is passionately Welsh. Perhaps it's not possible to be dispassionately Welsh because, as he stated in one of his essays, the Welsh are 'nurtured on a diet flavoured by the conviction that all would be perfect if it wasn't for the English'. All of Gareth's essays are marked by the combined power of rhetoric and lyricism. Maybe his formative years of going to chapel, two or sometimes three times each Sunday, instilled him with both. We can see this early influence in his description of his father's funeral service; Gareth was just 21 when his father died:

> The minister took a worn copy of the Gospel of St John, held it up and spoke, as only Welsh Non-conformist ministers can speak, of how my father had carried it through the War, of how important his family was to him and I struggled to choke back the tears. His voice was quiet with an almost palpable quality of restrained emotion and the slow pace quickened with each sentence, and the English and Welsh merged into a special language of grief.

Clause after clause the prose rolls off the page, building on itself in a swell of emotion able to contain 'a special language of grief'. Now compare this passage with the opening of Gareth's essay on identity:

> We emigrated from the land of our fathers, our childhood, adolescence and early adulthood and were excited at the thoughts of a new life in a new land. But no matter how far the Welsh travel they always remain Welsh and, perhaps, the further they travel the more Welsh they become. We pay New Zealand taxes, have New Zealand passports and our children have New Zealand accents but our upbringing has branded us with our Welshness.

The passage unfolds with the triple clause at the beginning and closes with the powerful anaphora invoking New Zealand three times in the final sentence, exactly the sort of rhetorical device the non-conformist ministers might have used. It's not surprising, then, to learn that Gareth wrote his drafts out longhand, revising them several times before typing them up. His essays are eloquent and exemplary of the genre, poised and at ease, intelligent and heartfelt. I often asked him to read aloud in class for the pleasure of his accent and his prose marked by his inimitable Welsh self. As one of his migrant classmates joked, if he came upon an essay in the middle of Cathedral Square in downtown Christchurch, he would recognise Gareth's writing because, like all successful essays, his prose is marked by 'a strong sense of personal presence'.[29]

The above passage opens with the collective 'we' and an almost biblical invocation: 'We emigrated from the land of our fathers, our childhood, adolescence and early adulthood and were excited at the thoughts of a new life in a new land.' Gareth progresses from the ancestral link of 'the land of our fathers' through his own lifetime up to the point of migration in 'early adulthood'. Then, as though distrusting or perhaps mocking the universalising promise of the new land, his own national identity immediately asserts itself: 'But no matter how far the Welsh travel they always remain Welsh and, perhaps, the further they travel the more Welsh they become.' Here the triple use of 'Welsh' in one sentence insists on a collective Welsh identity as much as the sentence itself does.

Gareth has no doubt the Welsh have an enduring sense of who they are: 'they always remain Welsh', an identity that is concentrated, not diluted, by the distance from Wales. He states his connection to New Zealand: 'We pay New Zealand taxes, have New Zealand passports and our children have New Zealand accents.' But despite those three ties, including citizenship, 'our upbringing has branded us with our Welshness'. That branding is more than in name, as he explains: '[I]t is the sum total of upbringing, culture, an ancient history, attitudes, tolerances and intolerances.' But what is curious is that all he treasures about 'Being Welsh in Wales', where he is 'bolstered by the past, sheltered by the sacrifices of the Rebecca rioters, the Chartists, the unions and the Labour Party, conformed by the Non-Conformist chapels', creates 'an enormous pressure to be *Welsh*' (italics the author's). To escape that pressure his family 'took a leap into the dark and came to Aotearoa. And having come twenty thousand kilometres we have, strangely, become even more Welsh.' Once more we see how distance from the place of origin concentrates his sense of identification of being Welsh.

Perhaps we cannot escape our life story in some core fashion, and we are, as Gareth put it, 'branded' by our upbringing. He returns to this image of branding in the close of his essay:

> I am a New Zealander and am proud to be so but I will always, always be filled with an unquenchable *hiraeth* [longing, yearning] which brands me indelibly as Welsh. I am incredibly fortunate that I now have two tūrangawaewae and have a whakapapa that is Welsh but has Pākehā and Rangitane branches. If I did not love Wales who would I be? A castaway afloat on a sea of uncertainty constantly searching for a cultural identity and the security of ancestry.

Now in his seventies, Gareth has lived in New Zealand half his life and declares that both his cultural identifications are here. He doesn't see being a New Zealander or being Welsh as mutually exclusive. His sense of self is not fragmented, hybrid, negotiated, or any of those critical terms

used 'to construct' post-structural identity. On the contrary, he identifies
with both in the same sentence because, as a migrant, 'To live "elsewhere"
means to continually find yourself in a conversation in which different
identities are recognized, exchanged and mixed, but do not vanish.'[30]

Gareth considers himself and is proud to be a New Zealander, while
avowing: 'I will always, always be filled with an unquenchable *hiraeth*
which brands me indelibly as Welsh.' The use of future tense and the
repetition in 'I will always, always' emphasise his enduring sense of
Welsh identity. The choice of *hiraeth*, Welsh for yearning or longing
to describe both what fills him and what brands him, seems entirely
appropriate. His identification is both internal and unquenchable,
as well as external and indelible. For Gareth, the ability to identify
simultaneously with New Zealand and Wales is not contradictory but
coexistent. Migration enriches his sense of self rather than disrupts it,
an outcome that echoes Cixous' idea that experience of other enriches
and confirms our identity: 'The other in all his or her forms gives me *I*.'[31]
Migration is thus an encounter with other – other landscapes, languages,
cultures *and* of other people who are unlike ourselves.

Gareth also sees his migration in a very positive light: 'I am incredibly
fortunate that I now have two tūrangawaewae and have a whakapapa that
is Welsh but has Pākehā and Rangitane branches.' He enriches his sense
of Welsh and New Zealand identity by invoking two core and interrelated
Māori concepts, tūrangawaewae and whakapapa. Māori scholar Hirini
Mead defines the former as 'the right to a place for the feet to stand,
that is, tūrangawaewae. It is a place where one belongs by right of birth.
Tūrangawaewae represents one spot, one locality on planet earth where
an individual can say, 'I belong here. I can stand here without challenge.
My ancestors stood here before me. My children will stand here.' … It
is a place associated with the ancestors and is full of history.'[32] Though
Pākehā and migrants cannot claim tūrangawaewae for themselves,
Gareth recognises that he now belongs in both Wales and New Zealand.

Likewise the term whakapapa, which is often translated as 'genealogy',
has a complex meaning for Māori: 'Whakapapa is a taxonomic
framework that links all animate and inanimate, known and unknown

phenomena in the terrestrial and spiritual worlds. Whakapapa therefore binds all things. It maps relationships so that mythology, legend, history, knowledge, tikanga (customs), philosophies and spiritualities are organised, preserved and transmitted from one generation to the next.'[33] Gareth's grandchildren will have whakapapa from the Rangitane branch of their family.

Gareth's embrace of these core Māori concepts exemplifies the idea that 'rather than movement from one place to another uprooting or deterritorialising migrants' identities – as has been intimated – what scholars witness among contemporary migrants is a strengthening and deepening of ties to multiple places.'[34] Gareth acknowledges the deepening of those ties through his grandchildren's whakapapa in New Zealand and feeling 'incredibly fortunate' to have two tūrangawaewae. The use of Welsh and Māori terms inscribes his sense of identification in the language of each place.

In the final sentences of his essay Gareth addressed the idea of cultural identity directly: 'If I did not love Wales who would I be? A castaway afloat on a sea of uncertainty constantly searching for a cultural identity and the security of ancestry.' Here, his original homeland and ancestry, embodied by his love for Wales, anchor his sense of who he is on the far side of the world and half a lifetime away. He remains Welsh even as he's declaring, 'I am a New Zealander.'

Gareth's inclusive sense of belonging and his reconciliation of dual nationalities are not shared by all migrants. Instead of feeling their identities blend, some migrants are torn by their far-flung attachments to people and place. Amelia, the Englishwoman married to a New Zealander who migrated in 1995, is one such: 'The disengagement from my UK family and heritage comes at a personal cost,' she wrote. 'Of late I feel a foreigner in this land. I had given up the closeness with my extended family and had taken on the responsibilities of my New Zealand relatives as if they were my own.' While she does not mind the caregiving she provides her in-laws, 'I ask myself should I have given up so much?' And although she has lived in New Zealand for over 20 years, she feels, 'Of late ... a foreigner in this land.' Separated from what and who she loves, especially her aging parents far away in England, in her writing she provides us with a sense of the emotional cost of distance on her sense of well-being and belonging. On the one hand, she recognises that 'Leaving the traditional square of upbringing freed me physically and mentally to create a new path in life.' But on the other, stepping outside the square has had a cost: 'I do not have the supporting nest of my upbringing living here in New Zealand.'

The ability to entertain contradiction is central to the essay and perhaps the human mind. Migrants are particularly aware of contradiction in their lives, having left places and people they love to live elsewhere. Since 'the essay lives in tension, pulled formally and historically in contrary directions: paradox abounding',[35] the genre's penchant for holding contrary and conflicting emotions and thoughts is ideally suited to what migrants themselves experience in their divided loyalties between people and place. Amelia's closing image in her last essay depicts that divided self perfectly: 'I do not feel like a New Zealander! Rather the image of a person standing in outsized black shiny wellington boots with one foot on the South Island of New Zealand and the other foot planted in the UK. Because truly, I still feel outside the square.'

Amelia declares, adamantly, who she is not: 'I do not feel like a New Zealander!' She then shifts the focus to outside herself, portraying herself suspended above the globe, straddling her two sets of islands, New Zealand and the British Isles. She remains outside the square of home and upbringing yet envisions herself from an external perspective wearing the outsized black Wellington boots of her homeland (gumboots in New Zealand parlance), thus showing her English sense of identification even there.

For some migrants, identification with where they originated from prevents them from forming any connection with New Zealand. Elizabeth, another Englishwoman, expressed this perfectly: 'I missed, and still miss, England terribly. There I knew what to expect in every which way and I long to navigate my life again by familiar landmarks. Radio 4, stately homes, Bath streets, Cotswold hills, Marks and Spencer food, and a snobbery that is explicit and doesn't pretend to be an egalitarian hero.' She lists what she misses about England in concrete detail, from radio station to landscape, from food to class snobbery, but what is even more important is 'There I knew what to expect in every which way and I long to navigate my life again by familiar landmarks.' She both recognises and identifies with these landmarks, the dear familiar, revealing how 'narratives and strategies of identity and belonging are constructs which are produced relationally'.[36] We form relationships with people, places and customs, but migration disrupts and dislocates the context for these connections.

One of the reasons we miss familiar things we know and love when we migrate is that our brain is mapped with them: 'The *sine qua non* of a neural network is its penchant for strengthening neuronal patterns in direct proportion to their use. The more often you do or think or imagine a thing, the more probable it is that your mind will revisit its prior stopping point.'[37] What we miss is something both rooted and routed in the brain. Thus, our sense of identity and belonging becomes engrained over years of association.

Elizabeth experienced this on a visit back to England: 'When I returned to England for a holiday in August 2009, I walked Bath streets with eager knowing. Streets I have walked time and again since I was a child. Forty years of walking pathways that are the same, but with a slightly different me each time.' Her identification with the Bath streets remains constant even while her self ages as it walks along them. For Elizabeth, identification and identity, England and being English, are entwined: 'I am not Pākehā. Neither am I New Zealand European, which I take to mean a second generation European migrant, rather than a European wanting to be a New Zealander. I am neither. I am English.'

When her marriage ended Elizabeth returned to England, where she has such a strong sense of connection and self-understanding. I visited her when I was there, my studies having been relocated courtesy of the earthquakes and Oxford University. She and I walked in the Cotswold Hills, toured the stately home of Dyrham Park near Bath and drank countless cups of tea. Her writing embodied her happiness: 'I love home, I love stability, I love routine.' And there it is: 'I love home.' Home concretises our identity.

Migrant roots

Our sense of where and with whom we belong is central to who we are. Belonging constellates around our most profound and enduring connections to people, culture, language, landscape and self. As such, our past informs our present. All the migrants in this narrative said that their original roots contributed significantly to their sense of self, for 'when one begins to explore one's identity it is both surprising and shocking to learn how the roots of one's personality inevitably lead back to the unsuspecting home.'[38]

Theresa, the Indian nurse, concurred with this idea when she concluded: 'the truth is we are just the reflection of our old meanest parents. The involuntary actions and words can be clearly traced back to those days. There is a saying, which translates as what is written on your forehead by your birth cannot be erased by hand or covered by makeup.' Birgitta, the Swedish migrant, summed up the extent to which the past had shaped her: 'To wish for another past than the one we have, wish for another family than the one that gave us the genes and the home atmosphere that shaped us and set us up for the lives we were to lead, is to wish to *be* somebody else. It was the family that made me feel I had a rightful place in life.' She credits her sense of identity and belonging to her genetics, family and home atmosphere. In two separate essays, In Suk from Korea wrote: 'my daily life practices remain deeply rooted in Korea', and 'the foundation of my thinking is deeply rooted in my culture'. The neuronal patterns formed by her daily life in Korea remain, keeping her 'deeply rooted' and culturally bound in thought and practice.

Roots are such a universal and essential metaphor that when we speak of them we often do not feel the need to explain. 'They have always been there,' writes Hélène Cixous. 'I have never looked at them. I "know" they are there. Their presence. Roots. Mine? My so strange roots.'[39] The idea that we 'know' our roots are there, even after we've migrated (as Cixous herself did from Algeria to France), is critical. Roots provide a sense of continuity amidst the radical displacement of migration. Pull hard on any taproot and it breaks off in the ground of our being: first language, first landscape, the first people who've known and loved us. Our original frame of reference – a combination of emotion, culture, family and language – becomes internalised when we migrate. What was rooted becomes uprooted and comes with us as part of our identity, a truism acknowledged by Ghassan Hage: '… they are not roots that keep you grounded, they are roots that stay *with* you as you move'.[40]

The portable nature of roots is vitally important to migrants, as Mary, the Scottish psychotherapist, observed: 'I was leaving the place but that land is always home – in my inner landscape if not under my feet. I was leaving people but taking them with me in that I can conjure them up in my head and have imaginary conversations – if not real ones'. Here, both the people and the place are carried within her because 'To know who you are means knowing where you are. Your world has a centre you carry with you'.[41] Even if we move across the world, we bring our language, our memories and our cultural traditions with us.

Renowned American author and poet Gertrude Stein lived in France for 30 years before returning to the States for a visit. She elaborated on the concept of the enduring and portable nature of one's roots in an interview she gave in the US before she travelled back to France:

> Our roots can be anywhere and we can survive, because if you think about it, we take our roots with us. I always knew that a little and now I know it wholly. I know because you can go back to where they are and they can be less real to you than they were three thousand, six thousand miles away. Don't worry about your roots so long as you worry about them. The essential thing is to have the feeling that they exist, that they are somewhere. They will take care of themselves, and they will take care of you, too, though you may never know how it has happened.[42]

The migrant essays attest to Stein's claim that 'we take our roots with us'. In short, roots migrate, if only metaphorically. Yet that makes perfect sense because metaphor, 'in its classical usage, means being at home in a strange place'.[43] The migrant, as the stranger who comes to town, must learn to be at home in a strange place if he or she wishes to feel welcome and have a sense of belonging.

The idea that roots migrate nonetheless seems contradictory: we tend to see roots as settled, fixed, permanent, rooted in a place, both a noun and a verb. Yet the migrants in my classes managed to successfully address this seemingly contradictory phenomenon in their writing. Noki, who has not been back to the Netherlands in over 30 years, agrees that his 'background is as Dutch as can be, but I feel no current connections to the Low Countries'. He may not feel any current connection to the Netherlands, but he cannot dispute that his 'background is as Dutch as can be'. His self-understanding of being Dutch endures.

Nor does time diminish a migrant's identification with roots, as evidenced by Cathrine, the elderly Dane, in a passage I quoted earlier from one of her essays: 'I never felt a stranger. To me I have always been as much part of the landscape as any New Zealander. But my whole outlook on life is that of a Dane with a background formed by the Danish educational system as well as by family and genetics.' Cathrine has a strong sense of both a New Zealand and a Danish identity, with neither cancelling the other out. Her words give credence to the idea that 'identity is a confluence, not a simple matter of subjectivity'.[44]

The idea that identity is a confluence, something that flows together like a braided river with different channels, is particularly well suited to migrant identity informed by more than one language and culture. Cathrine understands this intuitively when she embeds herself in the landscape and identifies with her second country: 'I have always been as much part of the landscape as any New Zealander.' Yet, in her perception, her self-understanding remains that of a Dane: 'But my whole outlook on life is that of a Dane with a background formed by the Danish educational system as well as by family and genetics.' Clearly, Cathrine's strong sense of Danish identity does not preclude her from feeling she belongs in the landscape of her chosen country. Her roots have stayed with her, informing her whole outlook on life 50 years on.

The migrant personal essays explore this concept of roots still being part of migrants' sense of self, much as Gertrude Stein claimed: 'The essential thing is to have the feeling that they [roots] exist, that they are somewhere.'[45] For example, Piet, the Dutch migrant who has been in New Zealand for over 50 years, observed: 'Even if we put down firm roots in a new country, there will always be something that we leave behind in our country of origin. I think we are untrue to ourselves if we are denying our original roots altogether. As emigrants we will never be quite 100% New Zealanders, even though we are happy to be in New Zealand and have a real sense of belonging here.' Piet does not name the 'something' migrants always leave behind, but in the next sentence he claims: '... we are untrue to ourselves if we are denying our original roots altogether'. And should roots be metaphorically left behind in the country of origin, they continue to inform a sense of self. Denying those roots therefore means being 'untrue to ourselves'. Perhaps the idea 'there will always be something that we leave behind in our country of origin' is why Piet feels '[as] emigrants we will never be quite 100% New Zealanders'. But this feeling does not prevent him from being happy in New Zealand or from having 'a real sense of belonging here'.

Piet returned to the roots metaphor in his final essay on identity, declaring, 'So who am I here? How do I see myself? I am someone who had his original roots in a far off land, with still some sentimental feelings for that place. But I am also someone who has put down firm roots in New Zealand now and is happy to be here.' Piet's declaration as to where his original roots and current roots are bears the weight of long experience and reflection: 'Kiwis, some perhaps only a fraction of my age, might still perceive me as a foreigner, even though I have lived in this country for over 52 years now ... My perception of my own identity is of an immigrant who feels at home in New Zealand and who has integrated well.' He balances his own self-understanding with the identity he thinks Kiwis accord him. He sees himself not as other, 'as a foreigner', even though some still do, but as someone who is 'at home in New Zealand'.

Migrant identity is closely bound to who and what migrants identify with: people, place, culture, landscape, all resonant with meaning and attachment. For some migrants these prior attachments far outweigh anything found in the new country, which means a sense of belonging or feeling at home never takes hold. Their earlier sense of identity is strong enough to make the acceptance of other identities difficult, even as it pertains to citizenship. For example, Theresa, the Indian nurse, had to forfeit her Indian citizenship when she became a New Zealand citizen. The decision to do so filled her with regret. Her email to me, unedited, is intense with her sense of loss:

> i am 100% indian … all the indians are my brothers and sisters i love my culture … i love my country with all its problems … with all its poverty. i don't know why i chose this but this is the reality knowing that i won't be buried with all the traditional mourning, among my family members … it hurts, it hurts deep down, especially when i know i don't really belong here.

Given her core identification with her own country and culture, the reason why Theresa chose to forfeit her citizenship might seem inexplicable. Her anguish is evident in her frantic, broken prose, all the more grievous when she admits, 'it hurts, it hurts deep down, especially when i know i don't really belong here'. Eva Hoffman, who migrated from Poland to Canada at age 14 and therefore experienced first-hand what non-native speakers undergo, warns that when we privilege 'uncertainty, displacement, marginality, the decentered identity … [this] underestimates the deep costs of uprootedness and transculturation, a process that involves not a willful positioning of ourselves between cultures or "on the borders", but a deep upheaval in the very fabric of self'.[46] Theresa's external identification of citizenship counters who she believes she is: '100% indian'. She gives both the country and the pronoun a small 'i' throughout her note, and while this could be because of the looser conventions in email, it may also reflect a diminished sense of identity and importance, one not strong enough to assert itself with respect to choice of citizenship.

The passport is an external symbol of identity, an official recognition of citizenship in a nation. I have two passports, one American, one New Zealand. I am fortunate to be allowed citizenship in two countries. Unlike Theresa, I didn't have to forfeit my first citizenship, and I'm not torn by a sense of disloyalty to the United States. When I swore the oath of allegiance to a monarch on the other side of the world to become a New Zealand citizen, I realised I had never sworn an oath before and that I took my own citizenship for granted, because I could. I didn't give up anything to become a New Zealand citizen, and indeed one of the best things we could have given our children is the right to live in a country where they feel they belong.

'Nationalism,' wrote Edward Said, 'is an assertion of belonging to a place, a people, a heritage. It affirms the home created by a community of language, culture, and customs; and by doing so it fends off the ravages of exile.'[47] Theresa clearly considers her standing place to be in India, as her passionate identification with her country and culture confirms: 'all the indians are my brothers and sisters i love my culture … i love my country with all its problems'. These claims offset and perhaps contribute to her sense of not belonging in New Zealand.

Theresa's feeling of loss is not unfounded, as one of her essays revealed. While she considers life in New Zealand to be 'happy and comfortable', it has cost her 'the price of our [India's] rich culture and traditions. Family gatherings and celebrations are unknown here [in New Zealand]. There are times I long for some loved ones company. I do miss the warmth of that extended family and the closeness of the village community where everyone knew each other and cared for each other.' New Zealand offers Theresa none of that, so it's hardly surprising she refers to herself as 'a case of lost identity'. She's lost everything she identifies with: language, culture, traditions, extended family and 'the closeness of the village community where everyone knew and cared for each other'. I felt a similar sense of lost identity in Sweden, stripped as I was of language, connection, knowing and being known. In mirroring my own sense of displacement, Theresa's words provided me with that moment of recognition between text and reader. Her self-understanding grounded my own, although I acknowledge that recognition is not the preserve of only those who migrate.

Embracing the unknown

The personal essays written by migrants address their own self-understanding as well as how they are identified and perceived by others. Perhaps no genre is better suited to wrestling with questions of identity than one where the writer 'becomes the crucible in which experience is tried and tested and meaning extracted. The essay's subject is not then, the self, contrary to popular opinion, although the essayist's soil, or laboratory, is nothing but the self.'[48] In the essay, the individual's consciousness mediates, through the writing, whatever it dwells upon or within. The text reflects the writer's habit of attention; what arrests it and emerges from that is a rooting out of what is essential. The text, furthermore, reveals the unexpected, unknown and otherwise undiscovered until the writer sets out to sift through and pursue where thought leads.

Aldous Huxley pointed out that the essay exists in three possible worlds: the personal, the universal and the abstract, with the best essays inhabiting all three.[49] Essayists discover what they think and know in the midst of writing, reflecting upon it simultaneously, even as migrants discover the new country moment by moment and over time. The premise that the unknown manifests in writing seems inherent when we regard the essay as a method of inquiry, a genre capable of both revelation and recognition. Hélène Cixous describes the process thus: 'When one has faith in what is not knowable: in the unknown in ourselves that will manifest. This is something so strange that to speak about it always seems to me almost illegal. It is the secret of the *ability-to-write*.'[50] The unknown is the appearance of the other within ourselves and on the page, made welcome, resonant and manifest, like the migrant who feels at home, no longer estranged in the new country.

People who embrace the unknown and other live in a larger world, a world not circumscribed by their own national or cultural identities. The contact zone becomes fruitful and engaging, not contentious. For migrants, as well as for the inhabitants of the host country, the awareness of identity occurs in the contact zone. Where the other meets,

identity coalesces: 'Discovery or recognition of identity lives not so much
in cultures as in the meeting of cultures.'[51] Amama, a doctor in her sixties
who has lived in New Zealand half her life, described this meeting of
cultures:

> A frequent conversation when I meet someone new goes as follows:
> 'Where do you come from, you look Greek or Turkish, but you speak
> English very well.'
>
> I sigh inwardly and think, here we go again. I tell them of my African
> origin, Indian genes, Scottish education, English husband, Kiwi children
> and residence in Christchurch for thirty years. 'You are international and
> that must be wonderful.' Or others will say, 'You are now one of us.'

This anecdote relating a repeated experience in her life – 'here we go
again' – shows not only the close link between identity and life story, as
Adriana Cavarero points out, but also that migrant identity is mapped
in multiple places and connections. Amama's narrative reveals that roots
and routes are 'two sides of the same coin: roots, signifying identity
based on stable cores and continuities; routes suggesting identity based
on travel, change, and disruption.'[52] Her identity is rooted in genetics
and routed in movement: from Uganda, where she was born to Indian
parents who migrated there, to Edinburgh, where she studied medicine,
and on to her marriage to an English doctor and their joint migration
to New Zealand. Small wonder that her Indian ethnicity and fluent
English, albeit sounding slightly different to a Kiwi ear, leaves native New
Zealanders unable to 'place' her. If ever there is an example of identity as
a confluence of roots and routes, Amama embodies it.

Amama also showed in her essay how others identify her by their
response to her life story. The first, 'You are international and that must
be wonderful,' implies she doesn't belong in New Zealand but is part of
some larger world that is 'international'. The second, 'You are now one
of us,' accepts her as someone who belongs in New Zealand. These two
responses reveal more about the interlocutor than about Amama, who
has, after all, identified herself in terms of ethnicity, place of origin,
education, profession, marital status, children and residence of 30 years
in New Zealand.

Perhaps the statement 'you are now one of us' is characteristic of the individual who recognises that New Zealand is a country of migrants, whose roots/routes differ and converge, whether they arrived on waka from the Pacific islands or ships and planes from everywhere else in the centuries since. As previously mentioned, census data tell us that one quarter of all New Zealanders were born abroad, and that twenty per cent of New Zealanders live overseas.[53] Migration is woven through New Zealand's historical and social fabric. Every migrant encounter occurs in the contact zone, which corresponds with Hélène Cixous' premise that the experience of other confirms our own sense of I. Resonating in any encounter are prior connections to people, place, language and culture, as well as who migrants become in response to the new country.

While a sense of one's roots remains within migrants, even long after they leave their origin country, migration will change each of them. Birgitta, the migrant from Sweden, wrote: 'The "I" goes through changes, though. Changing language, culture and climate all in one foul swoop was a bit of a thump on the head for the normal "I".' Even as fell swoop is changed to foul, whether by chance or choice, so the migrant sense of self will be altered. That change, moreover, is ongoing, as Taegen, the Englishwoman in her seventies who migrated in 1980, came to understand: 'I had underestimated my sense of belonging to an ancient culture and the "newness" that New Zealand was to offer me. It took time to adapt and it still does after all the years.' Allowing for that adaptation is vital to the migrant's sense of identity: 'It is crucial that the migrant should be able to find a space to construct an identity that can accommodate what he or she once was and is now supposed to be.'[54] For migrants, the roots inform the routes as a core frame of reference. But migrants are also changed by the routes they've taken and by what they've learned and adopted in their new frame of reference.

Sabina, who came alone to New Zealand in her thirties from the Netherlands in 2004, described a positive interaction between these two frames of reference in one of her essays:

> After five years I no longer feel like an alien, I've learned to love both worlds and how rich am I to know and enjoy those two. I'm glad that I

wasn't born here, my youth would have been boring and I think I definitely gained a better education and a sense of history, I've enjoyed the easy opportunity to travel to other countries by car and train and to have roots in two very distinctive places in Holland. That I can enjoy reading Dutch books but also sing along to the latest Kiwi band. That I have improved my English and Kiwi accent and that I've changed for the better.

Feelings of alienation, dislocation and displacement are common among migrants when they arrive, and some never adapt, yet Sabina can say she no longer feels like an 'alien' after five years in the new country. She has 'learned to enjoy both worlds' rather than pining for the one left behind or forgetting it completely by over-identifying with her adopted homeland.

Although realising 'how rich am I to know and enjoy those two' worlds, Sabina remains enthusiastic about her origins and smacks New Zealand roundly when she declares: 'I'm glad that I wasn't born here, my youth would have been boring and I think I definitely gained a better education and a sense of history.' She claims roots in two parts of the Netherlands, with a nod to her own ancestry and places to stand: 'I myself am a mix of two different people from different places but very, very Dutch/Frisian. I'm very much the product of my parents, one born in Dokkum and the other in Rotterdam, two different cultures in themselves.' She revelled in the proximity and ease of travel while growing up and living in Europe, a place accessible only to those in New Zealand who have the money and time to travel there. Then, in a telling move, she fuses her two senses of self and achieves harmony: 'That I can enjoy reading Dutch books but also sing along to the latest Kiwi band. That I have improved my English and Kiwi accent and that I've changed for the better.'

Shining throughout the passage is Sabina's joy in both worlds, the roots/routes reinforcing her sense of who she is and fostering her belief that she has 'changed for the better'. In the final sentence of this essay, which she titled 'Alien', she wrote: 'This new country of mine is not yet in my blood but surely familiar enough to be under my skin.' The sense of connection is close enough that she can claim New Zealand as her own.

'Migrants – borne-across humans'

A sense of blended identity is often evident in the migrant narratives. Chris, who migrated at age eight from England, explained her identity in terms of food: 'I see my life today as a blend of my heritage and the modern New Zealand lifestyle, typified by the Christmas pudding and white sauce sitting alongside the pavlova on the Christmas dinner table.' Here, two classic desserts served at Christmas embody the braided strand of her life: one the Christmas pudding, very English; the other the pavlova, which Australians like to claim as their concoction, but which New Zealanders vehemently insist is their own.

The traditions Chris celebrates are those she learned from her mother, who migrated in her forties and did not settle well in New Zealand: 'Spending hours over a hot stove making Christmas dinner in the middle of summer was unnatural and uncomfortable, but not celebrating this special day in a traditional way was unthinkable.' As a child, Chris might not have been aware of her mother's unhappiness and her pining for home, but in one of Chris's most moving essays she imagines how her mother must have felt. 'Most of all,' Chris wrote in her mother's voice, 'I missed my friends, those people who had shared my joys and sorrows over the decades. I did not transplant well and even though the soil was richer and the climate milder in my new home, I did not flourish.'

Now in her sixth decade, Chris can look back not only on her life but also on her mother's to see what the long-term effects of the migration were. American memoirist Patricia Hampl observes that when we write our lives we live them twice, 'and the second living is both spiritual and historical'.[55] Coming as a child to New Zealand, Chris adapted readily and easily, was teased briefly for her Lancashire accent but quickly made friends with the local children. She noted the same ease with locals was not possible for her mother and that almost all her parents' friends 'came from "somewhere else", not just England but Scotland, Rhodesia, and Czechoslovakia. Looking back I think this didn't help my mother to assimilate into the New Zealand way of life and she never really became a "Kiwi".' Her mother's identification with both fellow migrants and the country left behind may have prevented her from acquiring a New Zealand identity.

Sometimes a sense of blended identity originates even before the individual's migration to New Zealand, thus showing the migrant's inclination to embrace other. An excellent example of this came from the young Slovakian, Kornel, who arrived in New Zealand intent on improving his English but then fell in love with a Kiwi just before he left to go home. He migrated to be with his Kiwi partner and lived in New Zealand for 10 years before they moved to Slovakia in 2015. In his essay on identity he wrote:

> So who am I? A bastard. A European bastard and this is a compliment, because bastard is what we call back at home a mongrel. A street-mix dog, which in comparison to a pure breed has the qualities of all the inherited breeds and therefore is strong and resistant. I am all of these: a Hungarian Slovak, a Hungarian, a Slovak or a Czechoslovak; although, here in New Zealand the first guess is that I am German or Scandinavian due to the blue-eye-blond combination. Well, all this is in my blood thanks to my ancestors and many of the true Kiwi blokes are just as mixed up. I have got multiple identities and one saying has it: you are as many times human as [the] many languages you speak.

Kornel uses the analogy of the bastard, a European bastard, a mongrel, but rather than being disparaging this metaphor of the mongrel in comparison with purebreds is positive because the mongrel has 'the qualities of all the inherited breeds and therefore is strong and resistant'. Kornel then lists all the possible combinations of his nationalities that make up his mongrel identity: 'a Hungarian Slovak, a Hungarian, a Slovak or a Czechoslovak'.

When in New Zealand, Kornel is misidentified as German or Scandinavian because of his blonde hair and blue eyes. The mistaken external identification bears no relationship to either his national affiliation or his sense of mongrel identity: 'all this is in my blood thanks to my ancestors and many of the true Kiwi blokes are just as mixed up'. Now he identifies and draws parallels with 'true Kiwi blokes', who are 'just as mixed up' and therefore, by extension, also mongrels. He ends by summing himself up: 'I have got multiple identities.' He affirms not only hybrid vigour but linguistic and emotional breadth as well. He considers himself enriched, his humanity broadened by the fact that he speaks five languages.

Kornel's personal essay reveals something even more compelling than the multilingual mongrel identity he ascribes to himself. That something is his ability to mediate his self-understanding through both metaphor and language. He uses the Slovakian expression for bastard translated into English, but glosses over its original meaning, again in English, as mongrel. Now his identity is not only cast in metaphor but also translated into another language. His identity migrates literally, figuratively and linguistically.

Migration and metaphor indeed share an essential feature, as Salman Rushdie explains: 'The very word *metaphor*, with its roots in the Greek words for *bearing across*, describes a sort of migration, the migration of ideas into images. Migrants – borne-across humans – are metaphorical beings in their very essence; and migration, seen as a metaphor, is everywhere around us.'[56] The metaphor of migrants as borne-across humans applies not only to language, identity and location but also to the transformative nature of migration upon the individual. Metaphor draws upon the similar and the different simultaneously, and the sudden recognition and surprise they evoke in us when they resonate together. At its most essential level, recognition of what is similar and different informs the entire migration experience. Migrants must look past surface differences and similarities to find a deeper correspondence between self and the new country if they are to achieve any sense of resonance and belonging.

'Understanding nourishes belonging'

The one constant apparent to all migrants is that they have been changed by their migration. Theresa, the Indian nurse, distilled this idea when she wrote, 'Change was inevitable for survival.' A pervasive and potent example of this change is evident in the experiences of migrants from the Netherlands who came to New Zealand in the 1950s and often quit speaking Dutch in favour of English, even within their homes. As Piet recalled: 'The school discouraged us from speaking Dutch at home, as their thinking at the time was that it would confuse the children too much, having to cope with two languages.' However, although he's lived in New Zealand for 50 years, Dutch can still be a fall-back position: 'The interesting thing is that we easily revert back to Dutch when we discuss someone or something Dutch.' It makes sense that he associates his native language with people and things Dutch. Noki, who came to New Zealand 20 years later, notes: 'Living with Kiwi-kids day and night certainly gets the language up to speed!' His children's rapid acquisition of English shaped the parent's language use.

In Suk observed that Korean parents risk losing their children to the host culture because 'Even though the children have an English language barrier at the beginning, they quickly and easily adjust at school, where they learn the dominant NZ values and beliefs through education. They go through their lives independently like their New Zealand peers, while most of their mothers expect to care for their children a lot longer than New Zealand parents.' The children identify more closely with New Zealand culture and less with that of their parents. As a single parent alone in New Zealand, In Suk's loss of her daughter to the dominant culture could have been grievous, but she did her best to ensure this did not happen: 'Learning English and supporting my daughter to keep the mother tongue were a spirit of despair. I have bestowed on my daughter a crown of bilingualism.' What is striking in this extract from her essay is the dissonance between the 'spirit of despair' in learning English while trying to keep the mother tongue alive, and the wonderful metaphor of bestowing 'a crown of bilingualism' upon her daughter. It's as though In Suk skips over all the years of struggle: the awkwardness in the first sentence recalling the early years, and the 'crown of bilingualism' the reward for those efforts. But she doesn't claim the crown of bilingualism for herself, only for her daughter, who was nine when they migrated.

Twenty years after arriving in New Zealand, In Suk still feels limited in her ability to express herself in her second language: 'The few sisterly Kiwi friends who I have gained here are precious, but I think the rest

of life would not suffice to master English like being able to share my
deep emotion and intimacy to them.' Perhaps she is right, and 'the rest
of life' is not long enough to master English, as the awkward phrasing
unintentionally reveals. The absent pronoun in 'the rest of [my] life'
seems symbolic of the one thing she cannot express fully: herself. Even
with her dearest friends, she is unable 'to share my deep emotion and
intimacy to them'. That slight error in preposition, 'to' instead of 'with',
which implies a closer connection, seems emblematic of the gap that
remains between her and her 'sisterly Kiwi friends'.

Despite her self-perceived shortcomings in a second language, In
Suk raises an essential consideration that Freud stressed: 'the one point
which the emigrant experiences so particularly painfully: It is – one
can only say: the loss of the language in which one lived and thought
and which one will never be able to replace with another, for all one's
efforts at empathy.'[57] I knew I would never be able to express a fraction
of what I felt in Swedish, just as In Suk feels she cannot express herself
fully in English to her closest friends even after 20 years in New Zealand.
No wonder I felt voiceless and unhappy while living in Sweden, bereft
of my native language, despite English being a compulsory subject in
schools and with nearly all Swedes speaking some English. I remember
my disbelief when I learned that alone and lonely were the same word
in Swedish: *ensam*. But they are not the same state or emotion for the
English-speaking migrant who experiences them.

Our ability to understand and be understood is crucial to our sense of
well-being wherever we are in the world. John O'Donohue underscored
this idea: 'Where you are understood, you are at home. Understanding
nourishes belonging.'[58] If non-native speakers are to secure a sense of
identity in their chosen country outside that of being a migrant, then an
ability to speak the local language is critical. Language gives migrants
access to work, friendship, the daily interactions involving language
– in short, the country and culture in which they live. I understood
this intuitively when I lived in Sweden. I felt I had no identity outside
of English, and my ability to understand Swedish was so limited and
limiting it was crushing to my sense of self and world.

The effect of understanding the local language on the migrant's identification with the new country cannot be underestimated, and in this regard migrants 'are defined by and through the other place'.[59] Huang, from Taiwan, who married an Englishman and migrated to New Zealand in 2004, gives non-native speakers sound advice in one of her essays: 'Language is important in getting to know the culture in which you find yourself living and if you do not make an effort to learn the language then it is difficult to get an appreciation of the people you live with.'

One rainy winter evening all the migrant writers in my class concluded that language embodied culture more than any other aspect of their lives, and they discussed this in a language most of them had had to learn, each of them having crossed the incredible distance from incomprehension to understanding, and between them having come to New Zealand from Chile, China, Korea, Kiribati, the Netherlands and India. I remember feeling great humility in the face of their fluency, both around the table and on the page, as I realised that for all non-native speakers who migrate 'an essential part of survival … [is] language'.[60] Barbara, the elderly German who teaches English voluntarily to migrants, understands the importance of language better than most: 'Basic communication is no real problem to any of them, but it is to speak with fluency and articulately. Finding work for people who are new here in a climate of high unemployment is crucial and for most a question of survival. Language is so often the key.' Without that key in Sweden, I went from fluency to silence as I wrote about the one thing that would help me to live and work there.

My loss of identity became even more symbolic after I left my wallet on the bus one night when returning from my Swedish class in Gothenburg and had to replace all my forms of identification. I spent half an hour on hold, slowly advancing in the phone queue to speak with the police. The woman took my statement in English, making jokes while we spoke, and explained she had to translate everything back into Swedish in the police report. She had the immense advantage of being bilingual, able to make jokes, and I knew that achieving a corresponding level of fluency in Swedish would take me years and a strong commitment to learning its tricky vowels and pile-up words, like *Rättshjälpsmyndigheten* (legal aid). Along with my wallet, my identity seemed to have disappeared with language.

The move to Sweden was the real migration, not the previous one to New Zealand, and it would test everything I thought about being a migrant. Salman Rushdie states: 'To migrate is certainly to lose language and home, to be defined by others, to become invisible, or even worse, a target; it is to experience deep changes and wrenches in the soul.'[61] The sense of invisibility is a trope for non-native speakers, and Damira, the Croatian migrant, captured this feeling accurately: 'I felt as invisible as I did when learning rudimentary English amongst those who were using it since birth. It was their language, not mine.' In 20 years Damira has gone from feeling invisible to working as a lawyer for the Minister of Immigration and writing a blog in English, where she observes: 'In my years of learning English out of necessity, I often asked myself whether it is indeed possible to have any feelings, any thoughts at all if one cannot name them, cannot describe them. How does one recognise its world, and find one's place in it if one cannot name it, ask for it, call for it, curse for it?' And yet within 20 years she has found words to express that idea, and herself, in English.

The wrong road

The way that language transforms and transmits our identity is subtle and profound. In Sweden my identity seemed to contract because my fledgling Swedish limited my ability to interact on myriad and mundane levels. Amelia, the English migrant who lived in the Netherlands at one time, was able to capture this feeling perfectly in her writing: 'The sense of loss was acute. It was as though I was deaf. For what I heard I could not understand.' This diminished sense of self and world is understandable given that 'Empathy, connectedness, is a function of language itself, because [it is] a function of human subjectivity, but not always acknowledged as such.'[62] Bereft of language and connection in

Sweden, I became depressed and sought counselling at our local clinic. My counsellor was Swedish, although his father was English, and I felt a sense of kinship with him, split at the root as he was. Even his name was not Swedish: Thomas Wright. After our first appointment I asked him if he saw many migrants and he nodded, saying there were so many he had thought of forming a support group for them.

Thomas listened with the careful attention of someone trained to focus on stories, on what the speaker tells and does not tell. He was listening for the river beneath the river, for the deeper narrative beneath the surface story of a depressed migrant living in Sweden. We talked for months, or rather I talked, he listened. But now and then, he pointed things out to me in my narrative, a parallel process to the one I was using as I studied migrant essays for what they revealed.

One morning, in a moment of rare disclosure, Thomas said: 'You can't live here. I can't think of a single country where you belong less than this one.' I asked him where he would place me. 'I don't know,' he replied, 'but not here.' I knew he was right. No part of me wanted to be in Sweden, and yet this was where we lived. *Ensam*, alone and lonely. That same morning he explained that if words are missing to describe colours or flavours in a language, it is as though those colours and flavours don't exist for the individual. I thought more about the word *ensam* and its meanings of lonely, alone, sole, desolate, lonesome, lone – just one word for six different states of being in English – and I wondered what else was missing here. Aside from my family and a handful of Swedish friends, I realised there was not enough for me to love in Sweden, and never would be. Not words, not landscape, not warm-hearted people, not sunlight. Who and what we love is an elemental part of identity and grounds our being in ways that are ineffable and irreplaceable, which is why migration is such a rupture. Only the migrants who form strong and lasting attachments to the new country thrive and have a sense of identity that fuses who they were before with who they are now. The root meeting the route.

As someone who swims in language, living in Sweden was, for me, like losing my habitat. I knew I would never have in Swedish what I had in English, 'an inexplicable grace that makes one not be condemned and chained to the linear, univocal, reduced use of language; but rather, right away, one is in this milieu: one is in the middle of language.'[63] I would never be in the middle of Swedish. Maybe if my husband had been Swedish, maybe if my children had been younger and chattered away to me all the time in Swedish, I could have learned to be somewhat fluent. Instead, in public I felt both mute and invisible, and I understood I had lost what Eva Hoffman calls 'our psychic home', the intangible elements that give us a sense of identity: 'for the first vivid lessons of my uprooting were in the essential importance of language and of culture, and in the inseparability of these large and supra-personal entities from our most inward and intimate selves.'[64] But it was not just me; my entire family had lost its psychic home.

In New Zealand our children's lives had been unfurling like the silver fern from its spiral coil, and they were flourishing when we uprooted them to Sweden. Stripped of language and friendship, they were placed in the local school. Our son told me he now understood how the Korean and Chinese students in his New Zealand school felt. I thought a crash course in empathy was no bad thing for him, but an adolescence riddled with exclusion is. Unlike in New Zealand, our children were the only migrants in their Swedish school. They were outside and other in a culture that is subtly and quietly conforming. Our outgoing and buoyant daughter had only one friend, a girl who had lived in England for five years and been bullied at her former school in the area. At 11 and 14 our children were independent and direct, unafraid of the contact zone scrupulously avoided in the land where the ombudsman originated. Meanwhile, my husband navigated the academy in Swedish, with its pile-up words and underlying desire for consensus and stasis at all costs. He realised he would never possess the cultural and linguistic ability to effect positive changes amidst the bureaucratic inertia.

In Sweden our family was like one of the small uninhabited islands near the coast where we lived. The culture lapped around us, but we were isolated in it. When I looked out at the water I had the same thought over and over again: leave. I thought of my Swedish teacher, a cheerful and effervescent Hungarian woman fluent in Swedish, who had lived in Sweden for five years but had only one Swedish friend. I remembered the first thing Thomas ever said to me: that migrants from Mediterranean cultures could not adjust to living in Sweden because they found the people too closed off and the weather too overcast. For our fifteenth wedding anniversary my husband gave me a beautiful silk scarf made in India. The shop owner had been living in Sweden for 25 years and still didn't like living there. She longed to retire in India. I couldn't fathom living half my life somewhere I did not like – it seemed soul-destroying.

Perhaps it's no accident that *sol*, Swedish for sun, echoes 'soul' in English. Spring came cold and reluctant, a month late, the Baltic choked with more ice than it had seen in 70 years. The deer drifted into the garden and ate the tulips right down to the ground when they were still in bud. I looked at the trees still leafless in May and thought: 'Say this when you return, "I came by the wrong road and saw the starved woods burn."'[65]

We came by the wrong road. Suddenly, an essential piece of the migration equation fell into place. Migrants must want to live where they migrate if they are to adapt and settle. Everything else is secondary. If migrants want to live in the chosen country, they can learn the language, they can find work, they can forge the friendships and connections that bind them and make their lives meaningful there. Many of the migrant essays attest to this resilience and pluck in the face of difficulty, uncertainty and radical adjustment. For these migrants, New Zealand had not been the wrong road. One spring morning, when class finally resumed after the first earthquake, one of its members mused: 'Lately I have been wondering where I want to die.' The room became silent. I could feel all of us thinking: where do I want to die? It was an arresting question for a migrant to ask, but the more important question, for any of us, is where do we want to live?

Language was the key that broke off in the lock of Sweden. Perhaps my husband and I came there too late in life to make the transition, perhaps the exhausted faces of our two children reproached us when they came home from school, but we soon realised we didn't belong in Sweden. We could survive, yes; live, no. No matter how fluent our Swedish became we would remain outsiders in ways we never felt in New Zealand, a country of migrants and the most recently settled land in the world. We couldn't identify with Sweden, and that too seems to be a key to identity: not simply how the country identifies you as citizen, migrant or illegal alien, but whether you identify with the country – its culture, its language, its people.

Within four weeks of moving to Sweden, my husband began looking at job listings in New Zealand and within six months had an interview. When asked why he wanted to accept a position back in New Zealand, he said simply: 'I want my family to be able to speak English again.' Where you are understood, you are at home. We knew by then that we had been uprooted from where we felt at home. In Sweden the cultural and linguistic distances far outweighed the geographical isolation of New Zealand and were more difficult to bear. Unlike migrants who are forced to leave the place they love, we could choose friendship, language, landscape, the impossible clarity of the southern skies, knowing and being known. We could return to New Zealand where we belonged to live under brighter, more numerous stars, facing the other half of the universe.

Chapter 6
The Gift of Return

'Chaque homme porte la forme entière de l'humaine condition.'

– MONTAIGNE, *Essais*, Book 3, Chapter 2

When I think of the headwaters of *The Braided River*, I know an infinite number of drops melted, fell and were collected unseen beneath stones to form a trickle that only later appeared in the first glimmering of an idea. I think of all the different channels and tributaries that have carried me here, entwining my narrative with others, and how could I know, except by looking back to see what design emerged.

The braided rivers that arise in the Southern Alps of New Zealand to snake and twine their way across the plains to the Pacific tell a deeper story than their interwoven pattern reveals. Underneath the crisscrossing of oceans, the ongoing migrations, the sojourns in other countries that have made up my life until now, there has always been the search for home. We live forwards but understand backwards, and only by tracing the route of our migration can we discover the root of it, as T.S. Eliot understood:

And the end of all our exploring
Will be to arrive where we started
And know the place for the first time.[1]

I had to leave New Zealand and migrate to Sweden where I was truly foreign and other to grasp how essential it is to belong, to feel connected, to have meaning and give meaning to others. But when we left that winter afternoon, flying away from Christchurch, a city devastated by earthquakes, I had no idea we would come back to the country where I first realised I was a migrant and had been one all my life, when all I ever longed for was home.

We cannot know how the journey will unfold or where it will end because the river of our lives is still flowing, but in the personal essay we can chart a version of its course thus far. When we stop and look back in writing, we can see the river was shimmering in this direction all along, that the bends it made, the eddies, the branching off and rejoining, the movement underground, were all part of its journey to this moment in time.

All the migrants in this narrative shared a journey of both migration and writing. Each found that 'writing opens up a space that invites movement, migration, a journey'.[2] Tracing that journey in the personal essay allowed these migrants to explore living forwards and understanding backwards. It revealed how a deeper narrative could emerge in writing – the river under the river. The genre's method of inquiry brings this deeper narrative into awareness because 'in the essay, experience is weighed and assayed for its value and meaning, which derive from reflection, meditation, or contemplation'.[3] The essay lets us take a reflective and insightful measure of individual experience, capture much of what slips through the larger categories of analysis, and explore abstractions that resist articulation – home, belonging, identity, connection – abstractions intrinsic to our sense of self and world.

Bearing witness in the personal essay

The personal essay bears direct witness to the migrant experience and does so in a genre committed to writing as inquiry. Other critical lenses have been used to explore migration, but the personal essay is uniquely poised to access individual experience in ways those forms do not. Oral histories and interviews don't provide the drive towards the reflective self-inquiry of the personal essay. '[F]ew other genres,' argues Leonard Kriegel, 'commit the writer's "I" so relentlessly and few other genres are able to force the writer to confront himself so absolutely … Among the legacies of the personal essay is that it has been used to describe so many different kinds of pain and self-discovery.'[4] Rigorous inquiry combined with reflection make this genre a powerful tool for assessing what migrants actually experience.

The personal essay also resonates on more than the individual level because it purposely reaches out to readers. Unlike the diary, journal or letter, the personal essay is written for a larger audience, even while it preserves the sense of intimacy of these forms: 'It's an intimate journey of self-examination and self-reflection undertaken with a reader on your shoulder. But it is more than that. It seeks to reveal the self in relation to the world; to broader, social, cultural, or political themes or issues; to an event or series of events; to a person, government, culture.'[5] Given the essay's dynamic between the self and the world, exploring the many connections that self makes – social, cultural, emotional – the personal essay provides a rich matrix for studying how migrants negotiate that contact zone both in the world and on the page.

In the personal essay, moreover, the power of language forges connection and meaning in ways that bind us to people, places and the stories we tell. This book is a migrant's story – mine, interwoven with those of 37 others to reveal the emotional and existential landscape of migration that we have traversed in our lives. For migrants, the two archetypal narratives of a man going on a journey and a stranger coming to town are central to the migration experience. Migration, embodying those two master narratives, is also an archetypal story, as universal as it is individual. Migrants arrive in a country not yet known or familiar to them, where they must come to grips with everything their life touches: work, home, family, language. How migrants navigate that journey, both in life and in the essay, encapsulates how strangers experience a new environment, both at first and over the long term. Migration has a lifelong effect on the individual, though ideally that feeling of being a stranger diminishes over time. Migrant essays reveal that mutual acceptance and a willingness to try to understand the new culture and country lead to a sense of connection and familiarity, such that migrants are no longer the strangers who came to town.

As we journey towards understanding our own lives, one another and our world, we embark on a life that is unique and unrepeatable, and that is both the beauty and pathos of human existence. 'Your life,' wrote poet and philosopher John O'Donohue, 'is a totally unique story and only you really know it from within. No one knows what your experience is like.'[6] The personal essay, designed to access and share what is known only to the individual, constantly references Michel de Montaigne's question, '*Que sais-je?*' What do I know? Migrants can reflect on their own story as they strive to answer that question in the personal essay. In a genre dedicated to discovery, especially self-discovery, the writer weighs and tests experience for its value to reveal the true cost and effect of migration on the individual.

The idea of finding one's way through writing as a method of inquiry has a long tradition of both outward- and inward-directed discovery from Montaigne to the present, with clear parallels for how migrants navigate a new country and culture. As Phillip Lopate observes, 'the personal essay represents a kind of basic research on the self, in ways that are allied with science and philosophy', thus making it an ideal genre to study the complex experience of migration.[7]

The migrant and the personal essay both set out on a journey of discovery as they move from the known to the unknown, from the familiar to the unfamiliar, and what they both find, if and where possible, are meaning and understanding. The synergy between the migrant and the genre comes from the shared endeavour to inquire into and assess what things mean. In the personal essay, 'The doing, the writing itself, is both a path *to* knowing and a path *of* knowing.'[8] The migrant comes to understand where he or she lives, and the writer comes to understand what he or she has experienced. Both the world and the essay test and are tested by the individual migrant, and these strands are brought together in the essay: not just the experience, but the meaning derived from that experience.

The contact zone between self and other, self and world, and self and writing is where incidents, issues, experiences and details resonate, connect and acquire meaning, and the personal essay captures that exchange. Studying personal essays is elemental to developing our sense of shared humanity, for as British-born Ghanaian-American philosopher Kwame Anthony Appiah reminds us: 'evaluating stories together is one of the central human ways of learning to align our responses to the world.

And the alignment of responses is, in turn, one of the ways we maintain the social fabric, the texture of our relationships.'[9] As Earth becomes more crowded, aligning our responses to the world will become an even more pressing concern on all fronts. Migrants have crossed frontiers that are geographical, cultural, linguistic, existential and emotional, and their experiences in these contact zones of self and other are vital to our understanding of what is essential to the social fabric and what maintains it.

The real journey of the migrant, both in life and in the essay, is one of understanding. Only by understanding and finding meaning can migrants connect and feel at home in the world. As they journey towards understanding their individual migrations in writing, they find the personal essay yielding unexpected moments of recognition and revelation about lived experience that might not otherwise have manifested themselves in larger categories of analysis.

Writing, according to Hélène Cixous, forms a passage between two shores, just as migration acts as a passage between countries, languages and cultures. The personal essay explores the migrant passage between two or more shores, in writing and in life: the migrant moves from the known to the unknown, from the familiar to the unfamiliar and, in a vital and essential reversal, from stranger to friend. The experience of self meeting other, the importance of reciprocal acceptance, and the role of understanding in all forms of exchange have implications with ethical, real-world applications, a claim Montaigne understood: 'Every man has within himself the entire human condition.'[10] The migrant personal essay testifies to our shared humanity in a world that is becoming increasingly mobile, where more and more we find connection and meaning in contact with the other.

The road taken

Most of the world's seven billion inhabitants never leave the country of their birth. Others, that rare three per cent, prove that 'Migration is the exception, not the rule.'[11] Given how migration disrupts and dislocates people from everything that is known and familiar to them – roots, culture, perhaps language – determining why individuals choose to migrate, to take the road *not* taken by so many others, is an elemental question. The stock answers migrants give for leaving can be gleaned from any survey. However, the real reasons are often unexplored and less straightforward, and roots always precede routes, an understanding congruent with exiled Polish Nobel laureate Czeslaw Milosz's recognition that 'a given person has usually been pushed to migrate by a tangle of reasons'.[12] The personal essay's method of inquiry untangles the reasons, some long buried, for why migrants leave to find the headwaters of a river that leaps oceans to course elsewhere in the world.

The story of our lives is not predetermined but unfolds from everything that happens, both chosen and accidental. A migrant's route is rarely straightforward and defies the ready narrative of the conventional novel. 'Life,' Adriana Cavarero agrees, 'cannot be lived like a story, because the story always comes afterwards, it results; it is unforeseeable and uncontrollable, just like life.'[13] No one foresees becoming a migrant, and yet, as the personal essays in this narrative have revealed, the migration often begins long before the individual arrives in New Zealand.

Sabina, the Dutchwoman, traced the beginning of her migration back to childhood: 'After my New Zealand trip I had that feeling of homesickness again. It lasted longer this time; it was the voice of the little girl inside me. She was reminding me about my dreams. What would it be like to live in another country?' The pāua-heart charm bracelet Amelia received as a child set off, inadvertently perhaps, her route from England to marriage to a New Zealander. When Russian national Anton's company went bankrupt, he became stranded 'in an amazing green country with a culture and lifestyle that I had never imagined', but 'the story my father told me about the beautiful place inspired me to travel as much as possible while here'. YaYa, a Chinese migrant, became fascinated with New Zealand when a Kiwi team defeated China in football in 1982, and in 1986 she seized the opportunity to study there: 'I wanted to experience the difference, the freedom of thinking.' She went on to marry a sheep farmer and declares: 'New Zealand is a country full of adventures which suits me.'

Early disruptions and displacements feature in the migrant narratives, as though loosening the soil around their roots. Some are historic, like World War II, which led Gareth, the Welsh doctor, to ask: 'Did the war time atmosphere of excitement, anxiety, restriction, deprivation and fear foster a desire for escape into a new world?' Other disruptions are more personal but equally transformative. Dorothy, the Scottish migrant who was sent to boarding school in England, speculated: 'I was very home sick in the first term. But I did get used to being away. And I was there for five years. I often wonder if this influenced me to live abroad as I knew I could cope.' Mary, the Scottish psychotherapist, felt 'boarding school instilled the attitude of ignoring clearly ridiculous insecurities and feeble excuses, of being independent and having gumption (a lovely word, little used now)'. Werapong, who came from Thailand by himself at age 15 to attend high school in New Zealand, concluded: '[M]y hope and optimism carried me throughout my most difficult times in this country. Without these two strengths – I would probably remain in Thailand, in my comfort zone – cruising my way in the rat race.' His mother confessed after she visited that had she known how far away New Zealand was, she never would have let him go.

Migrants often possess a curious and risk-taking attitude. Hugh, the Irish doctor, wrote: '[I]f I was willing to look over the other side of the mountain, or lose sight of the land and take a bit of a risk, there was a whole other world out there which was both exciting and stimulating again'. Taegen, the Englishwoman, asked: 'What is it about the sense of "belonging" and staying within the corral versus stepping outside and searching and seeking?' Migrants indeed step outside the corral, and sometimes it's because they have a desire for freedom not understood by their countrymen, which was Dutchman Noki's experience: 'And why emigrate, while life has never been better here!? In short we were told what to do.' Voluntary migrants may display an affinity for what is foreign and other, Teuaneti from Kiribati being a case in point: 'I preferred somewhere far away with no Kiribati face in sight.' Marcela, from Chile, recorded a similar preference: 'And every time I found myself most comfortable among the aliens.'

What emerges in the personal essays is that the choice to migrate is often an active decision, often years in the making. If the decision happens more spontaneously, as with Anton, the Russian who found himself washed up in New Zealand, there is still a choice made, a decision to stay and give it a go. Even the most reluctant and conflicted of migrants still opt to leave their beloved homeland as Beth, the South African migrant, admitted: 'I know now what I should have said and how I should have stuck to it. But I did not.'

Because migrants move from the known and familiar to a world that is unknown and other, their migration mirrors the personal essay: 'in more than one manner the essay moves outward, the essay and its writer connecting with the world, with otherness'.[14] When migrants set out on their journey of the stranger who comes to town, they move outwards, connecting with the world and otherness. The migrant's willingness to risk and explore parallels the work of the writer. According to Phillip Lopate, 'There is something heroic in the essayist's gesture of striking out toward the unknown, not only without a map but without certainty that there is anything worthy to be found.'[15] Migrant and writer will both discover something in the new country and on the page, though it may not be what they wanted, expected or found worthy.

Navigating the route

Few migrants consider themselves in a heroic light, yet they all cross frontiers that those who remain at home have not: linguistic, cultural, existential. Salman Rushdie argues that 'to see things plainly you have to cross a frontier'.[16] All migrants do just that. And they can show what it takes to cross that frontier in their personal essays.

The importance of the frontier cannot be underestimated. The frontier is where the self meets other, routes meet roots, and where the stranger who comes to town may encounter resistance. Through navigating the route of migration migrants learn to live in and understand their new country, culture and perhaps language, thus providing them with a lifelong and ongoing lesson in what has meaning for them. In the course of both their lives and their writing, the migrants who participated in my classes realised 'the route is mapped in the going'.[17] What they learned en route was how to adapt and adjust to their new environment, and their personal essays document and detail that process. In an increasingly overpopulated and mobile world, no lesson may be more pressing than how to adapt and adjust to where we live and those we live among. No genre maps that route of inquiry and assessment better than the personal essay with its ability to make first-hand tested knowledge available to others in a form that is immediate, accessible and reflective.

The personal essay has remained resilient and versatile for over four centuries (or longer if we date it back to Seneca and Plutarch). Part of its ongoing appeal and versatility is that it's 'a form of discovery … [and] what one discovers in writing such essays is where one stands on complex issues, problems, questions, subjects. In writing the essay, one tests one's feelings, instincts, thoughts, in the crucible of composition'.[18] The genre allows writers to choose any subject, chart any course, reveal matters both incidental and elemental to their experience – what is known, what is not – driven by the desire to inquire and understand, weigh and assess. The personal essay allows migrants to step into the river anywhere they choose, from the hidden headwaters where their migration began to the route of its unwinding and what they have learned, or indeed to any section of the river they wish to explore, thus giving the form range and depth.

Yet beyond this freedom to choose, the essay is a powerful motivator because 'the impulse to write essays, as to tell stories, grows consistently out of a single source: the individual confrontation with the hard facts and particularities of the world – of place, of any aspect of life – and the resulting effort of the imagination to seek meaning in what it confronts'.[19] In their essays migrants confront the hard facts of migration as they document the challenges posed by the particulars of their new and different world: language, culture, new social mores, a world that touches every aspect of their migrated lives. The migrant's journey towards understanding a new country, culture and language therefore has relevance that radiates beyond the personal to embrace the larger concerns of our world.

In my classes, migrants of all ages and nationalities took to the personal essay readily, and the genre proved invaluable for mining their experience for its significance and worth. When the migrants read one another's essays, they shared in the narrative journey and saw examples that resonated with their own experience. As the writer and editor William Maxwell pointed out, 'what they read will in some way make their own experience available to them'.[20] Week after week, emboldened by one another's writing, they went into deeper water, finding more and more courage to write about their experiences. Livingston, the Scottish doctor, captured this phenomenon in his final essay when he referred to 'this happy band of ex-pats who have been brave enough to bare their souls to me and who have indulged me in the same'.

When migrants reflect upon their journey in the personal essay, their experience reverberates past their own lives to become shared and accessible. The importance of this endeavour is therefore not just individual, because 'to write one's life enables the world to preserve its history'.[21] From the arrival of the earliest Polynesians to subsequent waves of migrants, New Zealand's history has been rooted/routed in migration. Through the personal essay, contemporary migration to New Zealand can be accorded reflective, concrete attention and illuminate what otherwise might never be given such considered and thoughtful expression. More than just a route to individual understanding, the personal essay preserves and shares each migrant's unique place in history, making that experience available and lasting.

Living with distance

Migrants to New Zealand live in one of the most remote and beautiful parts of the world, surrounded by thousands of kilometres of ocean, at a considerable distance from the friends, family and places they love in their country of origin or even other countries where they have lived. Distance remains permanent spatially and grows temporally with each passing year that migrants live in New Zealand. Distance is perhaps the most painful consequence of migration because it attenuates and stretches migrants' emotional connection to those they know, love and have left behind. The words Kornel the Slovakian migrant vented in one of his essays merit repetition here: 'Oh yes, this bloody distance, it does not create any nearness, it's a myth. Sure, absence can make hearts grow fonder, but then in the same fashion grows the frustration, that those hearts find it hard to hug whenever they want to.'

How migrants negotiate and compensate for the geographical, temporal and emotional distance is an ongoing dynamic throughout their lives. Here is where the root, route and effect of migrating and perhaps belonging in New Zealand are most keenly felt. Closing the distance is an ongoing challenge for migrants, and the personal essay reveals its impact on their prior, now distant, relationships: the need to stay in touch; the fallout from adopting a new language; and, most importantly, the reality of never ceasing to long for and miss those they left behind.

My fellow migrants all described the painful fact of distance in their lives. Their essays show the ongoing cost of missing significant life events, the celebrations of weddings and births, the aging and death of parents, and the simple, daily nearness of being with friends and family. The burden to stay connected seems to fall on those who leave. Many migrants make considerable efforts to call, write and visit in order to close the distance between themselves and those they love. They also find it validating when family and friends visit, for their lives now have context and meaning, affirming why they chose to live in New Zealand. Each return visit ends with fewer farewells, a cruel fact of time's inexorable passage. As Gareth, absent from Wales for 35 years, wrote so poignantly, 'My Wales no longer exists.'

The personal essay can also bring near what is distant and remembered, can summon presence from absence, and can conjure up a world left behind. Anna, unable to attend her mother's funeral in Switzerland, could nevertheless find comfort imagining herself seated at her dying mother's bedside, the snow falling, despite it being summer in New Zealand. The essay thus works against the separation and distance all migrants feel. As G. Douglas Atkins notes, the essay 'functions as one agent of the holy tension that works against separation.'[22] What greater gift could a genre give to those who live at such a remove from the people they know and love?

Belonging: The deepest current

The deepest current in the river of our lives is the need to belong. Belonging is an elemental human need and the one most severely challenged by migration. Migrants leave behind an entire world that holds meaning for them: family, friends, language, culture, place, the ties to what matters most to humans. How migrants cope with such loss and establish a sense of connection and meaning in their new country is crucial to whether they will remain a stranger. Each migrant narrative is a braided river, with the surface channels tracing a journey from one country to the other, and the much deeper current denoting learning to live and perhaps belong in the new country. Belonging, as all the migrant personal essays revealed, is predicated on mutual acceptance of the other, an axiom in keeping with John O'Donohue's observation that 'True belonging is hospitable to difference.'[23]

Being hospitable to difference is at the heart of what it means to welcome and be welcomed as the stranger who comes to town. If migrants do not feel welcome in the new country, or do not in turn welcome what that country has to offer, they will never gain a sense of belonging. The migrant personal essays confirm the dynamic nature of belonging and bring a new resonance to migration theories when 'the very subjects these theories are built upon and around are allowed to speak, interrupt, deny, forget, forge and remember their multiple modes of belonging and dislocation.'[24] The personal essay grounds the abstraction of belonging in first-hand experience, addressing its fundamental importance to whether a migrant settles and feels at home in the host country.

How the other perceives and is perceived is at the centre of cultural exchange and resilience, reflecting an effort to impart and to understand what has meaning for each of us. The migrants I collaborated with as they wrote their essays were well aware of the importance of their role in this cultural exchange. Huang, the Taiwanese migrant, for example, stated that 'Any expatriate carries a heavy burden of responsibility because they may be the sole representative of their country or culture which somebody in their newly adopted country meets and they must portray themselves in a way which would make their stay-at-home country-men and -women proud.'

The migrant personal essays established the essential reciprocity of this encounter, and the accounts revealed different levels of acceptance in New Zealand. Audrey, the retired English psychiatrist observed: 'It is reassuring to know that we can have contact with a multitude of experiences world wide, and that barriers are only as high as we make them.' Not all barriers are of the migrant's own making, however. At one end of the spectrum of acceptance is Theresa, the nurse from India, whose accent and ethnicity presented a barrier: 'Here I felt like a zero.' Cathrine, who migrated from Denmark some 50 years earlier, claimed, however: 'I never felt a stranger. To me I have always been as much part of the landscape as any New Zealander.' Theresa remains alienated, unacknowledged and unaccepted in the host country while Cathrine feels she is accepted and belongs.

For migrants to cease feeling like strangers, they must both adapt *and* be accepted. While it's implicit that migration requires adaptability, given that 'going away teaches the lability of the subject, precisely because the object world poses new contexts and models', acceptance is what allows migrants to feel they belong.[25] Even as the migrant perspective is potentially enlarged and enriched by the journey of being a stranger coming to town, much depends upon how the migrant perceives and is received by the host country. Some of the migrants in my classes experienced few barriers. Doug, the American sculptor, discovered as his 'mission, slowly turning Christchurch into a small town. I honestly don't think it has a chance. After all, my story is now part of the fabric. It's mine for the weaving.' By weaving his story into where he now lives, Doug showed that choosing to belong is a proactive, integrative force.

Daisy, the Irish nurse, also embraced her new life: 'I took to the new ways of doing without hesitation. I made friends and was befriended.' However, John, a Malaysian dentist who came to New Zealand as a teenager in 1986 with his family, found acclimating took time: 'I do feel that I do belong here now. Like a new pair of shoes, it took me a long time to get used to this new place initially, but I have now moulded myself into the lifestyle of this country and feel that I am fitting snugly in this country I now call home.'

For several of the migrants, being perceived as the stranger, as other, has persisted despite their efforts to integrate. In Suk from Korea experienced racism in her apartment complex, in the schools and on the streets, but it is a testament to her fair-minded nature that she now serves as a justice of the peace in her community. Her tolerance and willingness to accept the other is continually put into practice in her life and work: 'I am involved in the lives of others by supporting many people through my duties as a Justice of Peace. I must go to the extra mile and make a concerted effort to integrate into the Kiwis which are being formed in the midst of this soaring ethnic diversity.'

In Suk recognised that 'the soaring ethnic diversity' of which she is part didn't necessarily wish to include her and that she had to 'make a concerted effort' to integrate. The Polish migrant writer Eva Hoffman emphasises: 'The effort to understand an unfamiliar world happens against resistance, but it is also fueled by curiosity and desire to know, by the attempt to imagine, and to enter into other subjectivities, and the subjectivity of another language and culture.'[26] In Suk worked patiently against that resistance, entering into other subjectivities of language and culture as illustrated by her life and her essays. Essential to belonging is the desire to understand and be understood by the other, an exchange that is as ethical as it is necessary to well-being on both individual and global levels.

Migrant identity: Fluid dynamics

Identity is where roots, routes, distance and belonging come together to form the nexus through which the migrant sense of self constellates. As migrants adapt to life in their new country, their sense of identity changes as well. Their identity is both rooted, as in placed in a past landscape, culture and perhaps language, and routed, as in transitioned through and to another place. The personal essay, given its thirst to discover what one knows, is particularly adept at wrestling with the problematic concept of identity. What migrant essays reveal, therefore, is the fluid nature of identity, which depends not only on how migrants are identified by others but also on how they identify themselves. Identity, moreover, is not simply passive, a category marker like race or gender, but is intrinsic to what the migrant identifies with: people, places, language, culture – an entire array of connection and meaning. The personal essay can address this multi-stable and dynamic sense of identity and identification – those things that cannot be checked off easily in an immigration application. Who we are is a question central to our lives, and the answer is often a story, not a category.

The migrant's own sense of self-understanding is integral to personal identity, and that may change with time and place, just as the story of our life changes. As Cavarero so aptly says, 'the verbal response to *who* someone is always consists in the narration of his or her life-story'.[27] I was very conscious of being a migrant in Sweden, outside of the culture and language, a stranger in their midst. I have not felt my migrant identity nearly as keenly this second time in New Zealand, perhaps because the migrant's triple disruption is no longer in place. Sweden forced our family to confront what mattered to us and convinced us to return to a place where we had roots, language and familiarity with the social norms. We now identify with New Zealand, an important and vital consideration for deepening our sense of connection and belonging. My own essential sea change is that I accept rather than resist New Zealand. When people ask me where I'm from, I tell them I live here, since 'placedness can be most certainly found in staying put, but it can also be found in migrating'.[28] I have found my place by migrating back to it and choosing to stay.

As the migrant personal essays attest, the sense of belonging fostered through a sense of identification with the host country does not pre-empt a migrant's attachment or love for the place left behind. 'Our roots can be anywhere and we can survive,' Gertrude Stein said, 'because

if you think about it, we take our roots with us.'[29] Our roots come with us
in our language, memories and cultural affiliations, and their portability
is what allows those of us who are migrants to remain connected with
our past while bringing an enriched frame of reference and perspective
to our respective host countries.

Roots may travel, but whether the migrant transplant will thrive
is a more open-ended question. Some migrants continue to identify
with their place of origin to the exclusion of all else. They may, like
the Englishwoman Elizabeth, even return there. While living in New
Zealand, Elizabeth realised that she both longed for and belonged in
England. Other migrants may remain strongly tied to their country and
culture of origin if they migrated later in life or felt conflicted about
their choice to leave, as has been the situation for Livingston the Scottish
doctor, Theresa the Indian nurse, and Beth the South African. Their
identity and identification have remained grounded in the places where
they no longer live. They will always feel displaced, never feel they fully
belong, due to that stronger attachment elsewhere. Had my family and I
stayed in Sweden, this would have been our fate. Forever the outsider, the
stranger. I will never forget my Swedish friend Inger, whom I've known
for over 15 years, saying to me: 'I knew eventually you would leave. I
just didn't think it would be this soon.' And what I failed to say was, why
would we stay when we did not feel welcome?

When migrants embrace living in New Zealand but still maintain
a sense of connection with their country of origin, they are able to
reconcile their identification with more than one landscape, culture and
perhaps language. Gareth, the Welsh migrant, considers both Wales and
New Zealand his place to stand, for which he feels 'incredibly fortunate'.
Contrapuntal understanding does not prevent migrants from feeling they
are part of their new country and culture. Many of the migrants I have
had the good fortune to work with feel a sense of connection with both
countries and cultures, and their personal essays expressed this enriched
sense of identity. Sabina, the Dutchwoman, is one of them: 'I've learned
to love both worlds and how rich am I to know and enjoy those two.' In
Suk is another: 'We will carry Korean culture on our shoulders and bring

NZ culture in our arms.' Then there's our daughter, who identifies herself as a Kiwi but as an American beneath that.

Another feature the personal essay reveals is that identity is neither a fixed nor a rigid concept. Rather, like migrants themselves, identity is adaptable and fluid, a confluence whose depth and complexity resist categorisation. Who migrants are depends on their self-understanding and where and what they identify with, both in the host country and in the country of origin. The British-born ethnically Indian writer Pico Iyer, who has lived in Japan since 1992, observed in his TED talk that 'for more and more of us home has really less to do with a piece of soil than, you could say, with a piece of soul'.[30]

In over 200 personal essays, my fellow migrants bore witness to that piece of soul, having weighed and tested and been tested by the experience of living in a new country. Whether they came to New Zealand 50 years ago by ship or five years ago by plane, whether they spoke the language fluently or came with no language but with hope in their hearts, their writing charts what they have learned on the lifelong route to understanding a new country, culture and sometimes language. Montaigne's genre for exploring personal experience is a vital and valid means of documenting and assessing the actual stakes of migration. What the migrant and the writer both realise is that 'One must seek out the world one inhabits. This is the only obligation the essayist cannot get beyond.'[31] All of these migrant writers sought out the world they inhabited, some more willingly than others, some more accepted by others, but all of them tried.

The willingness to try is at the centre of the migration experience and of the personal essay. These twin endeavours of trial and assessment in order to achieve understanding are critical not only to individual well-being but also to a larger and more collective sense of what matters, for 'at the core of the personal essay is the supposition that there is a certain unity to human experience'.[32] Finding that unity in human experience is at the root of what it means to try to understand the other, which is the journey of every migrant as the stranger who comes to town. The migrant essays share what each of their writers learned on that journey: the lived consequences of what it means to migrate, not across categories, but across days, years and lifetimes. Able to witness and articulate their own migration, these 37 strangers have confirmed that we remain strangers to one another until we understand that 'the world is mistaken. It imagines that the other takes something from us whereas the other only brings to us, all the time.'[33] In this century of the migrant, the acceptance of the other is what flows past surface differences to reveal our deep and abiding common humanity, the river under the river that feeds all our lives.

Walking with the world in Newtown

For the first four decades of my life, home kept shifting and moving like the restless channels of a braided river coursing across shingle toward the sea. From the red Marco Polo stamp on my Italian birth certificate to my life in two continents, two hemispheres and five different countries, I kept crossing the ocean, never staying more than seven years in one place. When I look back at everywhere I have lived in this world, I can see how the search for home has been the underlying current, the river under the river that has carried me from one place to the next. The braided river of my life has a branching, interwoven pattern of circumstance, accident and choice, but it is carried forward by a deeper and more resonant current: the need to belong.

As a child who grew up in the military, constantly uprooted and thrown into a new environment, I knew movement, not permanence; I knew upheaval, not stability; and while my siblings settled and never moved again as adults, I kept moving: Iowa, Ireland, Colorado, Sweden, Nebraska, Idaho and then, a leap across the ocean to New Zealand with my husband and two children. Hating New Zealand at that time, lonely, bereft, grief-stricken, I yearned for everything we had given up to migrate: our family, our friends, our house, our garden, our jobs, our dog, the 10,000 radiant connections of a known world.

I resisted New Zealand, its sparkling sunlight shining on everything, its delicious water, its many more stars, the kind and curious interest of its people who wanted me to like their country as much as they did. I wanted insulation, double glazing, central heating, canned green chillies, drive-thru Mexican food, a proper job, and I whinged and complained like the worst of spoiled Americans living overseas.

But then, slowly, small webs of connection formed. A cup of tea blossomed into friendship, a community education course turned into this exploration of migration and the personal essay, and I began to understand that belonging, like meaning, would not happen without endeavouring to understand and appreciate where I was in the world. I could cease being the stranger who came to town by starting to live in that town: rooted, connected, engaged. I could voyage from what I knew towards what I did not, no longer as a sojourner or a grown-up army brat, always expecting to leave, but as a person learning to stay, settle and belong. I could choose to see what is in New Zealand, not what is missing. Instead of loss being the defining paradigm of a migratory life, I could see the immeasurable gain of having lived in more than one country in the world.

Throughout my life I've arrived as a stranger in each new place I've lived, and I know from my varied and informed frame of reference what makes the world a diverse, rich and welcoming place. I understand how being a stranger who accepts the other changes the dynamic through contact and exchange. Slowly, I wove my way into the lives of the people around me, and the two degrees of separation in New Zealand helped foster those connections. Lois, the grower at the Sunday market where I got my potted herbs, sourced Anaheim green chilli seeds and grew an entire flat of them for me in spring. Migrants from all over gathered to write and talk about their journey in my classes, and I had a purpose again. Friendship, barbecues, birthday parties, bumping into people we knew in the supermarket – the world had meaning, resonance, a density of connection and affection, and our family started to feel we belonged. And, then, as though to test our resolve to live in New Zealand, the ground wrenched apart, not once, but twice, destroying much of the town we had come to know and love in those five years.

The earthquakes displaced many people living in Christchurch and its environs, ruining homes and eliminating jobs. In one of the unseen bends in the river, our family headed to Sweden where we became full migrants, stripped of roots, language and familiar social norms. In Sweden I realised there are far colder countries that have triple glazing, central heating, even canned green chillies, but which would never accept my family as anything but strangers, as other. True, I arrived there too late in life, too full of somewhere else, but I have also come to know that we cannot thrive everywhere, that some places suit us better than others. There simply wasn't enough for us to love or identify with in Sweden. The unlooked-for gift was our return to New Zealand, as unexpected as it was welcome.

That afternoon when we flew out of Christchurch for Sweden, I looked back at the snow-capped spine of the Southern Alps glittering above the clouds, never imagining we would return. I thought New Zealand would remain cloud-hidden and lost to me, like so many other places in my past. But the route did not end there, and our journey was not over. 'The river is not / where it starts and ends.'[34] We still had one more ocean to cross to come home.

All braided rivers reach the sea, and our family again lives on the far side of the world, under the brightest, clearest stars. We have been graced with the gift of return, given a second chance to live in Aotearoa, the land of the long white cloud. Our lives unfurl like a koru frond in the warmth of a people, a language and a place we know and love, our chosen home. The yellow Wellington city buses celebrate where we live as they roll past, emblazoned with the words: 'Go walk with the world in Newtown.' And I do. I walk with the world in Newtown, home to more migrants than any other part of the capital city. We have come from all over the world to New Zealand: the Somalis at Peoples Coffee, the Cambodian checkout clerk at the supermarket, the Malaysian librarian, the Italian weighing out the Kalamata olives, the Indian grocer with the fragrant barrels of spice. No wonder I feel so welcome among the rich, vibrant texture of this place. All my life I wanted to be home, and it seems that at long last, I am. Here is the place to stand, here is its homeland, write and bear witness.

Notes

Introduction: The Headwaters of the River

1. Kristjana Gunnars, *Stranger at the Door: Writers and the act of writing* (Waterloo: Wilfrid Laurier University Press, 2004), p. 27.
2. Statistics New Zealand, '2013 Census quickstats about culture and identity': www.stats.govt.nz/Census/2013-census/profile-andsummary-reports/ quickstats-culture-identity/birthplace.aspx#
3. Jo Smith, 'Post-cultural hospitality: Settler–native–migrant encounters', *Arena*, 28, 2007, p. 79.
4. Atholl Anderson, Judith Binney and Aroha Harris, *Tangata Whenua: An illustrated history* (Wellington: Bridget Willams Books, 2014), p. 10.
5. Patricia Hampl, *I Could Tell You Stories: Sojourns in the land of memory* (New York: W.W. Norton and Company, 1999), p. 37.
6. Duncan Gray and Jon S. Harding, *Braided River Ecology: A literature review of physical habitats and aquatic invertebrate communities* (Wellington: Department of Conservation, 2007), p. 7.
7. Carl H. Klaus, *The Made-up Self: Impersonation in the personal essay* (Iowa City: University of Iowa, 2010), p. 1.
8. Adriana Cavarero, *Relating Narratives: Storytelling and selfhood* (London: Routledge, 2000), p. 1.
9. Clarissa Pinkola Estés, *Women Who Run with the Wolves: Myths and stories of the wild woman archetype* (New York: Ballantine Books, 1992), p. 304.
10. James Clifford, 'Notes on travel and theory', *Inscriptions 5*, 1989, p. 177.
11. Thomas Nail, *The Figure of the Migrant* (Stanford: Stanford University Press, 2015), p. 7.
12. John Berger, *And Our Faces, My Heart, Brief as Photos* (New York: Random House, 1984), p. 55.
13. Kristen Iversen, *Shadow Boxing: Art and craft in creative nonfiction* (Upper Saddle River: Pearson Education, 2004), p. 41.
14. G. Douglas Atkins, *Tracing the Essay: Through experience to truth* (Athens: University of Georgia Press, 2005), p. 150.
15. SanSan Kwan and Kenneth Speirs, 'Introduction', in *Mixing It Up: Multiracial subjects*, eds SanSan Kwan and Kenneth Speirs (Austin: University of Texas Press, 2004), p. 11.
16. O.B. Hardison Jr, 'Binding Proteus: An essay on the essay', *The Sewanee Review 96*, no. 4, 1988, p. 620.
17. Michael L. Hall, 'The emergence of the essay and the idea of discovery', in *Essays on the Essay: Redefining the genre*, ed. Alexander J. Butrym (Athens: University of Georgia Press, 1989), p. 82.

18. United Nations Educational, Scientific and Cultural Organization (UNESCO), 'Learning to live together: Migrant/migration': www.unesco.org/new/en/social-and-human-sciences/themes/international-migration/glossary/migrant/

19. United Nations Department of Economic and Social Affairs Population, Division, *International Migration Report 2017: Highlights* (New York: United Nations, 2017).

20. Rudyard Kipling, *Letters of Travel 1892–1913* (New York: Doubleday, 1920), p. 50.

21. Ingrid Horrocks and Cherie Lacey, eds., *Extraordinary Anywhere: Essays on place from Aotearoa New Zealand* (Wellington: Victoria University Press, 2016), p. 11.

22. Hélène Cixous and Mireille Calle-Gruber, *Hélène Cixous, Rootprints: Memory and life writing* (New York: Routledge, 1997), p. 71.

23. Perry Nodelman, 'Discovery: My name is Elizabeth', in *(Re)Imagining the World: Children's literature's response to changing times*, eds Yan Wu, Kerry Mallan and Roderick McGillis (New York: Springer, 2013); Max Bryd, 'This is not a map', *The Wilson Quarterly 33*, no. 3, 2009.

24. Salman Rushdie, *Imaginary Homelands: Essays and criticism 1981–1991* (Harmondsworth: Granta Books, 1991), p. 394.

25. Lydia Fakundiny, *The Art of the Essay* (Boston: Houghton Mifflin, 1990), p. 5.

26. Atkins, *Tracing the Essay*, p. 139.

27. Patricia Hampl, *I Could Tell You Stories: Sojourns in the land of memory* (New York: W.W. Norton & Company, 1999), p. 35.

28. Atkins, *Tracing the Essay*, p. 81.

29. Shamita Das Dasgupta, ed., *A Patchwork Shawl: Chronicles of South Asian women in America* (New Brunswick: Rutgers University Press, 1998), p. 15.

30. Austin Bradford Hill quoted in Carla De Tona, 'But what is interesting is the story of why and how migration happened: Ronit Lentin and Hassan Bousetta in conversation with Carla De Tona', *Forum: Qualitative Social Research 7*, no. 3, 2006: www.qualitative-research.net/index.php/fqs/article/view/143/315

31. Homi K. Bhabha, *The Location of Culture* (New York: Routledge, 2nd edn, 1994), pp. 7–8.

32. Atkins, *Tracing the Essay*, p. 45.

33. Rushdie, *Imaginary Homelands*, p. 280.

34. Smith, 'Post-cultural hospitality', p. 83.

35. Emmanuel Levinas, *Totality and Infinity: An essay on exteriority*, trans. Alphonso Lingis (Pittsburgh: Dusquesne University Press, 1969), p. 75.

36. Martin Buber, *I and Thou*, trans. Walter Kaufmann (New York: Charles Scribner's Sons, 1970), p. 67.

37. Chris Arthur, '(En)Trance', *The Literary Review 51*, no. 2, 2008, p. 33.

38. Kristen Iversen, 'Interview with Kristen Iversen', in *Metawritings: Toward a theory of nonfiction*, ed. Jill Talbot (Iowa City: University of Iowa Press, 2012), p. 203.

39. Cixous and Calle-Gruber, *Hélène Cixous, Rootprints*, p. 87.
40. Jennifer Sinor, 'Writing place', in *Placing the Academy: Essays on landscape, work, and identity*, eds Jennifer Sinor and Rona Kaufman (Logan: Utah State University Press, 2007), p. 6.
41. Alberto Manguel, *The City of Words* (Toronto: House of Anansi Press, 2007), p. 5.
42. Eva Hoffman, 'Between worlds, between words: Thoughts on self-translation', in *Lost Childhood and the Language of Exile*, eds Judit Szekacs-Weisz and Ivan Ward (London: IMAGO MLPC and Freud Museum Publications, 2004), pp. 58–59.
43. Pico Iyer, 'Where is home?' TED Talks: www.ted.com/talks/pico_iyer_where_is_home
44. Berger, *And Our Faces*, p. 56.
45. James Clifford, *Routes: Travel and translation in the late twentieth century* (Cambridge: Harvard University Press, 1997), p. 3.
46. Eudora Welty, *The Eye of the Story: Selected essays and reviews* (New York: Vintage, 1983), p. 130.
47. Brené Brown, *Daring Greatly: How the courage to be vulnerable transforms the way we live, love, parent, and lead* (New York: Gotham Books, 2012), p. 8.
48. Phillip Lopate, *The Art of the Personal Essay: An anthology from the classical era to the present* (New York: Anchor Books, 1994), p. *li*.
49. Gunnars, *Stranger at the Door*, p. 80.

Chapter 1: Roots – The River Under the River

1. Adriana Cavarero, *Relating Narratives: Storytelling and selfhood* (London: Routledge, 2000), p. 39.
2. James Clifford, *Routes: Travel and translation in the late twentieth century* (Cambridge: Harvard University Press, 1997), p. 3.
3. Ghassan Hage and Dimitris Papadopoulos, 'Migration, hope and the making of subjectivity in transnational capitalism: Ghassan Hage in conversation with Dimitris Papadopoulos', *International Journal of Critical Psychology 12*, 2004, p. 116.
4. Rina Benmayor and Andor Skotnes, 'Some reflections on migration and identity', in *Migration and Identity*, eds Rina Benmayor and Andor Skotnes (Oxford: Oxford University Press, 1994), p. 14.
5. Richard Sennett, 'Humanism', *The Hedgehog Review 13*, no. 2, 2011, p. 22.
6. Cavarero, *Relating Narratives*, p. 2.
7. Walter J. Ong, *Orality and Literacy* (New York: Routledge, 2nd edn, 2002), p. 82.
8. Cavarero, *Relating Narratives*, p. 34.
9. John O'Donohue, *Eternal Echoes: Exploring our hunger to belong* (London: Bantam Books, 1998), p. 174.
10. Kristen Iversen, *Shadow Boxing: Art and craft in creative nonfiction* (Upper Saddle River: Pearson Education, 2004), p. 40.

11. Susan Sontag, 'Introduction', in *The Best American Essays 1992*, ed. Robert Atwan (New York: Ticknor and Fields, 1992), p. *xvii*.
12. Nina Glick Schiller, Linda Basch and Cristina Szanton Blanc, 'From immigrant to transmigrant: Theorizing transnational migration', *Anthropological Quarterly* 68, no. 1, 1995, p. 51.
13. Paul Thompson, 'Between identities: Homi Bhabha interviewed by Paul Thompson', in *Migration and Identity*, eds Rina Benmayor and Andor Skotnes (Oxford: Oxford University Press, 1994), p. 198.
14. Nancy Mairs, 'Trying truth', in *Truth in Nonfiction: Essays*, ed. David Lazar (Iowa City: University of Iowa Press, 2008), p. 91.
15. Frank Barron, 'Diffusion, integration, and enduring attention in the creative process', in *The Study of Lives: Essays on personality in honor of Henry A. Murray*, ed. Robert W. White (Chicago: Atherton Press, 1963), p. 236.
16. Paul Ricoeur, *Time and Narrative* (Chicago: Chicago University Press, 1984), p. 45.
17. G. Douglas Atkins, *Tracing the Essay: Through experience to truth* (Athens: University of Georgia Press, 2005), p. 68.
18. Julia Creet, 'Introduction: The migration of memory and memories of migration', in *Memory and Migration: Multidisciplinary approaches to memory studies*, eds Julia Creet and Andreas Kitzmann (Toronto: University of Toronto Press, 2011), p. 9.
19. Jennifer Sinor, 'Writing place', in *Placing the Academy: Essays on landscape, work, and identity*, eds Jennifer Sinor and Rona Kaufman (Logan: Utah State University Press, 2007), p. 10.
20. Zygmunt Bauman, *Liquid Modernity* (Cambridge: Polity Press, 2000), p. 207.
21. Carla De Tona, 'But what is interesting is the story of why and how migration happened: Ronit Lentin and Hassan Bousetta in conversation with Carla De Tona', *Forum: Qualitative Social Research 7*, no. 3, 2006: www.qualitative-research.net/index.php/fqs/article/view/143/315
22. Rockwell Gray, 'Autobiographical memory and sense of place', in *Essays on the Essay: Redefining the genre*, ed. Alexander J. Butrym (Athens: University of Georgia Press, 1989), p. 59.
23. Cavarero, *Relating Narratives*, p. 11.
24. Gray, 'Autobiographical memory and sense of place', p. 55.
25. Sven Birkerts, *The Art of Time in Memoir: Then, again*, (Minneapolis: Graywolf Press, 2008), p. 8.
26. Gray, 'Autobiographical memory and the sense of place', p. 216.
27. Antonio Damasio, *Self Comes to Mind: Constructing the conscious brain* (New York: Pantheon Books, 2010), pp. 296–97.
28. Birkerts, *Art of Time*, p. 8.
29. Kent C. Ryden, *Mapping the Invisible Landscape: Folklore, writing, and the sense of place* (Iowa City: University of Iowa Press, 1993), p. 240.
30. T.S. Eliot, 'Burnt Norton', in *T.S. Eliot: Collected poems 1909–1962* (New York: Harcourt Brace & Company, 1963), p. 176.

31. Russell King, 'Towards a new map of European migration', *International Journal of Population Geography 8*, no. 2, 2002, p. 99.

32. Clarissa Pinkola Estés, *Women Who Run with the Wolves: Myths and stories of the wild woman archetype* (New York: Ballantine Books, 1992), p. 152.

33. Patricia Hampl, *I Could Tell You Stories: Sojourns in the land of memory* (New York: W.W. Norton & Company, 1999), p. 31.

34. Gray, 'Autobiographical memory and sense of place', p. 57.

35. International Association for the Study of Forced Migration: http://iasfm.org/

36. O'Donohue, *Eternal Echoes*, p. 213.

37. Estés, *Women Who Run with the Wolves*, p. 184.

38. Phillip Lopate, *The Art of the Personal Essay: An anthology from the classical era to the present* (New York: Anchor Books, 1994), p. *xxiii*.

39. Gray, 'Autobiographical memory and sense of place', p. 61.

40. Gaston Bachelard, *The Poetics of Space*, trans. Maria Jolas (Boston: Beacon Press, 1964), p. 10.

41. Anne Michaels, *The Winter Vault* (New York: Random House, 2009), p. 94.

42. Lopate, *The Art of the Personal Essay*, p. *xliii*.

43. Graham Good, *The Observing Self: Rediscovering the essay* (New York: Routledge, Chapman and Hall, 1988), p. 183.

44. Kurt Spellmeyer, 'A common ground: The essay in the academy', *College English 51*, no. 3, 1989, p. 264.

45. Rainer Maria Rilke, *Letters to a Young Poet*, trans. Stephen Mitchell (New York: Random House, 1984), pp. 84–85.

46. Leonard Kriegel, 'The observer observing: Some notes on the personal essay', in *Truth in Nonfiction: Essays*, ed. David Lazar (Iowa City: University of Iowa Press, 2008), p. 95.

47. Andre Dubus, *Broken Vessels: Essays* (Jaffrey: David R. Godine, 1991), p. *xiii*.

48. De Tona, 'But what is interesting is the story of why and how migration happened'.

49. Hélène Cixous and Mireille Calle-Gruber, *Hélène Cixous, Rootprints: Memory and life writing* (New York: Routledge, 1997), p. 43.

50. Greg Madison, 'Existential migration: Conceptualising out of the experiential depths of choosing to leave "home"', *Existential Analysis 17*, no. 2, 2006, p. 247.

51. Jeffrey Gray, *Mastery's End: Travel and postwar American poetry* (Athens: University of Georgia Press, 2005), p. *x*.

52. Atkins, *Tracing the Essay*, p. 139.

53. John Hyde Preston, 'A conversation with Gertrude Stein', in *Gertrude Stein Remembered*, ed. Linda Simon (Lincoln: University of Nebraska Press, 1994), p. 157.

54. Susan Stanford Friedman, *Mappings: Feminism and the cultural geographies of encounter* (Princeton: Princeton University Press, 1998), pp. 153–54.

55. Salman Rushdie, *Imaginary Homelands: Essays and criticism 1981–1991* (Harmondsworth: Granta Books), p. 278.

56. Keith W. Thomson, 'The Dutch', in *Immigrants in New Zealand*, eds Keith Thomson and Andrew D. Trlin (Palmerston North: Massey University, 1970), p. 152.
57. Madison, 'Existential migration', pp. 246–47.
58. Kriegel, 'The observer observing', p. 93.
59. Good, *The Observing Self*, p. 8.
60. Sarah Allen, 'Reading the other: Ethics of encounter', *Educational Philosophy and Theory 40*, no. 7, 2008, p. 892.

Chapter 2: Routes – Writing Between Two Shores

1. Hélène Cixous, 'From the scene of the subconscious to the stage of history: A writer's path', in *French Feminism: An Indian anthology*, eds Danielle Haase-Dubosc, Mary E. John, Marcelle Marini, Rama Melkote and Susie Tharu (New Delhi: Sage Publications India, 2003), p. 91.
2. Rockwell Gray, 'Autobiographical memory and sense of place', in *Essays on the Essay: Redefining the genre*, ed. Alexander J. Butrym (Athens: University of Georgia Press, 1989), pp. 53–54.
3. Lydia Fakundiny, *The Art of the Essay* (Boston: Houghton Mifflin, 1990), p. 12.
4. Adriana Cavarero, *Relating Narratives: Storytelling and selfhood* (London: Routledge, 2000), p. 2.
5. Sven Birkerts, *The Art of Time in Memoir: Then, again*, (Minneapolis: Graywolf Press, 2008), p. 8.
6. Susan Stanford Friedman, *Mappings: Feminism and the cultural geographies of encounter* (Princeton: Princeton University Press, 1998), p. 151.
7. Stephen Castles and Mark J. Miller, *The Age of Migration: International population movements in the modern world* (New York: The Guilford Press, 4th edn, 2009), p. 31.
8. Atholl Anderson, Judith Binney and Aroha Harris, *Tangata Whenua: An illustrated history* (Wellington: Bridget Williams Books, 2014), pp. 62–66.
9. Philippa Mein Smith, *A Concise History of New Zealand* (Port Melbourne: Cambridge University Press, 2012), p. 12.
10. Ha Jin, *The Writer as Migrant* (Chicago: University of Chicago Press, 2008), p. 86.
11. Michael L. Hall, 'The emergence of the essay and the idea of discovery', in *Essays on the Essay: Redefining the genre*, ed. Alexander J. Butrym (Athens: University of Georgia Press, 1989), p. 86.
12. Leonard Kriegel, 'The observer observing: Some notes on the personal essay', in *Truth in Nonfiction: Essays*, ed. David Lazar (Iowa City: University of Iowa Press, 2008), p. 95.
13. Robert Root, *The Nonfictionist's Guide: On reading and writing creative nonfiction* (Lanham: Rowman & Littlefield Publishers, 2008), p. 104.
14. Kent C. Ryden, *Mapping the Invisible Landscape: Folklore, writing, and the sense of place* (Iowa City: University of Iowa Press, 1993), p. 217.

15. John O'Donohue, *Eternal Echoes: Exploring our hunger to belong* (London: Bantam Books, 1998), p. 335.

16. George Orwell, 'Such, such were the joys', in *The Collected Essays, Journalism and Letters of George Orwell*, eds Sonia Orwell and Ian Angus (London: Secker & Warburg, 1952), p. 334.

17. Jane Hirshfield, *Nine Gates: Entering the mind of poetry* (New York: HarperCollins, 1997), p. 190.

18. Phillip Lopate, *The Art of the Personal Essay: An anthology from the classical era to the present* (New York: Anchor Books, 1994), p. *xxiv.*

19. Mary Besemeres, *Translating One's Self: Language and selfhood in cross-cultural autobiography* (Bern: Peter Lang, 2002), p. 34.

20. Mary Chamberlain and Selma Leydesdorff, 'Transnational families: Memories and narratives', *Global Networks* 4, no. 3, 2004, pp. 227–41.

21. Hélène Cixous, 'The school of the dead', in *Three Steps on the Ladder of Writing*, trans. Sarah Cornell and Susan Sellers (New York: Columbia University Press, 1993), p. 3.

22. G. Douglas Atkins, *Tracing the Essay: Through experience to truth* (Athens: University of Georgia Press, 2005), p. 50.

23. Eva Hoffman, 'Between worlds, between words: Thoughts on self-translation', in *Lost Childhood and the Language of Exile*, eds Judit Szekacs-Weisz and Ivan Ward (London: IMAGO MLPC and Freud Museum Publications, 2004), p. 55.

24. Azade Seyhan, *Writing Outside the Nation* (Princeton: Princeton University Press, 2001), p. 79.

25. Russell King, Tony Warnes and Allan M. Williams, *Sunset Lives: British retirement migration to the Mediterranean* (Oxford: Berg, 2000), p. 128.

26. Salman Akhtar, *Immigration and Acculturation: Mourning, adaptation, and the next generation* (Lanham: Jason Aronson, 2010), p. 62.

27. Kristen Iversen, 'Interview with Kristen Iversen', in *Metawritings: Toward a theory of nonfiction*, ed. Jill Talbot (Iowa City: University of Iowa Press, 2012), p. 207.

28. Salman Rushdie, *Imaginary Homelands: Essays and criticism 1981–1991* (Harmondsworth: Granta Books, 1991), p. 125.

29. O'Donohue, *Eternal Echoes*, p. 3.

30. Russell King, 'Towards a new map of European migration', *International Journal of Population Geography* 8, no. 2, 2002, p. 100.

31. Sam Scott and Kim H. Cartledge, 'Migrant assimilation in Europe: A transnational family affair', *International Migration Review* 43, no. 1, 2009, p. 70.

32. Edward Hoagland, *The Tugman's Passage* (New York: Penguin, 1983), p. 25.

33. Lopate, *The Art of the Personal Essay*, p. *xliii.*

34. Joseph Epstein, 'The personal essay: A form of discovery', in *The Norton Book of Personal Essays*, ed. Joseph Epstein (New York: W.W. Norton & Company, 1997), p. 11.

35. Birkerts, *The Art of Time in Memoir*, p. 6.

36. Lopate, *The Art of the Personal Essay*, p. *xxvi.*

37. Martin Heidegger, *Poetry, Language, Thought*, trans. Albert Hofstadter (New York: Harper & Row, 1971), p. 201.
38. Graham Good, *The Observing Self: Rediscovering the essay* (New York: Routledge, Chapman and Hall, 1988), p. 22.
39. Scott and Cartledge, 'Migrant assimilation in Europe', p. 66.
40. D. Roer-Strier and D. Ben Ezra, 'Intermarriage between western women and Palestinian men: Multidirectional adaptation processes', *Journal of Marriage and Family 68*, 2006, p. 52.
41. Cynthia Ozick, *Quarrel and Quandary* (New York: Vintage, 2001), p. 178.
42. Atkins, *Tracing the Essay*, p. 149.
43. Hoffman, 'Between worlds, between words', p. 58.
44. Ryden, *Mapping the Invisible Landscape*, p. 212.
45. Good, *The Observing Self*, p. 23.
46. Ryden, *Mapping the Invisible Landscape*, p. 214.
47. Patricia Hampl, *I Could Tell You Stories: Sojourns in the land of memory* (New York: W.W. Norton & Company, 1999), p. 33.
48. Ilya Kaminsky and Katherine Towler, 'Zen and the art of poetry: An interview with Jane Hirshfield', AGNI Online, 2008: www.bu.edu/agni/interviews/online/2006/towler.html
49. Fakundiny, *The Art of the Essay*, p. 678.
50. Joan Didion, *Slouching Towards Bethlehem: Essays* (New York: Farrar, Straus and Giroux, 1990), p. 136.
51. David Lazar, 'Occasional desire: On the essay and the memoir', in *Truth in Nonfiction: Essays*, ed. David Lazar (Iowa City: University of Iowa Press, 2008), p. 104.
52. O'Donohue, *Eternal Echoes*, pp. 25–26.
53. Ibid., p. 7.
54. Alberto Manguel, *With Borges* (London: Telegram Books, 2006), p. 71.
55. Hélène Cixous and Mireille Calle-Gruber, *Hélène Cixous, Rootprints: Memory and life writing* (New York: Routledge, 1997), p. 102.

Chapter 3: Closing the Distance

1. John Berger, *And Our Faces, My Heart, Brief as Photos* (New York: Random House, 1984), p. 91.
2. Jennifer Sinor, 'Writing place', in *Placing the Academy: Essays on landscape, work, and identity*, eds Jennifer Sinor and Rona Kaufman (Logan: Utah State University Press, 2007), p. 10.
3. G. Douglas Atkins, *Tracing the Essay: Through experience to truth* (Athens: University of Georgia Press, 2005), p. 56.
4. Philippa Mein Smith, *A Concise History of New Zealand* (Port Melbourne: Cambridge University Press, 2012), pp. 3–4.
5. John Dawson, *Forest Vines to Snow Tussocks: The story of New Zealand plants* (Wellington: Victoria University Press, 1988), p. 13.

6. Atholl Anderson, Judith Binney and Aroha Harris, *Tangata Whenua: An illustrated history* (Wellington: Bridget Willams Books, 2014), p. 16.; Michael King, *The Penguin History of New Zealand* (Auckland: Penguin Books, 2003), p. 8.

7. Anderson, Binney and Harris, *Tangata Whenua*, p. 85.

8. Parliamentary Commissioner for the Environment, *Possum Management in New Zealand* (Wellington: Parliamentary Commissioner for the Environment, 1994), p. 4.

9. Harry Ricketts, *How to Live Elsewhere* (Wellington: Four Winds Press, 2004), p. 24.

10. Nikos Papastergiadis, *The Turbulence of Migration: Globalization, deterrorialization and hybridity* (Cambridge: Polity Press, 2000), p. 20.

11. David Lazar, 'Interview with David Lazar', in *Metawritings: Toward a theory of nonfiction*, ed. Jill Talbot (Iowa City: University of Iowa Press, 2012), p. 55.

12. John O'Donohue, *Eternal Echoes: Exploring our hunger to belong* (London: Bantam Books, 1998), p. *xxii*.

13. Geoffrey Blainey, *The Tyranny of Distance: How distance shaped Australia's history* (Sydney: Macmillan, rev. edn, 1983).

14. Adrian Favell, 'Rebooting migration theory: Interdisciplinarity, globality and postdisciplinarity in migration studies', in *Migration Theory: Talking across disciplines*, eds Caroline Brettell and James Hollifield (New York: Taylor & Francis Group, 2007), p. 269.

15. Kent C. Ryden, *Mapping the Invisible Landscape: Folklore, writing, and the sense of place* (Iowa City: University of Iowa Press, 1993), p. 215.

16. Kristen Iversen, 'Interview with Kristen Iversen', in *Metawritings: Toward a theory of nonfiction*, ed. Jill Talbot (Iowa City: University of Iowa Press, 2012), p. 203.

17. Patricia Hampl, *I Could Tell You Stories: Sojourns in the land of memory* (New York: W.W. Norton & Company, 1999), p. 29.

18. Tennessee Williams and E.D. Williams, *The Glass Menagerie* (New York: Heinemann Plays, 1945), p. 75.

19. Francesca Battisti and Alessandro Portelli, 'The apple and the olive tree: Exile, sojourners, and tourists in the university', in *Migration and Identity*, eds Rina Benmayor and Andor Skotnes (Oxford: Oxford University Press, 1994), p. 48.

20. Scott Russell Sanders, *Staying Put: Making a home in a restless world* (Boston: Beacon Press, 1993), p. 14.

21. George Core, 'Stretching the limits of the essay', in *Essays on the Essay: Redefining the genre*, ed. Alexander J. Butrym (Athens: University of Georgia Press, 1989), p. 215.

22. Iversen, 'Interview with Kristen Iversen', p. 202.

23. Thomas Lewis, Fari Amini and Richard Lannon, *A General Theory of Love* (New York: Random House, 2000), p. 156.

24. Olena Nesteruk and Loren Marks, 'Grandparents across the ocean: Eastern European immigrants' struggle to maintain intergenerational relationships', *Journal of Comparative Family Studies 40*, no. 1, 2009, p. 92.

25. Loretta Baldassar, 'The guilt trip: Emotions and motivation in migration and transnational caregiving', paper presented at the meeting of the Migration Working Group, European University Institute, Fiesole, Italy, 8 December 2010, p. 1.
26. David Boyer, *Four Legs Good* (Christchurch: Author, 2013), p. 54.
27. Ha Jin, *The Writer as Migrant* (Chicago: University of Chicago Press, 2008), p. 31.
28. Loretta Baldassar, 'Transnational families and the provision of moral and emotional support: The relationship between truth and distance', *Identities 14*, no. 4, 2007, p. 406.
29. Norma Tilden, 'Nothing quite your own: Reflections on creative nonfiction', *Women's Studies 33*, no. 6, 2004, pp. 709–10.
30. John O'Neill, *Essaying Montaigne: A study of the Renaissance institution of reading and writing* (Liverpool: Liverpool University Press, 2nd edn, 2001), p. 210.
31. O'Donohue, *Eternal Echoes*, p. 313.
32. Atkins, *Tracing the Essay*, p. 51.
33. Iversen, 'Interview with Kristen Iversen', p. 201.
34. Loretta Baldassar, 'Missing kin and longing to be together: Emotions and the constructions of co-presence in transnational relationships', *Journal of Intercultural Studies 29*, no. 3, 2008, p. 254.
35. Lewis, Amini and Lannon, *A General Theory of Love*, p. 159.
36. Denise Spitzer, Anne Neufeld, Margaret Harrison, Karen Hughes and Miriam Stewart, 'Caregiving in transnational context: "My wings have been cut: Where can I fly?"', *Gender and Society 17*, no. 2, 2003, p. 269.
37. Venetia Evergeti and Louise Ryan, 'Negotiating transnational caring practices among migrant families', in *Gender, Generations and the Family in International Migration*, eds Albert Kraler, Eleonore Kofman, Martin Kohli and Camille Schmoll (Amsterdam: Amsterdam University Press, 2011), p. 365.
38. Louise Ryan, 'Navigating the emotional terrain of families "here" and "there": Women, migration and the management of emotions', *Journal of Intercultural Studies 29*, no. 3, 2008, p. 303.
39. Annick Masselot, 'Highly skilled migrants and transnational care practices: Balancing work, life and crisis over large geographical distances', *Canterbury Law Review 17*, no. 2, 2011, p. 303.
40. Loretta Baldassar, 'Transnational families and aged care: The mobility of care and the migrancy of ageing', *Journal of Ethnic and Migration Studies 33*, no. 2, 2007, p. 281.
41. Adriana Cavarero, *Relating Narratives: Storytelling and selfhood* (London: Routledge, 2000), p. 40.
42. Ibid., p. 92.
43. Maruška Svašek, 'Who cares? Families and feelings in movement', *Journal of Intercultural Studies 29*, no. 3, 2008, p. 219.

44. Cavarero, *Relating Narratives*, p. 73.
45. Ibid., p. 87.
46. Rockwell Gray, 'Autobiographical memory and sense of place', in *Essays on the Essay: Redefining the genre*, ed. Alexander J. Butrym (Athens: University of Georgia Press, 1989), p. 53.
47. Charles Brasch, 'The Islands', in *Collected Poems*, ed. Alan Roddick (Oxford: Oxford University Press, 1984), p. 9.

Chapter 4: The Second Cup of Tea – On Belonging

1. Salman Akhtar, *Immigration and Acculturation: Mourning, adaptation, and the next generation* (Lanham: Jason Aronson, 2010), p. 62.
2. Elena Liotta, *On Soul and Earth: The psychic value of place*, trans. Erika Pauli (New York: Routledge, 2009), p. 4.
3. Salman Rushdie, *Imaginary Homelands: Essays and criticism 1981–1991* (Harmondsworth: Granta Books, 1991), pp. 277–78.
4. Quoted in Azade Seyhan, *Writing Outside the Nation* (Princeton: Princeton University Press, 2001), p. 9.
5. Verena Andermatt Conley, *Hélène Cixous* (Hemel Hempstead: Harvester Wheatsheaf, 1992), p. 13.
6. Luz María Umpierre, 'Unscrambling Allende's *"Dos Palabras"*: The self, the immigrant/writer, and social justice', *MELUS 27*, no. 4, 2002, p. 135.
7. Rushdie, *Imaginary Homelands*, p. 278.
8. Sidonie Smith and Julia Watson, *Reading Autobiography: A guide for interpreting life narratives* (Minneapolis: University of Minnesota Press, 2nd edn, 2010), p. 276.
9. Ralph Waldo Emerson, *Emerson: Essays and lectures*, ed. Joel Porte (New York: Library of America, 1983), p. 98.
10. O.B. Hardison, Jr, 'Binding Proteus: An essay on the essay', *The Sewanee Review 96*, no. 4, 1988, p. 630.
11. William H. Gass, *Habitations of the Word: Essays* (New York: Simon and Schuster, 1985), pp. 19–20.
12. Greg Madison, 'Existential migration: Conceptualising out of the experiential depths of choosing to leave "home"', *Existential Analysis 17*, no. 2, 2006, p. 239.
13. Phillip Lopate, *The Art of the Personal Essay: An anthology from the classical era to the present* (New York: Anchor Books, 1994), p. li.
14. Svetlana Boym, *The Future of Nostalgia* (New York: Basic Books, 2001), p. 251.
15. David Boyer, *Four Legs Good* (Christchurch: Author, 2013), p. 52.
16. Edward W. Said, 'The mind of winter: Reflections on life in exile', *Harper's Magazine*, 1984, p. 55.
17. Roy F. Baumeister and Mark R. Leary, 'The need to belong: Desire for interpersonal attachments as a fundamental human motivation', *Psychological Bulletin 117*, no. 3, 1995, p. 522.

18. Sam Scott and Kim H. Cartledge, 'Migrant assimilation in Europe: A transnational family affair', *International Migration Review 43*, no. 1, 2009, p. 67.
19. Seyhan, *Writing Outside the Nation*, pp. 157–58.
20. Akhtar, *Immigration and Acculturation*, p. 68.
21. Patricia Hampl, *I Could Tell You Stories: Sojourns in the land of memory* (New York: W.W. Norton & Company, 1999), p. 33.
22. John O'Donohue, *Anam Čara: A book of Celtic wisdom* (New York: HarperCollins, 1997), p. 14.
23. G. Douglas Atkins, *Reading Essays: An invitation* (Athens: University of Georgia Press, 2008), p. 263.
24. Jeff Porter, 'Introduction: "A history and poetics of the essay"', in *Understanding the Essay*, eds Patricia Foster and Jeff Porter (Peterborough: Broadview Press, 2012), p. *xi*.
25. Kent C. Ryden, *Mapping the Invisible Landscape: Folklore, writing, and the sense of place* (Iowa City: University of Iowa Press, 1993), p. 240.
26. Porter, 'Introduction: "A history and poetics of the essay"', p. *xi*.
27. Adriana Cavarero, *Relating Narratives: Storytelling and selfhood* (London: Routledge, 2000), p. 92.
28. Sara Ahmed, 'Home and away: Narratives of migration and estrangement', *International Journal of Cultural Studies 2*, no. 3, 1999, p. 344.
29. Richard Sennett, 'Humanism', *The Hedgehog Review 13*, no. 2, 2011, p. 22.
30. Julia Chaitin, J.P. Linstroth and Patrick T. Hiller, 'Ethnicity and belonging: An overview of a study of Cuban, Haitian and Guatemalan immigrants to Florida', *Forum Qualitative Sozialforschung/Forum: Qualitative Social Research 10*, no. 3, 2009, para. 29: www.qualitative-research.net/index.php/fqs/article/view/1363/2856
31. Rainer Maria Rilke, *A Year with Rilke: Daily readings from the best of Rainer Maria Rilke*, trans. Anita Barrows and Joanna Macy (New York: HarperCollins, 2009), p. 37.
32. Pico Iyer, 'Somewhere man', *Modern Maturity*, May/June, 2001, p. 68.
33. Andrew D. Trlin, 'Change and continuity: New Zealand's immigration policy in the late 1980s', in *New Zealand and International Migration: A digest and bibliography*, no. 2, eds Andrew D. Trlin and Paul Spoonley (Palmerston North: Department of Sociology, Massey University, 1992), pp. 1–28.
34. David R. Cox, *Welfare Practice in a Multicultural Society* (Sydney: Prentice Hall, 1989), p. 147.
35. Chaitin, Linstroth and Hiller, 'Ethnicity and belonging', para. 34.
36. Floya Anthias, 'Belongings in a globalising and unequal world: Rethinking translocations', in *The Situated Politics of Belonging*, eds Nira Yuval-Davis, Kalpana Kannabiran and Ulrike M. Vieten (London: Sage Publications, 2006), p. 21.
37. Mary Louise Pratt, 'Arts of the contact zone', *Profession*, 1991, p. 34.
38. Ingrid Horrocks and Cherie Lacey, eds., *Extraordinary Anywhere: Essays on place from Aotearoa New Zealand* (Wellington: Victoria University Press, 2016), p. 11.

39. Pratt, 'Arts of the contact zone', p. 40.

40. Akhtar, *Immigration and Acculturation*, p. 74.

41. Floya Anthias, 'Where do I belong? Narrating collective identity and translocational positionality', *Ethnicities 2*, no. 4, 2002, p. 510.

42. Zlatko Skrbiš, 'Transnational families: Theorising migration, emotions, and belonging', *Journal of Intercultural Studies 29*, no. 3, 2008, p. 236.

43. Scott Russell Sanders, *The Force of Spirit* (Boston: Beacon Press, 2000), p. 3.

44. Avril Bell, 'Being "at home" in the nation: Hospitality and sovereignty in talk about immigration', *Ethnicities 10*, no. 2, 2010, p. 252.

45. Yi-Fu Tuan, 'Space and place: Humanistic perspective', in *Philosophy in Geography*, eds Stephen Gale and Gunnar Olsson (Dordrecht: D. Reidel Publishing Company, 1979), p. 419.

46. Scott Russell Sanders, *Staying Put: Making a home in a restless world* (Boston: Beacon Press, 1993), p. 14.

47. Cavarero, *Relating Narratives*, p. 92.

48. Atkins, *Reading Essays*, p. 12.

49. Scott Russell Sanders, 'The singular first person', *The Sewanee Review 96*, no. 4, 1988, p. 660.

50. E.B. White, *Essays of E.B. White* (New York: Harper, 1977), p. *viii*.

51. Sandra T. Sigmon, Stacy R. Whitcomb and C.R. Snyder, 'Psychological home', in *Psychological Sense of Community: Research, applications, and implications*, eds Adrian T. Fisher, Christopher C. Sonn and Brian J. Bishop (New York: Kluwer Academic/Plenum Publishers, 2002), p. 26.

52. Yi-Fu Tuan, *Space and Place: The perspective of experience* (Minneapolis: University of Minnesota Press, 2001), p. 33.

53. Robert Root, *The Nonfictionist's Guide: On reading and writing creative nonfiction* (Lanham: Rowman & Littlefield, 2008), p. 79.

54. Ahmed, 'Home and away', p. 341.

55. Julia Creet, 'Introduction: The migration of memory and memories of migration', in *Memory and Migration: Multidisciplinary approaches to memory studies*, eds Julia Creet and Andreas Kitzmann (Toronto: University of Toronto Press, 2011), p. 10.

56. Ha Jin, *The Writer as Migrant* (Chicago: University of Chicago Press, 2008), p. 72.

57. Kathleen Norris, 'Introduction: Stories around a fire', in *The Best American Essays 2001*, ed. Kathleen Norris (Boston: Houghton Mifflin, 2001), p. *xvi*.

58. Gaston Bachelard, *The Poetics of Space*, trans. Maria Jolas (Boston: Beacon Press, 1964), p. 5.

59. Robert Root, 'Interview with Scott Russell Sanders', *Fourth Genre 1*, no. 1, 1999, p. 129.

60. Harry Kreisler, 'Between memory and history: A writer's voice. Conversation with Eva Hoffmann', *Conversations with History*, Berkeley: University of California, 2000: http://globetrotter.berkeley.edu/conversations/people/Hoffman/hoffman-con0.html

61. Chaitin, Linstroth and Hiller, 'Ethnicity and belonging', para. 13.
62. Robert L. Root and Michael Steinberg, 'Creative nonfiction, the fourth genre', in *The Fourth Genre: Contemporary writers of/on creative nonfiction*, eds Robert L. Root and Michael Steinberg (New York: Longman, 2002), p. *xxv*.
63. Harry Ricketts, *How to Live Elsewhere* (Wellington: Four Winds Press, 2004), p. 33.

Chapter 5: The Migration of Identity

1. Herbert R. Renginbogin, *Faces of Neutrality: A comparative analysis of the neutrality of Switzerland and other neutral nations during WWII*, trans. Ulrike Seeberger and Jane Britten (Berlin: LIT Verlag, 2009), pp. 93–94.
2. Rogers Brubaker and Frederick Cooper, 'Beyond "identity"', *Theory and Society* 29, no. 1, 2000, p. 15.
3. Salman Rushdie, *Imaginary Homelands: Essays and criticism 1981–1991* (Harmondsworth: Granta Books, 1991), p. 124.
4. Jacques Derrida, *Specters of Marx: The state of the debt, the work of mourning and the new international*, trans. Peggy Kamuf (New York: Routledge, 1994), p. 83.
5. Stephen Castles and Alistair Davidson, *Citizenship and Migration: Globalization and the politics of belonging* (New York: Routledge, 2000), p. 82.
6. Hélène Cixous and Mireille Calle-Gruber, *Hélène Cixous, Rootprints: Memory and life writing* (New York: Routledge, 1997), p. 204.
7. Ibid., p. 13.
8. Martin Buber, *I and Thou*, trans. Walter Kaufmann (New York: Charles Scribner's Sons, 1970), p. 80.
9. Steven Vertovec, 'Transnationalism and identity', *Journal of Ethnic and Migration Studies* 27, no. 4, 2001, p. 573.
10. Ulf Hedetoft, 'Discourses and images of belonging: Migrants between new racism, liberal nationalism and globalization', in *Politics of Multiple Belonging: Ethnicity and nationalism in Europe and East Asia*, eds Flemming Christiansen and Ulf Hedetoft (Aldershot: Ashgate Publishing, 2004), p. 36.
11. James Clifford, *Routes: Travel and translation in the late twentieth century* (Cambridge: Harvard University Press, 1997), p. 12.
12. Adriana Cavarero, *Relating Narratives: Storytelling and selfhood* (London: Routledge, 2000), p. 73.
13. Paul Thompson, 'Between identities: Homi Bhabha interviewed by Paul Thompson', in *Migration and Identity*, eds Rina Benmayor and Andor Skotnes (Oxford: Oxford University Press, 1994), p. 199.
14. United Nations Department of Economic and Social Affairs: Population Division, *International Migration Report 2017: Highlights* (New York: United Nations, 2017).
15. Cavarero, *Relating Narratives*, p. 73.
16. Henry David Thoreau, *The Portable Thoreau*, ed. Jeffrey S. Cramer (New York: Penguin Books, 2012), p. 199.

17. Tracy Kidder and Richard Todd, *Good Prose: The art of nonfiction* (New York: Random House, 2013), p. 79.
18. Brubaker and Cooper, 'Beyond "identity"', p. 17.
19. Phillip Lopate, *The Art of the Personal Essay: An anthology from the classical era to the present* (New York: Anchor Books, 1994), p. *xxxviii*.
20. Michel de Montaigne, *The Complete Essays of Montaigne*, trans. Donald M. Frame (Palo Alto: Stanford University Press, 1958), p. 2.
21. Virginia Woolf, 'A book of essays', *Times Literary Supplement*, 17 January 1918, p. 31.
22. Cavarero, *Relating Narratives*, pp. 39–40.
23. Galway Kinnell, 'Freedom, New Hampshire', in *Selected Poems* (Boston: Houghton Mifflin, 1982), p. 8.
24. Susan Stanford Friedman, *Mappings: Feminism and the cultural geographies of encounter* (Princeton: Princeton University Press, 1998), p. 8.
25. Robin Hemley, 'Interview with Robin Hemley', in *Metawritings: Toward a theory of nonfiction*, ed. Jill Talbot (Iowa City: University of Iowa Press, 2012), p. 133.
26. Joseph Epstein, 'Introduction', in *The Best American Essays 1993*, ed. Joseph Epstein (New York: Ticknor, 1993), p. *xv*.
27. Theodor W. Adorno, Bob Hullot-Kentor and Frederic Will, 'The essay as form', *New German Critique 32*, Spring–Summer 1984, p. 159.
28. Rina Benmayor and Andor Skotnes, 'Some reflections on migration and identity', in *Migration and Identity*, eds Rina Benmayor and Andor Skotnes (New Brunswick: Transaction Publishers, 2005), p. 15.
29. Epstein, 'Introduction', p. *xv*.
30. Iain Chambers, *Migrancy, Culture, Identity* (London: Routledge, 1994), p. 18.
31. Cixous and Calle-Gruber, *Hélène Cixous, Rootprints*, p. 13.
32. Hirini Mead, *Tikanga Māori: Living by Māori values* (Wellington: Huia Publishers, rev. edn. 2016), p. 49.
33. Rāwiri Taonui, 'Whakapapa – genealogy: What is whakapapa?', Te Ara – the Encyclopedia of New Zealand: www.TeAra.govt.nz/en/whakapapa-genealogy/page-1
34. David Ralph and Lynn A. Staeheli, 'Home and migration: Mobilities, belongings, and identities', *Geography Compass 5*, no. 7, 2011, p. 521. [
35. G. Douglas Atkins, *Tracing the Essay: Through experience to truth* (Athens: University of Georgia Press, 2005), p. 114.
36. Floya Anthias, 'Intersectionality, belonging and translocational positionality: Thinking about transnational identities', in *Ethnicity, Belonging and Biography: Ethnographical and biographical perspectives*, eds Gabriele Rosenthal and Artur Bogner (Berlin: LIT Verlag, 2008), p. 244.
37. Thomas Lewis, Fari Amini and Richard Lannon, *A General Theory of Love* (New York, Random House, 2000), p. 143.
38. John O'Donohue, *Eternal Echoes: Exploring our hunger to belong* (London: Bantam Books, 1998), p. 44.
39. Cixous and Calle-Gruber, *Hélène Cixous, Rootprints*, p. 179.

40. Ghassan Hage, 'With the fig, the olive and the pomegranate trees: Thoughts on Australian belonging', in *Politics, Culture and the Lebanese Diaspora*, eds Paul Tabar and Jennifer Skulte-Ouaiss (Newcastle: Cambridge Scholars, 2010), p. 157.
41. James Clifford, 'Notes on travel and theory', *Inscriptions 5*, 1989, p. 187.
42. John Hyde Preston, 'A conversation with Gertrude Stein', in *Gertrude Stein Remembered*, ed. Linda Simon (Lincoln: University of Nebraska Press, 1994), p. 157.
43. Roger Bromley, *Narratives for a New Belonging: Diasporic cultural fictions* (Edinburgh: University of Edinburgh, 2000), p. 108.
44. Ibid., p. 78.
45. Preston, 'A conversation with Gertrude Stein', p. 157.
46. Eva Hoffman, 'Between worlds, between words: Thoughts on self-translation', in *Lost Childhood and the Language of Exile*, eds Judit Szekacs-Weisz and Ivan Ward (London: IMAGO MLPC and Freud Museum Publications, 2004), p. 65.
47. Edward W. Said, 'The mind of winter: Reflections on life in exile', *Harper's Magazine*, 1984, p. 51.
48. Atkins, *Tracing the Essay*, p. 6.
49. Aldous Huxley, *Collected Essays* (New York: Harper, 1960), p. *vii*.
50. Cixous and Calle-Gruber, *Hélène Cixous, Rootprints*, p. 39.
51. Jeffrey Gray, *Mastery's End: Travel and postwar American poetry* (Athens: University of Georgia Press, 2005), pp. 12–13.
52. Friedman, *Mappings: Feminism and the cultural geographies of encounter*, p. 153.
53. Statistics New Zealand, '2013 Census quickstats about culture and identity': www.stats.govt.nz/Census/2013-census/profile-and-summary-reports/quickstats-culture-identity/birthplace.aspx
54. Bromley, *Narratives for a New Belonging*, p. 66.
55. Patricia Hampl, *I Could Tell You Stories: Sojourns in the land of memory* (New York: W.W. Norton & Company, 1999), p. 37.
56. Rushdie, *Imaginary Homelands*, pp. 278–79.
57. Sigmund Freud, *The Diary of Sigmund Freud 1929–1939: A record of the final decade*, trans. Michael Molnar (London: Hogarth Press, 1992), p. *xvi*.
58. John O'Donohue, *Anam Ċara: A book of Celtic wisdom* (New York: HarperCollins, 1997), p. 14.
59. Gray, *Mastery's End*, p. 13.
60. Iván Jaksić, 'In search of safe haven: Exile, immigration, and identity', in *Migration and Identity*, eds Rina Benmayor and Andor Skotnes (Oxford: Oxford University Press, 1994), p. 20.
61. Rushdie, *Imaginary Homelands*, p. 210.
62. Julia Borossa, 'Languages of loss, languages of connectedness', in *Lost Childhood and the Language of Exile*, eds Judit Szekacs-Weisz and Ivan Ward (London: IMAGO MLPC and Freud Museum Publications, 2004), p. 34.
63. Cixous and Calle-Gruber, *Hélène Cixous, Rootprints*, p. 38.
64. Hoffman, 'Between worlds, between words', p. 55.

65. Richard Church quoted in Helen Humphreys, *The Lost Garden* (New York: W.W. Norton & Company, 2002), p. *v*.

Chapter 6: The Gift of Return

1. T.S. Eliot, *T.S. Eliot: Collected Poems 1909–1962* (New York: Harcourt Brace & Company, 1963), p. 208.
2. Iain Chambers, *Migrancy, Culture, Identity* (London: Routledge, 1994), p. 78.
3. G. Douglas Atkins, *Tracing the Essay: Through experience to truth* (Athens: University of Georgia Press, 2005), p. 68.
4. Leonard Kriegel, 'The observer observing: Some notes on the personal essay', in *Truth in Nonfiction: Essays*, ed. David Lazar (Iowa City: University of Iowa Press, 2008), p. 95.
5. Kristen Iversen, 'Interview with Kristen Iversen', in *Metawritings: Toward a theory of nonfiction*, ed. Jill Talbot (Iowa City: University of Iowa Press, 2012), p. 201.
6. John O'Donohue, *Eternal Echoes: Exploring our hunger to belong* (London: Bantam Books, 1998), p. *xxiii*.
7. Phillip Lopate, *The Art of the Personal Essay: An anthology from the classical era to the present* (New York: Anchor Books, 1994), p. *xlii*.
8. Lydia Fakundiny, *The Art of the Essay* (Boston: Houghton Mifflin, 1990), p. 678.
9. Kwame Anthony Appiah, *Cosmopolitanism: Ethics in a world of strangers* (New York: W.W. Norton & Company, 2006), p. 29.
10. Lopate, *Art of the Personal Essay*, p. *xxiii*.
11. Stephen Castles and Mark J. Miller, *The Age of Migration: International population movements in the modern world* (New York: The Guilford Press, 4th edn, 2009), p. 9.
12. Czeslaw Milosz, 'On exile', in Josef Koudelka, *Exiles* (New York: Aperture, 1988), n.p.
13. Adriana Cavarero, *Relating Narratives: Storytelling and selfhood* (London: Routledge, 2000), p. 3.
14. Atkins, *Tracing the Essay*, p. 50.
15. Lopate, *Art of the Personal Essay*, p. *xlii*.
16. Salman Rushdie, *Imaginary Homelands: Essays and criticism 1981–1991* (Harmondsworth: Granta Books), p. 125.
17. Fakundiny, *The Art of the Essay*, p. 12.
18. Joseph Epstein, 'The personal essay: A form of discovery', in *The Norton Book of Personal Essays*, ed. Joseph Epstein (New York: W.W. Norton & Company, 1997), p. 15.
19. Kent C. Ryden, *Mapping the Invisible Landscape: Folklore, writing, and the sense of place* (Iowa City: University of Iowa Press, 1993), p. 216.
20. George Plimpton and John Seabrook, 'William Maxwell: The art of fiction', in *Conversations with William Maxwell*, ed. Barbara Burkhardt (Jackson: University Press of Mississippi, 2012), p. 41.

21. Patricia Hampl, 'The dark art of description', *The Iowa Review 38*, no. 1, 2008, p. 81.

22. Atkins, *Tracing the Essay*, p. *ix*.

23. O'Donohue, *Eternal Echoes*, p. 59.

24. Reshmi Dutt-Ballerstadt, *The Postcolonial Citizen: The intellectual migrant* (New York: Peter Lang, 2010), p. *ix*.

25. Jeffrey Gray, *Mastery's End: Travel and postwar American poetry* (Athens: University of Georgia Press, 2005), p. 13.

26. Eva Hoffman, 'Between worlds, between words: Thoughts on self-translation', in *Lost Childhood and the Language of Exile*, eds Judit Szekacs-Weisz and Ivan Ward (London: IMAGO MLPC and Freud Museum Publications, 2004), p. 64.

27. Cavarero, *Relating Narratives*, p. 73.

28. Jennifer Sinor, 'Writing place', in *Placing the Academy: Essays on landscape, work, and identity*, eds Jennifer Sinor and Rona Kaufman (Logan: Utah State University Press, 2007), p. 15.

29. John Hyde Preston, 'A conversation with Gertrude Stein', in *Gertrude Stein Remembered*, ed. Linda Simon (Lincoln: University of Nebraska Press, 1994), p. 157.

30. Pico Iyer, 'Where is home?' TED Talks: www.ted.com/talks/pico_iyer_where_is_home

31. Kriegel, 'The observer observing', p. 98.

32. Lopate, *Art of the Personal Essay*, p. *xxiii*.

33. Hélène Cixous and Mireille Calle-Gruber, *Hélène Cixous, Rootprints: Memory and life writing* (New York: Routledge, 1997), p. 13.

34. Jim Harrison, 'Walter of Battersea', in *The Shape of the Journey: New & collected poems* (Port Townsend: Copper Canyon Press, 1999), p. 298.

Bibliography

Adorno, Theodor W., Bob Hullot-Kentor and Frederic Will, 'The essay as form', *New German Critique 32*, Spring–Summer 1984, 151–71

Ahmed, Sara, 'Home and away: Narratives of migration and estrangement', *International Journal of Cultural Studies 2*, no. 3, 1999, 329–47

Akhtar, Salman, *Immigration and Acculturation: Mourning, adaptation, and the next generation* (Lanham: Jason Aronson, 2010)

Allen, Sarah, 'Reading the other: Ethics of encounter', *Educational Philosophy and Theory 40*, no. 7, 2008, 888–99

Anderson, Atholl, Judith Binney and Aroha Harris, *Tangata Whenua: An illustrated history* (Wellington: Bridget Williams Books, 2014)

Anthias, Floya, 'Belongings in a globalising and unequal world: Rethinking translocations', in *The Situated Politics of Belonging*, eds Nira Yuval-Davis, Kalpana Kannabiran and Ulrike M. Vieten (London: Sage Publications, 2006)

———, 'Intersectionality, belonging and translocational positionality: Thinking about transnational identities', in *Ethnicity, Belonging and Biography: Ethnographical and biographical perspectives*, eds Gabriele Rosenthal and Artur Bogner (Berlin: LIT Verlag, 2008)

———, 'Where do I belong? Narrating collective identity and translocational positionality', *Ethnicities 2*, no. 4, 2002, 491–514

Appiah, Kwame Anthony, *Cosmopolitanism: Ethics in a world of strangers* (New York: W.W. Norton & Company, 2006)

Arthur, Chris, '(En)Trance', *The Literary Review 51*, no. 2, 2008, 23–37

Atkins, G. Douglas, *Reading Essays: An invitation* (Athens: University of Georgia Press, 2008)

———, *Tracing the Essay: Through experience to truth* (Athens: University of Georgia Press, 2005)

Bachelard, Gaston, *The Poetics of Space*, trans. Maria Jolas (Boston: Beacon Press, 1964)

Baldassar, Loretta, 'The guilt trip: Emotions and motivation in migration and transnational caregiving', paper presented at the meeting of the Migration Working Group, European University Institute, Fiesole, Italy, 8 December 2010

———, 'Missing kin and longing to be together: Emotions and the constructions of co-presence in transnational relationships', *Journal of Intercultural Studies 29*, no. 3, 2008, 247–66

———, 'Transnational families and aged care: The mobility of care and the migrancy of ageing', *Journal of Ethnic and Migration Studies 33*, no. 2, 2007, 275–97

———, 'Transnational families and the provision of moral and emotional support: The relationship between truth and distance', *Identities 14*, no. 4, 2007, 385–409

Barron, Frank, 'Diffusion, integration, and enduring attention in the creative process', in *The Study of Lives: Essays on personality in honor of Henry A. Murray*, ed. Robert W. White (Chicago: Atherton Press, 1963), 234–48

Battisti, Francesca and Alessandro Portelli, 'The apple and the olive tree: Exile, sojourners, and tourists in the university', in *Migration and Identity*, eds Rina Benmayor and Andor Skotnes (Oxford: Oxford University Press, 1994), 25–54

Bauman, Zygmunt, *Liquid Modernity* (Cambridge: Polity Press, 2000)

Baumeister, Roy F. and Mark R. Leary, 'The need to belong: Desire for interpersonal attachments as a fundamental human motivation', *Psychological Bulletin 117*, no. 3, 1995, 497–529

Bell, Avril, 'Being "at home" in the nation: Hospitality and sovereignty in talk about immigration', *Ethnicities 10*, no. 2, 2010, 236–56

Benmayor, Rina and Andor Skotnes, 'Some reflections on migration and identity', in *Migration and Identity*, eds Rina Benmayor and Andor Skotnes (Oxford: Oxford University Press, 1994), 1–18.

Berger, John, *And Our Faces, My Heart, Brief as Photos* (New York: Random House, 1984)

Besemeres, Mary, *Translating One's Self: Language and selfhood in cross-cultural autobiography* (Bern: Peter Lang, 2002)

Bhabha, Homi K., *The Location of Culture* (New York: Routledge, 2nd edn, 1994)

Birkerts, Sven, *The Art of Time in Memoir: Then, again* (Minneapolis: Graywolf Press, 2008)

Blainey, Geoffrey, *The Tyranny of Distance: How distance shaped Australia's history* (Sydney: Macmillan, rev. edn, 1983)

Borossa, Julia, 'Languages of loss, languages of connectedness', in *Lost Childhood and the Language of Exile*, eds Judit Szekacs-Weisz and Ivan Ward (London: IMAGO MLPC and Freud Museum Publications, 2004), 29–40

Boyer, David, *Four Legs Good* (Christchurch: Author, 2013)

Boym, Svetlana, *The Future of Nostalgia* (New York: Basic Books, 2001)

Brasch, Charles, *Collected Poems*, ed. Alan Roddick (Oxford: Oxford University Press, 1984)

Bromley, Roger, *Narratives for a New Belonging: Diasporic cultural fictions* (Edinburgh: University of Edinburgh, 2000)

Brown, Brené, *Daring Greatly: How the courage to be vulnerable transforms the way we live, love, parent and lead* (New York: Gotham Books, 2012)

Brubaker, Rogers and Frederick Cooper, 'Beyond "identity"', *Theory and Society 29*, no. 1, 2000, 1–47

Bryd, Max, 'This is not a map', *The Wilson Quarterly 33*, no. 3, 2009, 26–32

Buber, Martin, *I and Thou*, trans. Walter Kaufmann (New York: Charles Scribner's Sons, 1970)

Castles, Stephen and Alistair Davidson, *Citizenship and Migration: Globalization and the politics of belonging* (New York: Routledge, 2000)

Castles, Stephen and Mark J. Miller, *The Age of Migration: International population movements in the modern world* (New York: The Guilford Press, 4th edn, 2009)

Cavarero, Adriana, *Relating Narratives: Storytelling and selfhood* (London: Routledge, 2000)

Chaitin, Julia, J.P. Linstroth and Patrick T. Hiller, 'Ethnicity and belonging: An overview of a study of Cuban, Haitian and Guatemalan immigrants to Florida', *Forum Qualitative Sozialforschung/Forum: Qualitative Social Research 10*, no. 3, 2009: www.qualitative-research.net/index.php/fqs/article/view/1363/2856

Chamberlain, Mary and Selma Leydesdorff, 'Transnational families: Memories and narratives', *Global Networks 4*, no. 3, 2004, 227–41

Chambers, Iain, *Migrancy, Culture, Identity* (London: Routledge, 1994)

Cixous, Hélène, 'From the scene of the subconscious to the stage of history: A writer's path', in *French Feminism: An Indian anthology*, eds Danielle Haase-Dubosc, Mary E. John, Marcelle Marini, Rama Melkote and Susie Tharu (New Delhi: Sage Publications India, 2003), 87–103

———, 'The school of the dead', in *Three Steps on the Ladder of Writing*, trans. Sarah Cornell and Susan Sellers (New York: Columbia University Press, 1993), 1–55

Cixous, Hélène and Mireille Calle-Gruber, *Hélène Cixous, Rootprints: Memory and life writing* (New York: Routledge, 1997)

Clifford, James, 'Notes on travel and theory', *Inscriptions 5*, 1989, 177–86

———, *Routes: Travel and translation in the late twentieth century* (Cambridge: Harvard University Press, 1997)

Conley, Verena Andermatt, *Hélène Cixous* (Hemel Hempstead: Harvester Wheatsheaf, 1992)

Core, George, 'Stretching the limits of the essay', in *Essays on the Essay: Redefining the genre*, ed. Alexander J. Butrym (Athens: University of Georgia, 1989), 207–20

Cox, David R., *Welfare Practice in a Multicultural Society* (Sydney: Prentice Hall, 1989)

Creet, Julia, 'Introduction: The migration of memory and memories of migration', in *Memory and Migration: Multidisciplinary approaches to memory studies*, eds Julia Creet and Andreas Kitzmann (Toronto: University of Toronto Press, 2011), 3–26

Damasio, Antonio, *Self Comes to Mind: Constructing the conscious brain* (New York: Pantheon Books, 2010)

Dasgupta, Shamita Das, ed., *A Patchwork Shawl: Chronicles of South Asian women in America* (New Brunswick: Rutgers University Press, 1998)

Dawson, John, *Forest Vines to Snow Tussocks: The story of New Zealand plants* (Wellington: Victoria University Press, 1988)

Derrida, Jacques, *Specters of Marx: The state of the debt, the work of mourning and the new international*, trans. Peggy Kamuf (New York: Routledge, 1994)

De Tona, Carla, 'But what is interesting is the story of why and how migration happened: Ronit Lentin and Hassan Bousetta in conversation with Carla De Tona', *Forum: Qualitative Social Research 7*, no. 3, 2006: www.qualitative-research.net/index.php/fqs/article/view/143/315

Didion, Joan, *Slouching Towards Bethlehem: Essays* (New York: Farrar, Straus and Giroux, 1990)

Dubus, Andre, *Broken Vessels: Essays* (Jaffrey: David R. Godine, 1991)

Dutt-Ballerstadt, Reshmi, *The Postcolonial Citizen: The intellectual migrant* (New York: Peter Lang, 2010)

Eliot, T.S., *T.S. Eliot: Collected poems 1909–1962* (New York: Harcourt Brace & Company, 1963)

Emerson, Ralph Waldo, *Emerson: Essays and lectures*, ed. Joel Porte (New York: Library of America, 1983)

Epstein, Joseph, 'Introduction', in *The Best American Essays 1993*, ed. Joseph Epstein (New York: Ticknor, 1993), *xiii–xviii*

————, 'The personal essay: A form of discovery', in *The Norton Book of Personal Essays*, ed. Joseph Epstein (New York: W.W. Norton and Company, 1997), 11–24

Estés, Clarissa Pinkola, *Women Who Run with the Wolves: Myths and stories of the wild woman archetype* (New York: Ballantine Books, 1992)

Evergeti, Venetia and Louise Ryan, 'Negotiating transnational caring practices among migrant families', in *Gender, Generations and the Family in International Migration*, eds Albert Kraler, Eleonore Kofman, Martin Kohli and Camille Schmoll (Amsterdam: Amsterdam University Press, 2011), 355–73

Fakundiny, Lydia, *The Art of the Essay* (Boston: Houghton Mifflin, 1990)

Favell, Adrian, 'Rebooting migration theory: Interdisciplinarity, globality and postdisciplinarity in migration studies', in *Migration Theory: Talking across disciplines*, eds Caroline Brettell and James Hollifield (New York: Taylor & Francis Group, 2007), 259–78

Freud, Sigmund, *The Diary of Sigmund Freud 1929–1939: A record of the final decade*, trans. Michael Molnar (London: Hogarth Press, 1992)

Friedman, Susan Stanford, *Mappings: Feminism and the cultural geographies of encounter* (Princeton: Princeton University Press, 1998)

Gass, William H., *Habitations of the Word: Essays* (New York: Simon and Schuster, 1985)

Good, Graham, *The Observing Self: Rediscovering the essay* (New York: Routledge, Chapman and Hall, 1988)

Gray, Duncan and Jon S. Harding, *Braided River Ecology: A literature review of physical habitats and aquatic invertebrate communities* (Wellington: Department of Conservation, 2007)

Gray, Jeffrey, *Mastery's End: Travel and postwar American poetry* (Athens: University of Georgia Press, 2005)

Gray, Rockwell, 'Autobiographical memory and sense of place', in *Essays on the Essay: Redefining the genre*, ed. Alexander J. Butrym (Athens: University of Georgia Press, 1989), 53–70

Gunnars, Kristjana, *Stranger at the Door: Writers and the act of writing* (Waterloo: Wilfrid Laurier University Press, 2004)

Hage, Ghassan, 'With the fig, the olive and the pomegranate trees: Thoughts on Australian belonging', in *Politics, Culture and the Lebanese Diaspora*, eds Paul Tabar and Jennifer Skulte-Ouaiss (Newcastle: Cambridge Scholars, 2010)

Hage, Ghassan and Dimitris Papadopoulos, 'Migration, hope and the making of subjectivity in transnational capitalism: Ghassan Hage in conversation with Dimitris Papadopoulos', *International Journal of Critical Psychology*, *12*, 2004, 95–117

Hall, Michael L., 'The emergence of the essay and the idea of discovery', in *Essays on the Essay: Redefining the genre*, ed. Alexander J. Butrym (Athens: University of Georgia Press, 1989), 73–91

Hampl, Patricia, *I Could Tell You Stories: Sojourns in the land of memory* (New York: W.W. Norton & Company, 1999)

———, 'The dark art of description', *The Iowa Review 38*, no. 1, 2008, 74–82

Hardison, O.B. Jr, 'Binding Proteus: An essay on the essay', *The Sewanee Review 96*, no. 4, 1988, 610–32

Harrison, Jim, *The Shape of the Journey: New & collected poems* (Port Townsend: Copper Canyon Press, 1999)

Hedetoft, Ulf, 'Discourses and images of belonging: Migrants between new racism, liberal nationalism and globalization', in *Politics of Multiple Belonging: Ethnicity and nationalism in Europe and East Asia*, eds Flemming Christiansen and Ulf Hedetoft (Aldershot: Ashgate Publishing, 2004), 23–44

Heidegger, Martin, *Poetry, Language, Thought*, trans. Albert Hofstadter (New York: Harper & Row, 1971)

Hemley, Robin, 'Interview with Robin Hemley', in *Metawritings: Toward a theory of nonfiction*, ed. Jill Talbot (Iowa City: University of Iowa Press, 2012), 133–37

Hirshfield, Jane, *Nine Gates: Entering the mind of poetry* (New York: HarperCollins, 1997)

Hoagland, Edward, *The Tugman's Passage* (New York: Penguin, 1983)

Hoffman, Eva, 'Between worlds, between words: Thoughts on self-translation', in *Lost Childhood and the Language of Exile*, eds Judit Szekacs-Weisz and Ivan Ward (London: IMAGO MLPC and Freud Museum Publications, 2004), 53–65

Horrocks, Ingrid and Cherie Lacey, eds., *Extraordinary Anywhere: Essays on place from Aotearoa New Zealand* (Wellington: Victoria University Press, 2016)

Humphreys, Helen, *The Lost Garden* (New York: W.W. Norton & Company, 2002)

Huxley, Aldous, *Collected Essays* (New York: Harper, 1960)

International Association for the Study of Forced Migration: http://iasfm.org/

Iversen, Kristen, 'Interview with Kristen Iversen', in *Metawritings: Toward a theory of nonfiction*, ed. Jill Talbot (Iowa City: University of Iowa Press, 2012), 202–07

———, *Shadow Boxing: Art and craft in creative nonfiction* (Upper Saddle River: Pearson Education, 2004)

Iyer, Pico, 'Somewhere man', *Modern Maturity*, May/June 2001, 67–69

———, 'Where is home?' TED Talks: www.ted.com/talks/pico_iyer_where_is_home

Jaksić, Iván, 'In search of safe haven: Exile, immigration, and identity', in *Migration and Identity*, eds Rina Benmayor and Andor Skotnes (Oxford: Oxford University Press, 1994), 19–33

Jin, Ha, *The Writer as Migrant* (Chicago: University of Chicago Press, 2008)

Kaminsky, Ilya and Katherine Towler, 'Zen and the art of poetry: An interview with Jane Hirshfield', AGNI Online: www.bu.edu/agni/interviews/online/2006/towler.html

Kidder, Tracy and Richard Todd, *Good Prose: The art of nonfiction* (New York: Random House, 2013)

King, Michael, *The Penguin History of New Zealand* (Auckland: Penguin Books, 2003)
King, Russell, 'Towards a new map of European migration', *International Journal of Population Geography 8*, no. 2, 2002, 89–106
King, Russell, Tony Warnes and Allan M. Williams, *Sunset Lives: British retirement migration to the Mediterranean* (Oxford: Berg, 2000)
Kinnell, Galway, *Selected Poems* (Boston: Houghton Mifflin, 1982)
Kipling, Rudyard, *Letters of Travel 1892–1913* (New York: Doubleday, 1920)
Klaus, Carl H., *The Made-up Self: Impersonation in the personal essay* (Iowa City: University of Iowa, 2010)
Knox, Elizabeth, *The Love School: Personal essays* (Wellington: Victoria University Press, 2008)
Kreisler, Harry, 'Between memory and history: A writer's voice. Conversation with Eva Hoffmann', *Conversations with History*, Berkeley: University of California, 2000: http://globetrotter.berkeley.edu/conversations/people/Hoffman/hoffman-con0.html
Kriegel, Leonard, 'The observer observing: Some notes on the personal essay', in *Truth in Nonfiction: Essays*, ed. David Lazar (Iowa City: University of Iowa Press, 2008), 93–99
Kwan, SanSan and Kenneth Speirs, 'Introduction', in *Mixing It Up: Multiracial subjects*, eds SanSan Kwan and Kenneth Speirs (Austin: University of Texas Press, 2004), 1–10
Lazar, David, 'Interview with David Lazar', in *Metawritings: Toward a theory of nonfiction* (Iowa City: University of Iowa Press, 2012), 55–59
———, 'Occasional desire: On the essay and the memoir', in *Truth in Nonfiction: Essays*, ed. David Lazar (Iowa City: University of Iowa Press, 2008), 100–13
Levinas, Emmanuel, *Totality and Infinity: An essay on exteriority*, trans. Alphonso Lingis (Pittsburgh: Dusquesne University Press, 1969)
Lewis, Thomas, Fari Amini and Richard Lannon, *A General Theory of Love* (New York: Random House, 2000)
Liotta, Elena, *On Soul and Earth: The psychic value of place*, trans. Erika Pauli (New York: Routledge, 2009)
Lopate, Phillip, *The Art of the Personal Essay: An anthology from the classical era to the present* (New York: Anchor Books, 1994)
Madison, Greg, 'Existential migration: Conceptualising out of the experiential depths of choosing to leave "home"', *Existential Analysis 17*, no. 2, 2006, 238–60
Mairs, Nancy, 'Trying truth', in *Truth in Nonfiction: Essays*, ed. David Lazar (Iowa City: University of Iowa Press, 2008), 89–92
Manguel, Alberto, *The City of Words* (Toronto: House of Anansi Press, 2007)
———, *With Borges* (London: Telegram Books, 2006)
Masselot, Annick, 'Highly skilled migrants and transnational care practices: Balancing work, life and crisis over large geographical distances', *Canterbury Law Review 17*, no. 2, 2011, 299–315
Mead, Hirini, *Tikanga Māori: Living by Māori values* (Wellington: Huia Publishers, rev. edn. 2016)

Mein Smith, Philippa, *A Concise History of New Zealand* (Port Melbourne: Cambridge University Press, 2012)

Michaels, Anne, *The Winter Vault* (New York: Random House, 2009)

Milosz, Czeslaw, 'On exile', essay in Josef Koudelka, *Exiles* (New York: Aperture, 1988)

Montaigne, Michel de, *The Complete Essays of Montaigne*, trans. Donald M. Frame (Palo Alto: Stanford University Press, 1958)

Nail, Thomas, *The Figure of the Migrant* (Stanford: Stanford University Press, 2015)

Nesteruk, Olena and Loren Marks, 'Grandparents across the ocean: Eastern European immigrants' struggle to maintain intergenerational relationships', *Journal of Comparative Family Studies 40*, no. 1, 2009, 77–95

Nodelman, Perry, 'Discovery: My name is Elizabeth', in *(Re)Imagining the World: Children's literature's response to changing times*, eds Yan Wu, Kerry Mallan and Roderick McGillis (New York: Springer, 2013), 43–54

Norris, Kathleen, 'Introduction: Stories around a fire', in *The Best American Essays 2001*, ed. Kathleen Norris (Boston: Houghton Mifflin, 2001), *xiv–xvi*

O'Donohue, John, *Anam Ċara: A book of Celtic wisdom* (New York: HarperCollins, 1997)

———, *Eternal Echoes: Exploring our hunger to belong* (London: Bantam Books, 1998)

O'Neill, John, *Essaying Montaigne: A study of the Renaissance institution of reading and writing* (Liverpool: Liverpool University Press, 2nd edn, 2001)

Ong, Walter J., *Orality and Literacy* (New York: Routledge, 2nd edn, 2002)

Orwell, George, 'Such, such were the joys', in *The Collected Essays, Journalism and Letters of George Orwell*, eds Sonia Orwell and Ian Angus (London: Secker & Warburg, 1952), 330–69

Ozick, Cynthia, *Quarrel and Quandary* (New York: Vintage, 2001)

Papastergiadis, Nikos, *The Turbulence of Migration: Globalization, deterrorialization and hybridity* (Cambridge: Polity Press, 2000)

Parliamentary Commissioner for the Environment, *Possum Management in New Zealand* (Wellington: Parliamentary Commissioner for the Environment, 1994)

Plimpton, George and John Seabrook, 'William Maxwell: The art of fiction', in *Conversations with William Maxwell*, ed. Barbara Burkhardt (Jackson: University Press of Mississippi, 2012), 35–58

Porter, Jeff, 'Introduction: "A history and poetics of the essay"', in *Understanding the Essay*, eds Patricia Foster and Jeff Porter (Peterborough: Broadview Press, 2012), *ix–xxiv*

Pratt, Mary Louise, 'Arts of the contact zone', *Profession*, 1991, 33–40

Preston, John Hyde, 'A conversation with Gertrude Stein', in *Gertrude Stein Remembered*, ed. Linda Simon (Lincoln: University of Nebraska Press, 1994), 153–71

Ralph, David and Lynn A. Staeheli, 'Home and migration: Mobilities, belongings and identities', *Geography Compass 5*, no. 7, 2011, 517–30

Renginbogin, Herbert R., *Faces of Neutrality: A comparative analysis of the neutrality of Switzerland and other neutral nations during WWII*, trans. Ulrike Seeberger and Jane Britten (Berlin: LIT Verlag, 2009)

Ricketts, Harry, *How to Live Elsewhere* (Wellington: Four Winds Press, 2004)

Ricoeur, Paul, *Time and Narrative* (Chicago: Chicago University Press, 1984)

Rilke, Rainer Maria, *A Year with Rilke: Daily readings from the best of Rainer Maria Rilke*, trans. Anita Barrows and Joanna Macy (New York: HarperCollins, 2009)

———, *Letters to a Young Poet*, trans. Stephen Mitchell (New York: Random House, 1984)

———, *The Selected Poetry of Rainer Maria Rilke* (New York: Random House, 1982)

Roer-Strier, D. and D. Ben Ezra, 'Intermarriage between western women and Palestinian men: Multidirectional adaptation processes', *Journal of Marriage and Family 68*, 2006, 41–55

Root, Robert, 'Interview with Scott Russell Sanders', *Fourth Genre 1*, no. 1, 1999, 119–32

———, *The Nonfictionist's Guide: On reading and writing creative nonfiction* (Lanham: Rowman & Littlefield, 2008)

Root, Robert and Michael Steinberg, 'Creative nonfiction, the fourth genre', in *The Fourth Genre: Contemporary writers of/on creative nonfiction*, eds Robert L. Root and Michael Steinberg (New York: Longman, 2002)

Rushdie, Salman, *Imaginary Homelands: Essays and criticism 1981–1991* (Harmondsworth: Granta Books, 1991)

Ryan, Louise, 'Navigating the emotional terrain of families "here" and "there": Women, migration and the management of emotions', *Journal of Intercultural Studies 29*, no. 3, 2008, 299–313

Ryan, P.M., *The Raupō Dictionary of Modern Māori* (Auckland: Penguin, 2008)

Ryden, Kent C., *Mapping the Invisible Landscape: Folklore, writing, and the sense of place* (Iowa City: University of Iowa Press, 1993)

Said, Edward W., 'The mind of winter: Reflections on life in exile', *Harper's Magazine*, 1984, 49–55

Sanders, Scott Russell, *The Force of Spirit* (Boston: Beacon Press, 2000)

———, 'The singular first person', *The Sewanee Review 96*, no. 4, 1988, 658–72

———, *Staying Put: Making a home in a restless world* (Boston: Beacon Press, 1993)

Schiller, Nina Glick, Linda Basch and Cristina Szanton Blanc, 'From immigrant to transmigrant: Theorizing transnational migration', *Anthropological Quarterly 68*, no. 1, 1995, 48–63

Scott, Sam and Kim H. Cartledge, 'Migrant assimilation in Europe: A transnational family affair', *International Migration Review 43*, no. 1, 2009, 60–89

Sennett, Richard, 'Humanism', *The Hedgehog Review 13*, no. 2, 2011, 21–30

Seyhan, Azade, *Writing Outside the Nation* (Princeton: Princeton University Press, 2001)

Sigmon, Sandra T., Stacy R. Whitcomb and C.R. Snyder, 'Psychological home', in *Psychological Sense of Community: Research, applications, and implications*, eds Adrian T. Fisher, Christopher C. Sonn and Brian J. Bishop (New York: Kluwer Academic/Plenum Publishers, 2002), 25–42

Sinor, Jennifer, 'Writing place', in *Placing the Academy: Essays on landscape, work, and identity*, eds Jennifer Sinor and Rona Kaufman (Logan: Utah State University Press, 2007), 3–24

Skrbiš, Zlatko, 'Transnational families: Theorising migration, emotions and belonging', *Journal of Intercultural Studies 29*, no. 3, 2008, 231–46

Smith, Jo, 'Post-cultural hospitality: Settler–native–migrant encounters', *Arena Journal*, 28, 2007, 65–86.

Smith, Sidonie and Julia Watson, *Reading Autobiography: A guide for interpreting life narratives* (Minneapolis: University of Minnesota Press, 2nd edn, 2010)

Sontag, Susan, 'Introduction', in *The Best American Essays 1992*, ed. Robert Atwan (New York: Ticknor and Fields, 1992), *xiii–xix*

Spellmeyer, Kurt, 'A common ground: The essay in the academy', *College English 51*, no. 3, 1989, 262–76

Spitzer, Denise, Anne Neufeld, Margaret Harrison, Karen Hughes and Miriam Stewart, 'Caregiving in transnational context: "My wings have been cut; where can I fly?"', *Gender and Society 17*, no. 2, 2003, 267–86

Statistics New Zealand, '2013 Quickstats about culture and identity': http://archive. stats.govt.nz/Census/2013-census-profile-and-summary-reports/quickstats-culture-identity/birthplace.aspx

Svašek, Maruška, 'Who cares? Families and feelings in movement', *Journal of Intercultural Studies 29*, no. 3, 2008, 213–30

Taonui, Rāwiri, 'Whakapapa – genealogy: What is whakapapa?', Te Ara – the Encyclopedia of New Zealand: www.TeAra.govt.nz/en/whakapapa-genealogy/page-1

Thomson, Keith W., 'The Dutch', in *Immigrants in New Zealand*, eds Keith W. Thomson and Andrew D. Trlin (Palmerston North: Massey University, 1970), 95–105

Thompson, Paul, 'Between identities: Homi Bhabha interviewed by Paul Thompson', in *Migration and Identity*, eds Rina Benmayor and Andor Skotnes (Oxford: Oxford University Press, 1994), 183–99

Thoreau, Henry David, *The Portable Thoreau*, ed. Jeffrey S. Kramer (New York: Penguin Books, 2012)

Tilden, Norma, 'Nothing quite your own: Reflections on creative nonfiction', *Women's Studies 33*, no. 6, 2004, 707–18

Trlin, Andrew D., 'Change and continuity: New Zealand's immigration policy in the late 1980s', in *New Zealand and International Migration: A digest and bibliography*, no. 2, eds Andrew D. Trlin and Paul Spoonley (Palmerston North: Department of Sociology, Massey University, 1992), 1–28

Tuan, Yi-Fu, 'Space and place: Humanistic perspective', in *Philosophy in Geography*, eds Stephen Gale and Gunnar Olsson (Dordrecht: D. Reidel Publishing Company, 1979), 387–427

———, *Space and Place: The perspective of experience* (Minneapolis: University of Minnesota Press, 2001)

Umpierre, Luz María, 'Unscrambling Allende's "*Dos Palabras*": The self, the immigrant/writer, and social justice', *MELUS 27*, no. 4, 2002, 129–36

United Nations Department of Economic and Social Affairs: Population Division, *International Migration Report 2009: A global assessment* (New York: United Nations, 2011)

———, *International Migration Report 2017: Highlights* (New York: United Nations, 2017)

United Nations Educational, Scientific and Cultural Organization (UNESCO), 'Learning to live together: Migrant/migration': www.unesco.org/new/en/social-and-human-sciences/themes/international-migration/glossary/migrant/

———, 'Learning to live together: Glossary of migration related terms': www.unesco.org/new/en/social-and-human-sciences/themes/international-migration/glossary/

Vertovec, Steven, 'Transnationalism and identity', *Journal of Ethnic and Migration Studies 27*, no. 4, 2001, 573–82

Welty, Eudora, *The Eye of the Story: Selected essays and reviews* (New York: Vintage, 1983)

White, E.B., *Essays of E.B. White* (New York: Harper, 1977)

Williams, Tennessee and E.D. Williams, *The Glass Menagerie* (New York: Heinemann Plays, 1945)

Woolf, Virginia, 'A book of essays', *Times Literary Supplement*, 17 January 1918, 31

Index